PHILOSOPHY LOOKS AT THE ARTS

PHILOSOPHY
LOOKS AT THE ARTS
Contemporary Readings in Aesthetics

JOSEPH MARGOLIS

DEPARTMENT OF PHILOSOPHY
UNIVERSITY OF CINCINNATI

CHARLES SCRIBNER'S SONS　New York

Preface

This anthology took form almost spontaneously, while I was at work on a somewhat more ambitious project, also in aesthetics. In a sense, it proved to be surprisingly easy to select a dozen prime papers, from a large literature, that would at once suggest the range and force and outlook of contemporary analytic philosophy applied to the problems of aesthetics. Ideally, I should have liked to have a paper from every one of the leading writers active in the field today. But there were all sorts of reasons—not having to do with merit only—why this was not possible. At any rate, I am pleased to think that the collection offered here has uses that go beyond the usual textbook considerations of "equal time" for all views, nodding in the direction of classical authors, and the tactful avoidance of difficult essays.

J. M.

University of Cincinnati
July 23, 1962

CONTENTS

PHILOSOPHY LOOKS AT THE ARTS

INTRODUCTION

CONTEMPORARY philosophy is often accused of a certain unbecoming levity. Many people, to come at once to cases, are nonplussed to find philosophers cheerfully waiving their professional right to decide issues of right and wrong and public policy. I remember discussing some poems with a very charming lady who deferred to me somewhere in our conversation with an "Of course, as an aesthetician, you probably don't think these poems very good." I am reasonably sure she took my answer—"In a way, my opinion doesn't count"—to be a nice attempt at tact. I was of course trying to say something about the professional competence of aestheticians and not to hide my view of the poetry. Had she suspected, however, she might (much as people do with a philosopher's interest in moral and religious issues) have expressed some concern about the seriousness and importance of philosophy, the professional duty and public responsibility of philosophers.

I

Now, it is quite true that philosophers, at the present time, particularly those professionals associated with American and British universities, neither feel obliged nor qualified to decide the sort of issue mentioned. It is of course important to say at once that these issues deserve attention, everyone's attention, even the philosopher's attention. But one must say also that, when he addresses himself, for instance, to the evaluation of poetry, the philosopher (also, the aesthetician, the chemist, the mathematician, the historian, the architect, the mortician, the lawyer, the priest) cannot be performing in his professional role.

One somehow concedes the restricted interests of nearly all academic disciplines except philosophy. And the hesitation to do so for professional philosophy very likely depends on a popular way of speaking of the writings of admittedly wise and informed men as "philosophy." Also, many of the authors who have had impressive visions of the good life or of good taste in art or of piety have had worthwhile things to say (sometimes embedded in these other contributions) for the distinctive enterprise of philosophy. And of course, many professional philosophers, certainly in the older tradition or, today, largely outside the orbit of Anglo-American philosophy, insist that they are making discoveries about goodness, beauty, reality, God. There is a certain grandeur in such claims, and philosophers who may be supposed to have given up these topics must look a trifle pale by comparison. But of course, these have their reasons for not pursuing such matters. And I think one may, in all fairness to the great variety of methods that philosophers use, generalize about their disinclination. I should say that all contemporary philosophers who subscribe to the programs of Anglo-American philosophy (not at all always in harmony one with another) would accept the maxim (associated with Ludwig Wittgenstein) that "all the facts are in."

This maxim does not mean that no new discoveries will be forthcoming. It means merely that philosophers, as philosophers, raise their questions in a context in which the facts (whatever they may be) are not themselves in dispute. In short, the philosopher acknowledges whatever the admitted facts of science may be, whatever counts as an eligible judgment of conduct, or whatever may be admitted to express someone's appreciation or evaluation of a work of art. The philosopher simply is not in a professional position to dispute these facts; they are of course all open to dispute, sometimes by other professionals, sometimes by the man in the street. But philosophical questions, whatever they may be like, presuppose, and are debatable only on the admission of, such data.

The upshot is that philosophy is "vertically" related to all the usual comments people make in all the usual roles they take. For instance, if you claim that Ingmar Bergman's film *The Magician* is a much better film than his *The Seventh Seal,* the philosopher will not be at all concerned to dispute or vindicate your judgment. He would be interested rather in what sort of reasons might eligibly be put forward in defense, what sort of reasons another might advance against the judgment, whether there is a sense in which the dispute could be resolved, whether one or the other view could be taken to be correct. That is, *if* "all the facts are in," the philosopher's questions, such as they are, will be answered by a certain consulting of the facts conceded. He will not decide, say, which of two opposing opinions is justified but rather what we would mean by a justified opinion in the context given.

Once the matter is put this way, our confidence in philosophers may be restored. They are working seriously. In fact, their findings may have important implications for particular human endeavors. For instance, if it can be shown that, given the world we live in, goodness is not a quality that can be perceived in any sense resembling that in which redness can, certain attitudes regarding moral and political reform may very well be affected. Philosophers may be motivated by such possibilities. But the profession has its own clear sense of the sort of question it is prepared to entertain. And this is as it should be.

I have deliberately avoided characterizing *the* method of philosophy. There is no such creature. There is, rather, an impressive variety of methods, methods in fact that are more practiced and exhibited than fully formulated. But the prevailing methods, in the Anglo-American tradition, are generally described as *analytic,* which is to say, broadly, concerned with the sort of question already mentioned and implicitly committed to the maxim that "all the facts are in." The chief sources of this movement may be traced to the influence of such figures as Wittgenstein, Bertrand Russell, G. E. Moore, and the Positivists. But merely to mention such a varied group of thinkers is to advise would-be readers to attend to a philosopher's method as it is actually being employed in the analysis of some question. Frequently, philosophers do not describe their own methods of working; and when they do, it is not unusual that their actual practice departs from their own account. Still, these descriptive efforts would have no point if philosophers did not in fact practice in relatively stable and clear-cut ways (think for instance of someone who might wish to formulate the rules of some traditional game, as it is actually played). Also, philosophers clearly dispute one with another, though, on demand, they might very well characterize their ways of proceeding in strikingly different, possibly even incompatible, terms.

II

The essays in the present collection represent in a sense the most advanced thinking on the standard questions philosophers have raised about the arts. This is not to say that all (or any) of the papers included are invulnerable.

They are all of reasonably high calibre and they are all, so to say, on target. That is, they are all aimed at the very center of current philosophical disputes. To read them is to be correctly oriented to the trend of the most recent professional literature. This may be disputed, of course. But a number of these papers (for instance, those by Weitz, Wimsatt and Beardsley, Isenberg, Black) are, without any doubt, among the most discussed papers aestheticians have been interested in. The rest of the collection includes papers that have commanded considerable professional notice or are authored by philosophers who have been notably concerned with the problems of the field. So the collection is at once an introduction to a number of the most active professionals and the most actively debated questions in aesthetics.

All the papers may be broadly characterized as analytic. But it will be clear to the reader that various methods are being employed in the analysis of different questions. Not infrequently, these are dictated by the questions themselves. For instance, Weitz is interested in the very eligibility of a certain philosophical question, and Wimsatt and Beardsley are interested in certain proper limits of criticism. Weitz is therefore drawn to characterize the logical features of our use of terms, and Wimsatt and Beardsley are drawn to theorize about a professional activity. Or, thinking of the movement of so-called Oxford philosophy, or "ordinary-language analysis," we might say that Weitz's method derives mainly from Wittgenstein's own method, and Urmson's is associated with that of more recent leaders of the movement, say, J. L. Austin. But we should have to emphasize that it is already misleading to speak of "leaders" of this movement, except in the sense that, given not insignificant differences in philosophical method, certain writers among a group that work in fairly similar ways will have written the most influential papers among them. In any event, the best way of proceeding will be to compare the actual methods employed by our authors.

It is perhaps important to emphasize that philosophers quite regularly are forming methods of work at the same time they attack a particular question. There are analogies in other fields of course; one thinks for instance of the development of psychiatry. But philosophy is a uniquely reflexive enterprise. And because it is, as I have explained, only "vertically" related to other professional inquiries, one cannot simply speak of the accumulated findings of philosophy, as one can of the summaries in the chemical and physical handbooks. All of these findings are intimately related to the particular method particular philosophers have used. But as there is a certain virtuoso quality in pursuing a philosophical question that has to do with the very invention of methods of work, one cannot properly "detach" the findings and discuss these alone.

There is a much greater sense, debating philosophical questions, of subtle shifts in method than there is in any other professional inquiry, which perhaps best explains a certain limbo air (not of neglect or oblivion) that hovers over the philosophical tradition. Because one has the feeling of arguments endlessly rehearsed, arguments that we have been assured again and again lie defeated. There is indeed a reasonable sense in which these arguments may be said to have been defeated, namely, by construing the issues in accord with this or that method of working and demonstrating errors or difficulties from a given point of view. But since the methods themselves are constantly shifting, one finds the arguments subtly revived, reinterpreted, and reassessed. What is important to notice here is not so much a certain fussiness about professional methods of work as the nature of philosophical findings themselves. In a word, the tradition preserves the sense of a kind of attack on a question. We have, so to say, St. Anselm's way of proving the existence of God and Kant's way of disqualifying it. Quite naturally, we ourselves become partisans of this or that method (sometimes, different ones for different questions) and we speak more bluntly of correct and incorrect analyses.

So, as one might suspect, some of the papers herein included have been taken to be both definitive and absolutely wrongheaded. The point of including them is simply that they represent particularly forceful positions that would need to be considered in the contemporary setting for the questions of aesthetics; also, the alternatives one might be able to formulate will be positions in the same sense. So philosophy (and aesthetics, in particular) progresses by illuminating the strength or weakness of such positions seen from the vantage of others that embody distinctive as well as similar methods of working. This of course is not to say that philosophers cannot be found to have made blunders, given even their own particular way of working. And it is not to say that the criticism of one position seen from the vantage of another (employing a somewhat different method) may not be compelling.

III

Aesthetics, as a discipline, begins approximately with Kant's *Critique of Judgment*. There are interesting and worthwhile disputes about the arts among the ancients, of course, and Kant himself was heavily indebted to both English and Continental writers who preceded him. But it was Kant, as a major philosopher writing somewhat derivatively about taste and genius and the beautiful and the sublime, who gave a sense of philosophical importance to aesthetics and who set certain of its central questions. It is, I think, also, a professional cliché (and a true one) that, until relatively recent years (with important exceptions), treatises in aesthetics "rounded out" philosophical systems, and professional discussions were led by people not especially well-informed about the arts. Also, it is nothing more than honest reporting to say that professional philosophy has, in the past, been rather suspicious of the credentials of specialists in aesthetics.

All of this, however, has changed. The reasons are themselves worth noticing. Possibly, the single most important factor was the founding of the American Society for Aesthetics and the *Journal of Aesthetics and Art Criticism* (1942). What the *Journal* and the Society made possible was a sense of a repertory of fairly precisely formulated questions of an analytic sort and a sense of a continuing, responsible exchange on these questions. The result has been—I think no one would deny it—that philosophers of the first ranks have interested themselves in these and that methods enjoying the greatest philosophical respect have been brought to bear on the repertory. In fact, it is now not at all uncommon that younger philosophers of promise apply their most recently acquired techniques to questions of aesthetics first. Other sub-disciplines of philosophy, notably the philosophy of science, have also had to make their way slowly as distinctive endeavors (though not perhaps with quite the doubtful air that one remembers attached to aesthetics).

It was fashionable, only a few years ago, to speak of the "dreariness" of aesthetics. Today, all important questions have clustered about them a range of positions of striking deftness and force. Aesthetics now exhibits the same sense of a repertory of alternatives that one associates, say, with the questions of perception theory. And the pattern of debate in perception theory is probably as fair an index of the characteristic behavior of the profession as any that might be supplied.

As a matter of fact, aesthetics is enjoying a certain vogue among professional philosophers. Undoubtedly, one of the reasons for this is the impression that there are clean-cut questions that deserve to be investigated that are also not quite picked-over yet. The repertory of positions for, say, the question of sense data extends about as far back as philosophy itself. But in aesthetics, at the present fortunate moment, we find at once lively philosophical dispute of a high order and a relatively slim repertory to be mastered. The combination is irresistible. But also, it turns out that if one reviews ranges of standard philosophical issues from the vantage of detailed analyses of questions in aesthetics, strikingly new possibilities present themselves. For example, a theory of language, originally formulated for scientific statements, may be richly informed by a study of fiction and metaphor; the nature of moral judgments may be clarified by turning from considerations of duty and permission to considerations of appreciation; unsuspected problems concerning descriptive statements may appear if one seeks to distinguish between describing and interpreting poems and paintings. And on the mention of such questions, it is at once obvious that issues of the greatest philosophical importance are at stake.

Also, we may notice very strong evidence that contemporary aestheticians are reasonably well-informed about the arts. As a matter of fact, they obviously research the arts and the activities of professional critics, connoisseurs, and historians. The result is that where Kant (and countless others) analyzed "the judgment of taste" in his closet, contemporary aestheticians study Wölfflin, Berenson, Panofsky, Tovey, Blackmur, Richards, Matthiessen. Consequently, for the first time, in a sense, it pays people interested in the arts and outside professional philosophy to look in regularly on aesthetics. The point is that the aesthetician's questions have become the questions these other activities—art, criticism, appreciation—themselves closely suggest. The aesthetician is now interested in reviewing, in his special professional way, the implications of the actual world of art. And his remarks have come increasingly to be focussed on quite definite and "middle-sized" features of activities in that world. There is, for instance, a fair reason for someone interested in music to learn what professional philosophers have to say about the "logical" relationship between a musical notation and different performances of the same piece. And there is a reason for someone interested in literature to learn what may be said about the "logic" of figurative language.

IV

The collection of essays offered here is, inevitably, a sample. I take it to have, however, strategic importance. In twelve selections, it is intended to combine the widest representation of the most influential and active aestheticians of the analytic sort, papers that have attracted the greatest interest in professional circles, the freshest and most recent and most characteristic work of the philosophers represented, the greatest possible range of problems, minimal duplication, presentation of forceful and readily formulable positions close to the heart of particular problems, positions that are not merely odd or easily overthrown, statements enjoying relative autonomy, and items that have not been collected in previous anthologies. Necessarily, I have not included many important papers. But within the limits imposed, I believe the collection ranks very well on all the scales that had to be considered.

The only way to avoid possibly distorted impressions of the finality and importance of the papers included is to provide, as I have with each selection, a bibliography of the relevant literature and an introductory statement that at least suggests the kinds of questions one might wish to press in each area of investigation. In fact, given the conception of philosophical progress sketched above, a position of genuine interest is bound to be ringed about with alternatives. To understand these is to understand the ways in which a philosophical question is "answered."

One naturally comes to ask, however, what is the point of philosophical answers? It is difficult to say. Not because there is no point, but rather because it makes itself felt at a certain level of abstraction and because its special value is perfectly obvious there. One has to think first of professional and nonprofessional talk going about its business: critics interpreting poems, for instance, or spectators at the ballet turning to express their appreciation. One has to think then of critics using their authority to approve and disapprove of certain ways of working or certain works of art, of spectators judging one another's taste and declaring for or against criteria of preference. Inevitably, one reaches for comfortable generalities about what a work of art is, what the critic does, what constitutes taste, what beauty is. We are at once plunged into philosophical speculations. Answers of some sort are required to put our entire conceptual frame in order.

The trouble is that the answers come thick and fast. They are generated from vastly different points of view. They seem to rise and fall at an alarming rate. Yesterday, Croce held the field; today, he is an Example of what to avoid. Sartre tells us calmly that a work of art is not real; Susanne Langer says it is a symbolic form; Stephen Pepper says it is a nest of objects; Paul Ziff says it is not different from a physical object. And we wonder whom we are to believe.

The questions become philosophical questions. But the contributors are not necessarily philosophers. R. S. Crane turns from criticism to theorize about the nature of a poem. Wimsatt speculates about the proper bounds of criticism; Richards offers a theory of language; Panofsky defines the description and interpretation of a painting. Aesthetics, possibly more than any other branch of philosophy (except perhaps the philosophy of science, which makes an interesting parallel), gathers its contributions from a great many amateurs of philosophy. And this is worth our notice, because it suggests how quite spontaneous these philosophical questions are. No one imposes them; they arise simply from the interplay of our original talk about works of art.

But there are obvious dangers in these amateur contributions. Think of A. C. Bradley's suggestion that a poem has a distinctive kind of existence; or of Wellek and Austin's definition of a literary work as a "structure of norms"; or Roger Fry's insistence on an aesthetic emotion; or Tolstoy's division of real and counterfeit art. Philosophers are performing a service, then, seeking to sort out, in accord with prevailing professional standards, the answers to essentially philosophical questions posed by art itself. They are attempting to exhibit the relative strength and weakness of alternative positions on persistent questions, proposed by amateurs and professionals, that have caught the eye of everyone seriously concerned with the arts.

I submit that philosophers too have contributed to the confusion. But clarity is always relative to the present moment. And at the moment, analytic philosophy has its own striking views of the questions that have been asked. The entire tradition has been canvassed and answers precipitated piecemeal that have become the focus of new disputes. Here is the point of the present collection and the point of philosophical answers as well. Because here we have important specimens of the actual views that are leading professional aesthetics. And that means, simply, here we have the most recent handling of the old philosophical questions, provided by commentators who know the older answers and the latest methods for providing answers.

I

AESTHETICS

IT is notoriously difficult to define the boundaries of such large and lively interests as the scientific, the moral, and the aesthetic. Philosophers, at least since Immanuel Kant, have hoped to be able to mark out nice logical distinctions among the kinds of judgments corresponding to such interests as these. Quarrels have inevitably arisen about all particular proposals. This is not to say that questions that belong to the very heart of empirical science, moral judgment, and the appreciation and criticism of fine art are not easily identified. They are, of course. But the philosopher has been inclined to hope that when they are sorted out, these questions will exhibit certain nice differences which will in effect "justify" their being distinguished in these ways. Hence, there may be a certain embarrassment at stake in failing to discover the required distinctions.

On the other hand, one may very well question the effort to discover the difference between the scientific, the moral, and the aesthetic. What would such a discovery be like? It seems fairly clear that these distinctions may prove to be some philosopher's proposals, not findings at all. One need not deny that there are certain hard-core questions that belong unquestionably to each of these domains. But that hardly means that the boundaries of each are also open to inspection. Criticism shades into science, and moral considerations into appreciation. One suspects here the difficulty of neat categories.

The enthusiasm of philosophers to discover the distinction of the aesthetic domain may very well continue after it develops that no simple logical differences exist among scientific, moral, and aesthetic judgments. Inquiry turns then to another sort of distinction, speculation, for instance, on the controlling interest of each of these domains. So one may argue that reasons of certain sorts are regularly put forward to defend those sorts of judgments we call aesthetic, economic, or moral. The judgments themselves need not differ in their logical properties; it may be only that there are clusters or classes of reasons that would be relevant to each of these sorts of judgment. And the question arises whether these are overlapping clusters or classes and whether they may be sharply defined or only exhibited by way of admissible samples.

Underneath all such investigation lurks the question of the nature of such large category-terms as the aesthetic, the moral, and the scientific. It may be asked, for instance, whether philosophers are primarily explicating the meaning of "aesthetic" or whether, by an ellipsis, they are really generalizing about the properties of certain sorts of judgments or remarks that are taken without dispute (though they are not infrequently disputed) to belong within the scope of an aesthetic interest. That is, one may ask whether an analysis of the meaning of "aesthetic" will be fruitful independently of the second sort of issue, whether in fact it can even be undertaken. The point is not without some interest (given the professional literature), because it is well known that philosophers have quite regularly disputed among themselves whether this or that is *really* appropriate to the aesthetic point of view. It may then be that statements about the aesthetic point of view are actually elliptical summaries of findings upon this or that set of data (that some philosophers at least will have thought to be related in an important way to our concern with fine art), that other philosophers, appearing to dispute the meaning of the aesthetic, may either be disputing these findings or even providing alternative findings for other sets of data.

J. O. Urmson's contribution to the Aristotelian Society's symposium on "What makes a situation aesthetic?" threads through the sort of considerations mentioned in a way that is at once in accord with certain traditional conceptions of the central features of aesthetic interest and in accord with a certain powerful theme in recent Anglo-American philosophy (associated originally with the name of Wittgenstein), that the use of terms in actual usage in our language need not, and may not be able to, be defined by means of necessary and sufficient conditions.

What Makes a Situation Aesthetic?

J. O. URMSON

PHILOSOPHERS have hoed over the plot of aesthetics often enough, but the plants that they have raised thereby are pitifully weak and straggling objects. The time has therefore not yet come for tidying up some corner of the plot; it needs digging over afresh in the hope that some sturdier and more durable produce may arise, even if its health be rather rude. I therefore make no excuse for reopening what seems to me to be the central problem of aesthetics: I hope that by a somewhat new approach I may succeed in making a contribution, if but a small one, towards its solution.

We may refer to a person as, in a given situation, getting an aesthetic thrill or aesthetic satisfaction from something, or of his finding something aesthetically tolerable, or aesthetically dissatisfying, or even aesthetically hateful. In a suitable context the adjective 'aesthetic' and the adverb 'aesthetically' may well be superfluous, but it is sometimes necessary to introduce one of

From *Proceedings of the Aristotelian Society,* Supplementary Volume XXXI (1957), 75-92 (now, with a new note). Reprinted by permission of the author and the Aristotelian Society.

these words in order to make it clear that when we refer, say, to a person's satisfaction we are not thinking of moral satisfaction, economic satisfaction, personal satisfaction, intellectual satisfaction, or any satisfaction other than aesthetic satisfaction. If we merely know that someone gained satisfaction from a play we do not know for sure that we are in the aesthetic field. Thus a play may give me moral satisfaction because I think it likely to have improving effects on the audience; economic satisfaction because it is playing to full houses and I am financing it; personal satisfaction because I wrote it and it is highly praised by the critics; intellectual satisfaction because it solves a number of difficult technical problems of the theatre very cleverly. But the question will still be open whether I found the play aesthetically satisfying. Though these various types of satisfaction are not mutually exclusive, it is clear that when we call a satisfaction aesthetic the purpose must be to mark it off from the other types.

The philosophical task to be tackled in this paper is therefore this: to make explicit what it is that distinguishes aesthetic thrills, satisfactions, toleration, disgust, etc., from thrills, satisfactions, etc., that would properly be called moral, intellectual, economic, etc. I put the question in this form because I think that it is tempting to consider the aesthetic as an isolated matter and within the field of the aesthetic to concentrate unduly upon the most sublime and intense of our experiences; but I am convinced that it is important to ensure that our account of the aesthetic should be as applicable to toleration as to our most significant experiences and should make it clear that in characterizing a reaction or a judgment as aesthetic the point is to distinguish it from other reactions and judgments that are moral, economic, and so on. Only thus can we hope to bring out the full forces of the term 'aesthetic.'

This is not intended to be a problem especially about the appreciation of works of art. No doubt many of our most intense aesthetic satisfactions are derived from plays, poems, musical works, pictures and other works of art. But to me it seems obvious that we also derive aesthetic satisfaction from artifacts that are not primarily works of art, from scenery, from natural objects and even from formal logic; it is at least reasonable also to allow an aesthetic satisfaction to the connoisseur of wines and to the gourmet. I shall therefore assume that there is no special set of objects which are the sole and proper objects of aesthetic reactions and judgments, and which are never the objects of an economic, intellectual, moral, religious or personal reaction or judgment. We may judge a power-station aesthetically and find economic satisfaction in a work of art that we own. We may take it, then, that we are not exclusively concerned with the

philosophy of art, and that whatever the criteria of the aesthetic may be
they cannot be found by trying to delimit a special class of objects.

If the aesthetic cannot be identified by its being directed to a special class
of objects, it might be more plausibly suggested that the criteria of the
aesthetic are to be sought by looking for some special features of objects
which are attended to when our reaction or judgment is aesthetic; beauty
and ugliness have often been adduced as the features in question. Alternatively it has often been suggested that aesthetic reactions and judgments
contain or refer to some unique constituent of the emotions of the observer,
either a special "aesthetic emotion" or an "aesthetic tinge" of some other
emotion. I think that most commonly theories elicited by our problem
have been variations on one or other of these two themes, a variation on
the first theme being called an objectivist theory and a variation on the
second being called subjectivist. I propose to give some reasons in this paper
for finding both these theories unsatisfactory as answers to our problem,
even if neither is wholly false as a mere assertion; in their place, I shall suggest that the correct answer is to be given in terms of the explanation of the
reaction or the grounds of the judgment. I shall make some tentative remarks
about what sort of grounds for a judgment make that judgment aesthetic,
but cannot even begin the systematic treatment of the subject.

Let us revert to an illustration already casually used, and suppose that
we observe a man in the audience at a play who is obviously beaming with
delight and satisfaction. If I now maintain that his delight is purely
economic, what have I to do in order to establish this contention? If the
question at issue were whether he was delighted or merely contented it
would no doubt be necessary to ascertain fairly accurately his emotional
state; but if it be agreed that he is delighted and the only issue is whether
his delight is properly to be called economic, it is surely clear that phenomenological study of his emotions is not necessary. If, however, we find him
to be the impresario, and he agrees that the complete explanation of his
delight is that there is a full house and the reaction of the audience indicates
a long run, what more could possibly be needed to justify us in describing
his delight as economic? It seems hard to dispute that in the case of
economic delight, satisfaction, disappointment and the like the criterion
of the reaction's being economic lies in the nature of the explanation of
the reaction. Similarly it would be beyond dispute that a man's delight
was wholly personal if it were conceded that its explanation was entirely
the fact that his daughter was acquitting herself well in her first part
as a leading lady; again his delight will be moral if wholly explained by

the belief that the play will have a good effect on the conduct of the audience. It would, I suggest, be very surprising if the way of establishing that delight, satisfaction and other reactions were aesthetic turned out to be quite different from the way in which we establish them to be moral, personal, economic, intellectual, etc. Nor would it be surprising merely as a novelty; it would be logically disturbing to find that one had suddenly to depart from a single *fundamentum divisionis,* which had sufficed for all the other types, when one came to the aesthetic.

We must now note a further point about the logical relation between the concepts of the moral, the aesthetic, the economic, the intellectual, and the personal, as applied to reactions, both because it is of some logical interest and because a misunderstanding of it has led to some silly theories. *Triangular, square* and *pentagonal,* as applied to surfaces, are clearly species of a single genus and as such are mutually exclusive; there is a single *fundamentum divisionis* which is the number of sides that the rectilinear surface has. The same applies, *mutatis mutandis,* to *bachelor, married* and *widowed* as applied to men. On the other hand *triangular, red* and *large* are three logically unconnected predicates of surfaces, and *bachelor, bald* and *wealthy* are similarly unconnected predicates of men. What then are we to say about the predicates *moral, economic* and *aesthetic* as applied to, say, satisfactions? Clearly they are not technically species of a genus for they are not mutually exclusive as are species of a single genus; I may be simultaneously satisfied by a single object aesthetically, morally and economically, just as well as a man may be simultaneously bald, wealthy and a widower. But on the other hand to ask whether a satisfaction is moral or aesthetic makes as good sense as to ask whether a surface is square or triangular, whereas only in a very odd context can one ask whether a man is bald or a widower; furthermore, if a satisfaction is wholly moral it is not at all aesthetic, whereas being wholly bald does not prevent a man from being a widower. Thus moral, aesthetic and economic satisfactions seem neither to be logically disconnected nor to be true species of a genus.

Aesthetic and moral satisfactions thus seem to be related as are business and sporting associates. A man may be both a business and a sporting asso-ciate, yet the point of calling a man a business associate is to distinguish his status from that of a sporting or other type of associate, as it does not distinguish him from, say, an associate first met at Yarmouth. In the same way, to call a satisfaction aesthetic has the point of distinguishing its status from that of being a moral or economic satisfaction, though a satisfaction may be both aesthetic and moral. It surely follows that the criteria for a reaction's being aesthetic cannot be wholly unrelated to the criteria for its being moral or economic—they must be connected in such a way that we can see how being wholly one excludes being also another and yet how a single reaction can be both moral and aesthetic.

If we find the criterion for distinguishing aesthetic from kindred reactions in the nature of the explanation of the reaction we can readily account for this logical situation. To say that a satisfaction is wholly aesthetic, for example, will be to say that the explanation or grounds of the satisfaction are wholly of one sort, which will necessitate that the satisfaction cannot rest also on moral grounds; on the other hand there is clearly nothing to prevent our satisfaction from being multiply-grounded and thus simultaneously aesthetic and moral, aesthetic and economic, and so on.

But if we were to accept different kinds of criteria of the aesthetic, the moral and the economic we should be in difficulties here. Thus if a philosopher were to hold (and some apparently do) that a moral judgment is one that asserts an object to have a certain character and an aesthetic judgment to be one that announces or expresses the special emotional state of the speaker he would be maintaining views which, however plausible when consistently adhered to in isolation, are poor bed-fellows. For one would expect a wholly moral judgment, interpreted as ascribing a moral character, to deny implicitly the presence of a special aesthetic or special economic character; similarly a wholly aesthetic judgment, interpreted as expressing a special aesthetic emotion, should deny implicitly the presence of a special moral or economic emotion. Consistency is required here.

So much for the logical point of being clear on the relation between the aesthetic, the moral, the economic, etc. Unclarity on the point can lead to other less philosophical confusions. Thus the belief that moral considerations are relevant to a thing's aesthetic rank seems to stem from an awareness that appreciation may be simultaneously based on aesthetic and moral considerations coupled with a blindness to the fact that to call an appreciation aesthetic has as part of its point the effect of ruling out the moral as irrelevant. At the opposite extreme those who rage at any moral comment on a work of art are so conscious that the moral is irrelevant to the aesthetic that they suppose some error in allowing one's general satisfaction to have both a moral and an aesthetic component.

I have illustrated sufficiently the dangers of considering aesthetic reactions and judgments in abstraction from moral, economic and other kindred reactions and judgments. Similarly we must not concentrate on aesthetic delight and neglect other aesthetic reactions. The view that delight is aesthetic when that emotion has some special aesthetic tinge is not unplausible in isolation; we can no doubt bring aesthetic disgust under the same theory easily enough. But what if I am asked for an aesthetic judgment on what seems to me a very ordinary building and I reply truthfully that I find it merely tolerable? Am I reporting an emotion of toleration which has an aesthetic tinge, or perhaps an absolute tinge with no emotion to be tinged? But if I be taken to report merely the absence of any emotion or tinge by what criterion can we say that I am making an aesthetic judgment at all? It is surely important that we should be able to distinguish an aesthetic judgment of toleration from merely refraining from any aesthetic judgment at all; to regard a thing with mere aesthetic toleration is quite different from not considering it in an aesthetic light at all.

Thus the view that what distinguishes the aesthetic reaction and judgment is the presence of a special emotion or a special emotional tinge has already proved unsatisfactory on two counts. First, we have seen that we require a similar type of criterion of the aesthetic, the moral, the intellectual and the economic reaction, whereas the emotional criterion is very unplausible in some of these cases. Secondly, we have seen that however plausible with regard to strong emotional reactions, the emotional view is most unplausible when we consider such cool aesthetic reactions as that of bare toleration. Even if these difficulties were overcome, it is perhaps worth noticing that on this view a single reaction which involved, say, simultaneous economic, moral, aesthetic and intellectual satisfaction might well be required to involve an emotion having a quite kaleidoscopic variety of tinges.

But apart from these more logical points it is surely clear that when we experience emotions that we should wish to call aesthetic they are often very different from each other. Thus Tovey (*Essays in Musical Analysis,* Vol. I, p. 200) speaks of a theme "which gives Mozart's most inimitable sense of physical well-being" precisely because most of even the most delightful musical themes are so different in emotional effect. Or again, is it so clear that aesthetic emotions are different in kind from others? Tovey, we have seen, compares a Mozart theme to a quite non-aesthetic delight, and Housman can be adduced as a still more striking, since unwilling, witness. Enumerating three types of "symptoms" of poetical delight in his lecture, *The Name and Nature of Poetry,* he says: "One of these symptoms was described in connection with another object by Eliphaz the Temanite: 'A spirit passed before my face; the hair of my flesh stood up'"; another he describes by using Keats' words about his feelings for Fanny Brawne, "Everything that reminds me of her goes through me like a spear"; the third, he says, "consists in a constriction of the throat and a precipitation of water to the eyes," an experience which is surely common to many emotional situations, and not confined to the aesthetic.

The objection to the view that what distinguishes the aesthetic judgment or reaction from others is that it alone involves the recognition or awareness of beauty and ugliness, if offered as a solution to our problem, is rather different. As a minor objection it is worth pointing out that we should hesitate to call many things for which we have a great aesthetic admiration "beautiful," that 'beautiful' is a relatively specialized word of aesthetic appraisal, though this will inevitably elicit the answer that here 'beauty' is being used with a wider meaning than is currently assigned to it. But granted that 'beauty' and 'ugliness' are being used with a wide enough significance, the trouble with this answer to our problem is not that it is false but that it is futile. Of course if I admire a thing aesthetically I must be aware of its beauty, or of its charm, or of its prettiness or some other "aesthetic characteristic"; this is true in the same way as it is platitudinously true that moral admiration must involve awareness of a thing's moral goodness or rectitude or of some other "moral characteristic." But the trouble is that we have no independent way of telling whether we are aware of beauty or ugliness on the one hand or rightness or wrongness on the other; to know this we must know whether our admiration is aesthetic or moral, or, more accurately, to try to discover whether our admiration is aesthetic or moral and to try to discover whether we are aware of beauty or rightness are not two distinct inquiries but a single inquiry described in two ways neither of which is more luminous than the other. To identify the aesthetic judgment by the aesthetic characters of which it involves awareness is therefore not helpful.

Let me now set out more generally and completely the view that I wish to urge. The terms 'good,' 'bad' and 'indifferent' are, I take it, among the widest terms of appraisal that we possess, and we do appraise things on the basis of criteria, criteria to be formulated in terms of the "natural" features of the things appraised. But usually we wish at any time to appraise a thing only from a restricted point of view. We may, for instance, wish to appraise a career from the restricted point of view of its worth as a means to earning a livelihood; to do so we restrict our attention to a special set of the criteria of a good career, all others being for the purpose irrelevant. I wish to suggest that the moral, the aesthetic, the economic, the intellectual, the religious and other special appraisals should all be understood as being appraisals distinguished by their concentration on some special sub-set of criteria of value. To say that something is good as a means is not to say that it is good in some special sense distinct from that of "good as an end" but to appraise it from a special point of view; similarly to judge a thing aesthetically good or first-rate is not to call it good in a sense different from that in which we call a thing morally good, but to judge it in the light of a different sub-set of criteria. We may if we wish choose to invent a special meaning for 'beautiful' in which it becomes shorthand for 'good from the aesthetic point of view,' but that is only a dubious convenience of no theoretical significance. The central task of the philosopher of aesthetics is, I take it, to clarify the principles on which we select the special set of criteria of value that are properly to be counted as relevant to aesthetic judgment or appraisal. We may recognize an aesthetic reaction by its being due to features of the thing contemplated that are relevant criteria of the aesthetic judgment, and the aesthetic judgment is one founded on a special sub-set of the criteria of value of a certain sort of thing.

It may justly be said that so far I have done little more than to assert this view dogmatically, though I should wish to claim that I have given it some *a priori* probability by showing that it is a view which will enable us to deal with some of the difficulties that other views cannot surmount. Certainly I have as yet done nothing to indicate on what principles the criteria of value relevant to the aesthetic judgment are selected.

This lacuna can only be properly filled by field-work, and then only filled completely by a full-scale work on aesthetics. By doing field-work I mean studying examples of people actually trying to decide whether a certain judgment is or is not aesthetic and observing how they most convincingly argue the matter. Unfortunately to do this on an elaborate scale in one paper of a symposium is hardly possible; I can but ask you to believe that this paper has been written only after a considerable amount of such work, and produce one or two examples of it to show more clearly what I have in mind.

In his more philosophical moments A. E. Housman tried to account for the peculiar nature of the aesthetic in terms of emotional, and even physical, reactions; but here is an example of what he has to say at a more literary and less philosophical level: "Again, there existed in the last century a great body of Wordsworthians, as they were called. It is now much smaller; but true appreciation of Wordsworth's poetry has not diminished in proportion: I suspect that it has much increased. The Wordsworthians, as Matthew Arnold told them, were apt to praise their poet for the wrong things. They were most attracted by what may be called his philosophy; they accepted his belief in the morality of the universe and the tendency of events to good; they were even willing to entertain his conception of nature as a living and sentient and benignant being; a conception as purely mythological as the Dryads and the Naiads. To that thrilling utterance which pierces the heart and brings tears to the eyes of thousands who care nothing for his opinions and beliefs they were not noticeably sensitive; and however justly they admired the depth of his insight into human nature and the nobility of his moral ideas, these things, with which his poetry was in close and harmonious alliance, are distinct from poetry itself."

It does not matter whether we agree with Housman about Wordsworth; but I do hope that all will agree that this is the right sort of way to set about showing that an appreciation is not aesthetic. Clearly Housman does not deny that what the nineteenth century admired in Wordsworth was admirable; but he says that if your admiration of Wordsworth is based on certain grounds (the philosophical truth and moral loftiness of the content of the poetry) it is not aesthetic admiration, whereas if it is based on what Housman calls the "thrilling utterance," by which the surrounding paragraphs abundantly show him to mean the sound, rhythm and imagery of the words used, then it is aesthetic admiration. Whether Housman is right about Wordsworth or not, whether he has selected the most important criteria of poetical merit or not, this is the type of argument to be expected in a competent discussion; but to have argued the case by adducing the claim that Wordsworthians tended to concentrate rather on traits other than beauty would in fact have been to have restated the case rather than to have argued it. Moreover, if some Wordsworthian had maintained that Wordsworth's pantheism did bring tears to his eyes it would clearly have made no difference to the argument; it is concentration on the utterance, rather than having tears in your eyes, that makes you truly appreciative of the poetry.

Housman's *The Name and Nature of Poetry* is a mine of similar examples. Though he says in a theoretical moment: "I am convinced that most readers, when they think that they are admiring poetry, are deceived by inability to analyze their sensations, and that they are really admiring, not the poetry of the passage before them, but something else in it, which they like better than poetry," in fact all the concrete examples are in accordance with my theory and not his own. Thus the later seventeenth century writers are said by Housman to have but rarely true poetic merit not on the basis of any analysis of sensations but because, for example, they aimed to startle by novelty and amuse by ingenuity whereas their verse is inharmonious.

If, then, Housman's practice is sound it vindicates my view and stultifies his; nor is the obvious fact that we would not rate highly poetry that did not move us, relevant to the question how we are to distinguish a high aesthetic rating from another type of high rating. If field work and reflection in general vindicate my contention as do these examples from Housman I cannot see what else can be relevant; but I freely own that it is the cumulative weight of a large collection of examples from a variety of fields that is necessary, and these I have not supplied; nor could we ever attain a strict proof.

But all this being granted we are still only on the periphery of our subject and the most difficult question remains to be dealt with. It is comparatively easy to see that there must be general principles of selection of evaluative criteria which determine whether our evaluation is to be counted as aesthetic, moral, intellectual or of some other kind; nor is it at all difficult to give examples of what anyone, who is prepared to accept this way of looking at the matter, can easily recognize as being a criterion falling under one or another principle. It would be a very odd person who denied that the sound of the words of a poem was one of the criteria of the aesthetic merit of a poem, or who maintained that being scientifically accurate and up to date was another; similarly it is clear that the honesty of a policy is a criterion of its moral goodness whereas, even if honesty is the best policy, honesty is not a direct criterion of economic merit. But it is by no means so easy to formulate these general principles.

This difficulty is by no means peculiar to aesthetics. Part of the general view of which the aesthetic doctrine given here is a fragment is that what determines whether a judgment is moral is what reasons are relevant to it; but everyone knows the difficulty of answering the question what makes a judgment a moral judgment. (In my terminology Kant's answer would be that the reasons must refer to the rationality or otherwise of consistently acting in a certain way.) Certainly it would be over-optimistic to expect to find very precise principles; probably there will be some overlap of criteria between the various spheres of evaluation in anybody's practice; certainly there are some overt border-line disputes whether this or that criterion is relevant to, say, aesthetic evaluation.

I think, however, that there is one peculiar difficulty in trying to find the principle, however vague, that determines what sort of reasons are relevant to a judgment if it is to be counted as aesthetic. When we think of giving reasons for an aesthetic judgment we tend at once to call to mind what we would give as reasons for our appreciation of some very complex works of art; rightly considering, for example, that the plays of Shakespeare are things intended especially for consideration from the aesthetic point of view (I believe that a work of art can most usefully be considered as an artifact primarily intended for aesthetic consideration), we tend to think that we can most usefully tackle our problem by examining what would be relevant to an appreciation of, say, *Hamlet,* merely leaving aside obvious irrelevancies like cost of production. But this is most unfortunate, because, dealing with things intended primarily for aesthetic appreciation, we are inclined to treat as relevant to aesthetic appreciation very much more than we would in the case of things not so officially dedicated to aesthetic purposes; for practical purposes it would be pedantic to do otherwise. Moreover it is obviously very difficult to get straight our grounds for appreciating anything so complex. I am inclined to think that if *Hamlet* were rewritten to give the essential plot and characterization in the jargon of the professional psychologist there could still be a lot to admire that we at present mention in our aesthetic appreciations, but we would no longer regard it as aesthetic appreciation but rather an intellectual appreciation of psychological penetration and the like.

For these and other reasons, it seems to me hopeless to start an inquiry into the nature of aesthetic grounds by concentrating our attention on great and complex works of art. Among the other reasons is that in evaluating great works of art the reasons proximately given will almost inevitably already be at a high level of generality and themselves evaluative—we will refer to masterly style, subtle characterization, inevitability of the action and so on. If we are to have any hope of success we must first set our sights less high and commence with the simplest cases of aesthetic appreciation; in this paper, at least, I shall try to look no further.

If we examine, then, some very simple cases of aesthetic evaluation it seems to me that the grounds given are frequently the way the object appraised looks (shape and color), the way it sounds, smells, tastes or feels. I may value a rose bush because it is hardy, prolific, disease-resistant and the like, but if I value the rose aesthetically the most obviously relevant grounds will be the way it smells; the same grounds may be a basis for aesthetic dislike. Though I might, for example, attempt to describe the shape to make you understand what I see in it these grounds seem to me to be really basic; if I admire a rose because of its scent and you then ask me why I admire its scent I should not in a normal context know what you want. These grounds are also those that we should expect to be basic in aesthetics from an etymological point of view, and while one can prove nothing philosophically from etymologies, etymological support is not to be despised. Things, then, may have sensible qualities which affect us favorably or unfavorably with no ulterior grounds. Surely there is no need to illustrate further these most simple cases of aesthetic evaluation.

But there are some slightly more sophisticated cases which need closer inspection. I have in mind occasions when we admire a building not only for its color and shape but because it looks strong or spacious, or admire a horse because it looks swift as well as for its gleaming coat. These looks are not sensible qualities in the simple way in which color and shape are. It is clear that in this sort of context to look strong or spacious or swift is not to seem very likely to be strong or spacious or swift. I might condemn a building for looking top-heavy when I knew very well that it was built on principles and with materials which insured effectively that it would not be top-heavy. It is no doubt a plausible speculation that if a building looks top-heavy in the sense relevant to aesthetics it would probably seem really to be top-heavy in the untutored eyes; but if an architect, who knows technically that a building is not top-heavy, judges it to look top-heavy when he considers it aesthetically he is in no way estimating the chances of its being blown over.

We are now considering the facts which, exclusively emphasized, lead to the functional view of aesthetics. The element of truth in that view I take to be that if a thing looks to have a characteristic which is a desirable one from another point of view, its looking so is a proper ground of aesthetic appreciation. What makes the appreciation aesthetic is that it is concerned with a thing's looking somehow without concern for whether it really is like that; beauty we may say, to emphasize the point, is not even skin-deep.

We have, then, isolated two types of aesthetic criteria, both of which are cases of looking (sounding, etc.) somehow; in the simpler type it is the sensible qualities, in the narrowest sense, that are revelant; in the slightly more complex type it is looking to possess some quality which is non-aesthetically desirable that matters. We like our motor-cars in attractive tones and we like them to look fast (which does not involve peering under the bonnet); we like, perhaps, the timbre of a bird's note and we like it also for its cheerful or nobly mournful character, but would not be pleased if it sounded irritable or querulous; the smell of a flower may be seductive in itself but it will be still better if it is, say, a clean smell. Both these elementary types of criteria go hand in hand and are constantly employed.

The most obvious criticism of these suggestions is not that they are wrong but that they are incapable of extension to the more complicated situations in which we appraise a work of art. I cannot try now to deal with this sort of objection in any full way. But I should like to make two small points. First, I would repeat my suggestion that we are inclined to allow in non-aesthetic criteria "by courtesy" when we are evaluating a work of art, so that we may even include intellectual merit. Secondly, the fact that such things as intellectual understanding are essential to an aesthetic appreciation of a work of art does not in itself establish the criticism. If for example we enjoy listening to a fugue it is likely that a part of our appreciation will be intellectual; no doubt intellectual understanding of what is going on is also necessary to aesthetic appreciation; but the fact that I cannot enjoy the sound of a theme being continually employed, sometimes inverted or in augmentation or in diminution, unless I have the theoretical training to recognize this, does not prevent my aesthetic appreciation from being of the sound. I am still appreciating the way a thing sounds or looks even when my intellect must be employed if I am to be aware of the fact that the thing does look or sound this way.

There remain many difficulties; above all the notion of "looking in a certain way," especially in such cases as when we say something looks strong or swift, needs more elaboration. But to carry out this task is beyond the scope of this paper. Apart from a short appendix, I shall now close with a brief summary, a summary of a paper which is intended to do no more than to distinguish the aesthetic judgment and reaction from others and perhaps to indicate the best way in which to proceed to the further problems of the philosophy of aesthetics.

Summary

1. The problem raised is how an aesthetic judgment, reaction or evaluation is to be distinguished from others.

2. We should expect to find a criterion which allows us to distinguish the aesthetic, the moral, the economic, the intellectual and other evaluations by a single *fundamentum divisionis*.

3. All evaluations are made on the basis of criteria for the merit of the kind of thing in question.

4. An aesthetic evaluation is one which is made on the basis of a selection from the total body of relevant criteria of merit.

5. In at least the simpler cases of aesthetic evaluation the relevant criteria appear to be those which are concerned with the way the object in question looks or presents itself to the other senses.

6. It is impossible to distinguish the aesthetic by a special object, by a special characteristic attended to, or by a special emotion.

Appendix

It may appear to some that too little importance has been accorded to the emotions in this paper. To avoid misunderstanding I will mention one or two ways in which I recognize the importance of considering the emotions in aesthetics.

First, I recognize that we would be very little interested in the aesthetic aspect of things but for their emotional effect upon us.

Secondly, I acknowledge that if we experience an emotional thrill when we look at a picture or hear a piece of music we do not normally have to examine our grounds and reasons to know that we are reacting aesthetically in a favorable way. But I do want to maintain that it is the nature of the grounds that makes our appreciation aesthetic and that if on an examination of our grounds we find, as sometimes happens, that our reasons are appropriate rather to moral evaluation or are erotic, or what you will, we will, if we are honest, recognize that our reaction was not after all aesthetic. Of course we have trained ourselves to a great extent to approach pictures and music from the aesthetic angle so that we shall not in general be mistaken if we rely on an unanalyzed impression.

Thirdly, there are a great number of terms that we use in aesthetic evaluation —*pleasant, moving, pretty, beautiful, impressive, admirable* and *exciting* among others. I do not know what makes one more appropriate than another in a given context; partly, perhaps, they are more or less laudatory, or are based on a still more restricted selection of criteria than a mere judgment of goodness or badness; but I suspect that the choice of word is at least in part determined by the precise character of the emotion experienced.

For these and other reasons I do not wish to belittle the importance of the emotions in the philosophy of aesthetics; but I do wish to deny most emphatically that the aesthetic field can be distinguished from others by an attempt to analyze the emotions involved therein: and that is all that the thesis of this paper requires.[1]

[1] [Mr. Urmson wishes to add the following note—Ed.]: "Though I would still approach the problems discussed in this paper in much the same way, I would now dissent from its positive contentions in some important ways. In particular I would now wish to say that when we judge a thing as of a kind we do so by criteria which are specially applicable to that kind whereas when we judge something from the economic point of view ('economically it is a good thing'), from the aesthetic point of view, from the butcher's, baker's, candlestick-maker's point of view, we are not judging it as of a kind at all but by criteria appropriate to the particular point of view, in the light of which anything can be judged, of whatever kind it may be. Thus I can judge that a certain concrete-mixer is of high (or low) aesthetic merit—by the criterion appropriate to the aesthetic point of view—even if being of aesthetic merit is not in any way a criterion of a good concrete-mixer. My confusion arose in part from the fact that for many things, such as dining room tables, being good from the aesthetic point of view is a criterion for being good of a kind."

Bibliography

A very recent summary of the historical development of aesthetics is provided in:

Ruth Saw and Harold Osborne, "Aesthetics as a Branch of Philosophy," *British Journal of Aesthetics,* Volume I (1960), 8-20.

General doubts about the fruitfulness of aesthetics may be found in:

William E. Kennick, "Does Traditional Aesthetics Rest on a Mistake?," *Mind* (1958), 317-334;

J. A. Passmore, "The Dreariness of Aesthetics," reprinted in William Elton (ed.), *Aesthetics and Language* (Oxford, 1954).

Specific doubts about Urmson's discussion (printed here) appears in a companion piece, by David Pole, in the Symposium, "What makes a situation aesthetic?" Various other attempts to explicate aspects of the aesthetic point of view are to be found in:

Henry Aiken, "The Aesthetic Relevance of Belief," *Journal of Aesthetics and Art Criticism,* Volume IX (1951), 301-315;

Virgil Aldrich, "Picture Space," *Philosophical Review,* Volume LXVII (1958), 342-352;

Monroe Beardsley, *Aesthetics* (New York, 1958), Chapter I;

W. B. Gallie, "The Function of Philosophical Aesthetics," reprinted in William Elton (ed.), *Aesthetics and Language* (Oxford, 1954);

Joseph Margolis, "Aesthetic Perception," *Journal of Aesthetics and Art Criticism,* Volume XIX (1960), 209-213;

I. A. Richards, *Principles of Literary Criticism* (London, 1925), Chapter II;

Vincent Tomas, "Aesthetic Vision," *Philosophical Review,* Volume LXVIII (1959), 52-67;

Eliseo Vivas, "A Definition of the Esthetic Experience," reprinted in his *Creation and Discovery* (New York, 1955).

II

EXPRESSION

O NE HEARS it regularly said that artists express themselves in their work. But the remark is deceptively simple, as the history of modern aesthetics attests. One has only to think of Croce and Tolstoy to be reminded of the tortuous investigations that have been made in the name of the theme of expression. We ask ourselves whether the artist does really express himself, whether he must be expressing himself, whether he expresses his society or age, whether works of art are merely expressive without "expressing" any one, whether art expresses what may otherwise be stated. The questions multiply and it soon becomes apparent that the theories advanced move in different directions. Sometimes, the issue at stake is the definition of fine art. Sometimes, it concerns the formulation of criteria of aesthetic merit. Sometimes, it concerns the psychology of creation. Sometimes, it concerns the catalogue of qualities distinctive in fine art. Sometimes, it concerns the morality of artistic endeavor. Sometimes, it concerns the description of different cultures.

Philosophically, the theory of expression has been most closely linked to the definition of fine art, aesthetic qualities, and aesthetic judgment. And each of these issues has its own very large puzzles. But all relevant inquiries here tend to converge on certain questions regarding the relation of the artist and his work. Those questions that philosophers have concentrated on ask, for instance, whether the emotion that may move an artist in his work is of the same sort as the emotion alleged to be found in works of art, whether the emotion originally in the artist may in some sense be incorporated into his work, whether what a work of art "expresses" may be identified with or in some important sense matched with the emotions the artist is alleged to be trying to "express." In short, the questions concern the similarity of certain psychological and critical distinctions.

The issue has larger ramifications, particularly for the theory of criticism. For instance, the status of psychoanalytic and Marxist criticism is at stake. And even here, there are well-known confusions that must be sorted out. Is it, for example, possible and critically legitimate to handle the analysis of works of art in terms of psychoanalytic and Marxist categories without making the judgment of art dependent on biography? Is a work of art open to analysis on its own terms, though with possible clues provided by the artist's life, or is the "meaning" or value of a work of art or both primarily decided by reference to elements of the artist's life? One may, as a matter of fact, consider Freud's *Leonardo da Vinci* as a prime specimen of art criticism suggesting all our questions.

An important by-product of the interest in the theory of expression is the developing classification of the qualities characteristically found in works of art. At the present time, so-called emotive or expressive qualities—one speaks of melancholy music, of a nervous style, of the excitement that is *in* a particular work—are being analyzed without reference to biographical considerations. These qualities form only a fraction of the total repertory of descriptive and evaluative terms we employ. But either they have distinctive logical features or they exhibit certain features more prominently or more accessibly than other ranges of terms, for their analysis provides us with a very clear sense of the variety and informality of the ways in which we characterize works of art.

Again, the theory of expression tends to encourage us to think of fine art and the appreciation of fine art in terms of a communicative pattern between artist and spectator. Considerations of this sort have typically affected the effort to define a work of art. Though, sometimes (as with Tolstoy), even the apparently neutral effort to define what we mean by a work of art has been turned into a prescription of aesthetic values (still expressed in terms of a communication between artist and spectator).

Vincent Tomas's contribution to the American Philosophical Association's symposium on the concept of expression unites, in an economical way, a reminder of the historical setting of the most central disputes and a philosophical analysis of them.

The Concept of Expression in Art

VINCENT TOMAS

Tolstoy, Santayana, Bosanquet, Ducasse, Reid, and Dewey, among many others, have exploited the concept of expression in their theories of art and aesthetic objects. They use the term "expression" to refer to (1) the creative activity of artists, (2) a characteristic of works of art, and (3) a characteristic of aesthetic objects. Let us refer to (1), the process, as artistic expression; to (2), the characteristic of products of art, as objective expression; and to (3), the characteristic of aesthetic objects, as aesthetic expression. As we shall see, (1) is defined in terms of (2), and (2) is defined in terms of (3).

The basic concept of expression, then, is (3), and in what follows I shall be mainly concerned with it. My main thesis will be that the "two terms theory" of aesthetic expression is untenable, and that if we want to be clear about (3), and therefore about (1) and (2), we must adopt some version of the theory that in aesthetic expression, "the expressive thing" and "the thing expressed" are really "one" thing, not "two."

1. Artistic expression. Theorists of art generally distinguish between artistic

From *Science, Language, and Human Rights* (Philadelphia: University of Pennsylvania Press, 1952) pp. 127-144 (now, with minor corrections). Reprinted by permission of the author and the University of Pennsylvania Press.

30

and nonartistic expression. When dogs and cats express their feelings in the manner described by Darwin, they are not engaged in artistic activity. Similarly, in man, behavior which is merely symptomatic of a feeling, such as blushing when one is embarrassed or swearing when one is angry, is not artistic expression of feeling. Collingwood says it is just a "betrayal" of feeling.[1] Dewey says it is "just a boiling over" of a feeling,[2] and Ducasse says it is "a merely impulsive blowing off of emotional steam."[3] As Hospers says, "A person may give vent to grief without expressing grief."[4] Unlike merely giving vent to or betraying a feeling, artistic expression consists in the deliberate creation of something which "embodies" or "objectifies" the feeling.

We should notice that the process of embodying or objectifying a feeling is one and the same as the process of expressing it. The definition of artistic expression is not circular, however, because according to it artistic expression is a consciously controlled making of a product which, in the *second* sense, expresses, embodies, or objectifies a feeling.

2. *Objective expression.* The expressiveness of a *product* of artistic expression is a disposition of it. A painted canvas or a piece of carved marble "embodies" a feeling, i.e., is objectively expressive, in the sense that it has the capacity to cause, under assigned conditions, an aesthetically expressive effect in a contemplative perceiver of it. This definition, of course, transfers the problem of analysis to the concept of aesthetic expression. But by adopting it, we gain two advantages.

First, we are able to avoid an unsatisfactory feature in what T. S. Eliot says about objective correlatives. According to Eliot, works of art are expressive in the sense that they are "such that when the external facts, which must terminate in sensory experience, are given, the emotion is immediately evoked."[5] But just as "a person may give vent to grief without expressing grief," so, too, a work of art may *evoke* grief without expressing it. What is lost on Eliot's view that the expressiveness of a work of art is merely its capacity to evoke a feeling in a spectator is the notion of embodiment, the same thing that would be lost if we were to think of the process of expression as being merely the process of betraying, or of giving vent to, a feeling. If we define both artistic and objective expression ultimately in terms of aesthetic expression, the notion of embodiment can be retained.

[1] R. G. Collingwood, *The Principles of Art* (The Clarendon Press, Oxford, 1938), pp. 121-124.

[2] John Dewey, *Art as Experience* (Minton, Balch and Co., New York, 1934), p. 61.

[3] C. J. Ducasse, *Art, the Critics, and You* (Oskar Piest, New York, 1944), p. 58.

[4] John Hospers, *Meaning and Truth in the Arts* (The University of North Carolina Press, Chapel Hill, 1946), p. 62.

[5] T. S. Eliot, *Selected Essays: 1917-1932* (Harcourt, Brace and Co., New York, 1932), p. 125.

The second advantage is that on this view we do not make the class of expressive things co-extensive with the class of works of art. There are many more things which embody or objectify feelings in the sense that they objectively express them than there are things which are products of artistic expression of feelings. Real landscapes, and not merely pictures of landscapes, are objectively expressive. Hence, if we hold that anything is objectively expressive if it has the capacity to cause, under assigned conditions, an aesthetically expressive effect in a contemplator of it, and do not specify the way in which it must have acquired this capacity, we leave room for those things which have the capacity by accident, as well as for those which have it by design. We should thus have no trouble in avoiding having to speak of a piece of driftwood, which is admittedly objectively expressive, as if it were a work of art, like a man-made carving, when in fact it is a product not of art but of the blind workings of water, wind, and weather.

3. Aesthetic expression. Possibly the majority of writers on the subject since Santayana agree with him that aesthetic expression is such that the following two propositions are true: (i) "In all expression we may thus distinguish two terms: the first is the object actually presented, the word, the image, the expressive thing; the second is the object suggested, the further thought, emotion, or image evoked, the thing expressed."[6] (ii) "Expression depends upon the union of two terms . . . The value of the second must be incorporated in the first."[7] Of course, as Santayana tacitly assumes, expression involves *three* terms, the third being the mind in which the presented object evokes "the thing expressed," or to which the value of the second term appears as being "incorporated" in the first.

The import of (i) and (ii) may be illustrated by the stock example of the music which some listener experiences as sad. When music expresses sadness, (i) the three terms involved are the listener, the music, and the sadness. But (ii) the listener apprehends the music and the sadness as *one* thing, not as two. The sadness is said to be incorporated or embodied in, or to be fused with, the music. This second defining condition is what serves to distinguish an expression from a sign. In the normal sign situation, something presented stands for or *represents* something which is not presented. Thus, the leitmotif we hear represents Siegfried, who has not yet made his entrance on the stage. But when music expresses sadness, it does not represent sadness. It *presents* it. In Dewey's terminology, the expressive object does not "lead" to an experience; it "constitutes one."[8]

[6] George Santayana, *The Sense of Beauty* (Charles Scribner's Sons, New York, 1936), p. 147.
[7] *Ibid.*, pp. 148-49.
[8] *Art as Experience*, p. 85.

4. Ambiguity of the "two terms." The contrast between an expression and a sign raises a so-called problem of expression. It is the problem of construing the defining conditions (i) and (ii) in such a way as to make them compatible with each other. For, it would seem, the concept of aesthetic expression is a concept of something such that if, for a contemplator C, A expresses B, B is presented "in" A, though A is something given, and B is not given, but suggested or evoked. The problem is to explain how this is possible. The "central problem of the aesthetic attitude," Bosanquet said, is "how a feeling can be got into an object."[9] As Reid puts it (his italics), "*How* do perceived characters come to *appear* to possess, for aesthetic imagination, qualities which as bare perceived facts they do not possess? How does body, a nonmental object, come to 'embody' or 'express,' for our aesthetic imagination, values which it does not literally contain? Why should colors and shapes and patterns, sounds and harmonies and rhythms, come to *mean* so very much more than they *are*?"[10]

This problem, to which Santayana, Reid, and others have devoted so much attention and ingenuity, is, I submit, a pseudo-problem. It presupposes something false, namely, that (Reid's italics) "The embodiment of value in the aesthetic object is of such nature that the value 'embodied' in the perceived object or 'body' is *not literally* situated in 'the body.' The 'joy' expressed in music is *not literally* in the succession of sounds."[11] To see why this is false, let us ask what exactly are the two terms of aesthetic expression: "the object actually presented . . . the expressive thing," on the one hand, and "the object suggested . . . the thing expressed," on the other.

a. The first term is not a physical thing or event. An interpretation of the two terms theory over which, I think, we will not need to linger is that the first term is a *physical* thing or event—the picture or statue which reflects light rays, or the plucking of a string which produces sound waves in the air. Santayana occasionally makes statements which lend themselves to this interpretation, as when he says, "The first term is the source of stimulation. . . ."[12] Similarly, Gotshalk says that "a person may assert that a certain non-representational painting expresses calmness and gentleness. . . . since the painting is the clear causal source of the feeling qualities evoked, these qualities are immediately taken as suggested by the painting, and their

[9] Bernard Bosanquet, *Three Lectures on Aesthetic* (Macmillan and Co., Ltd., London, 1915), p. 74.
[10] Louis Arnaud Reid, *A Study in Aesthetics* (The Macmillan Company, New York, 1931), pp. 62-63.
[11] *Ibid.,* p. 60.
[12] *The Sense of Beauty,* p. 54.

suggestion is taken as an integral feature of the painting's being."[13] Passages like these, in which paintings or music are regarded as "the source of stimulation" or "the clear causal source of the feeling qualities evoked," suggest that the first term is Eliot's objective correlative. If the objective correlative were indeed the first term in *aesthetic* expression, we should have to say, in accordance with Santayana's second defining condition, and as Gotshalk seems to say, that the emotion it has the capacity to evoke in a contemplator is incorporated in, or is "an integral feature of," the physical state of affairs which is the cause or the causal condition of the emotion. In other words, when music expresses sadness to a listener, (i) the three terms involved would be the listener, sound waves, and sadness, and (ii) the listener would apprehend the sound waves and the sadness as one thing, not as two. But the listener does not apprehend sound *waves* at all. Not these, but sound *qualities,* are "actually presented," i.e., are the content of his contemplative perception. What expresses sadness to him is an apparent or phenomenological object, not its presumed physical cause.

b. The two terms are equally "apparent" or "presented." The two terms theory might be interpreted in such a way as to make the first term, "the object actually presented," that which *appears* to us in aesthetic contemplation. The second term would then be, presumably, something that does not appear, but is "the object suggested."

What thus appears, it is often said, is the aesthetic surface, consisting of sense qualities (colors, sounds, smells, etc.) and their relations—in Santayana's terminology, sensuous material and form; and what is suggested by the surface is feeling import. On this view, the first term in the sad music we hear is a pattern of sounds, *devoid of feeling import;* and the second term is its sad-feeling import, *devoid of sensuous embodiment.*

The very attempt to state this view precisely makes it evident that the distinction between surface and feeling import (between "body" and "what is embodied," or between "the expressive thing" and "the thing expressed") can be made only by an effort of abstraction. The idea of what Reid refers to as "bare perceived facts" is, as Collingwood says, "the product of a process of sterilization."[14] An aesthetic surface does not *appear* to us stripped of its feeling import; on the contrary, in aesthetic contemplation, whatever appears is emotionally charged. Direct inspection of the content of aesthetic perception reveals no basis whatever for regarding its sterilized sensuous pattern as being something "actually presented" and its feeling import as

[13] D. W. Gotshalk, *Art and the Social Order* (The University of Chicago Press, Chicago, 1947), p. 138.
[14] *The Principles of Art,* p. 163.

being something "suggested." From the phenomenological point of view, feeling import is "literally in" aesthetic objects in precisely the same sense that colors are. "Body" and "what is embodied" are equally given in aesthetic experience, and Santayana's formulation of the criterion for distinguishing the two terms is, therefore, unsatisfactory.

c. A sense in which the two terms are equally "objective." If the two terms theory is reformulated so as to make the criterion to be used in distinguishing between the first and second terms the same as the one marking off the subjective from the objective elements in the phenomenological content, it seems to fare no better. Discussion of it, however, is complicated by the treacherous ambiguity and vagueness of the words "subjective" and "objective."

These sometimes mean "bodily" and "extra-bodily," respectively. When they do, those elements of a phenomenological content are subjective, or "in the subject," which are intuited as being situated in the body of the perceiver; and those elements are objective, or "in the object," which are intuited as being outside the body.[15] Reid sometimes uses these notions in formulating the two terms theory. In one place he writes:

> . . . in aesthetic experience we are not, normally, thinking about our bodies, but rather about the sounds and the colors. These are, in perception, taken as existing in the world external to the body. Now, though these objects are, in the sense just stated, but causes in us of values, we do not, aesthetically, regard them as causes, but as themselves "expressing" values. Our question is, How do the values get there? The only possible answer is that we put them there—in imagination. They are not, aesthetically, apprehended as belonging to the organism. The focus of interest is in the external object, and to the external object they become imputed.[16]

As will be indicated in (*d*) below, Reid also thinks of the subjective and the objective in other senses than the ones just specified. But in the sense specified, the second term is as objective a feature of the phenomenological object as aesthetic surface. Reid admits this when he writes that values "are not, aesthetically, apprehended as belonging to the organism." When music *expresses* sadness to us, we do not feel the sadness to be in us, the way we feel the nostalgic sadness *evoked* by a (possibly gay) popular song, which we knew in our youth, to be in us. Or, as O. K. Bouwsma says, in his playful but discerning "The Expression Theory of Art," when music expresses sadness, the sadness is to the music like the redness to the apple, not like the

---

[15] Compare Carroll C. Pratt, *The Meaning of Music* (McGraw-Hill Book Co., Inc., New York, 1931), pp. 157-59.
[16] *A Study in Aesthetics*, p. 79.

burp to the cider.[17] The endeavor to construct a version of the two terms theory in which the first term is objective and the second is subjective, in the senses just specified, leads away from our subject. We then cease to discuss the concept of expression and deal with that of evocation instead.[18] If we stick to our subject, and to the senses of "subjective" and "objective" that have been specified, there is no reason whatever for distinguishing two terms, one subjective, the other objective, in the aesthetic object.

d. A sense in which the two terms are equally "subjective." It will be said that the criterion by which we distinguish the two terms is an epistemological, not a phenomenological, criterion—that, on general epistemological grounds, we must distinguish between objective and subjective components in the aesthetic object. People and probably animals can literally be sad, but music cannot, no more than the sea-foam, if Ruskin was right, can be cruel or can crawl. Appearances to the contrary notwithstanding, then, feeling import is, in an epistemological sense, "in us," not "in the object." Thus, Ducasse says that it is true "that in ecpathy the object is not apprehended as out of us and the feeling as in us. . . . The feeling is apprehended as if it were a quality of the object. Nevertheless, when we are not actually going through the ecpathizing process, but describing it, we are well aware of the duality of object and subject, and of the fact that the feeling is experienced by the subject."[19] Similarly, Perry says, "That feeling does somehow color its object is an undeniable fact of experience, and a fact recognized by common speech in so far as all of the familiar feelings assume the form of adjectives." However, "It seems necessary at some point to admit that the qualities of feeling may be 'referred' where they do not belong, or that an object may for summary purposes of poetic suggestion be endowed with characters that accurate judgment will attribute to their effects or to the context."[20] And, still in the same vein, Reid says that although the hedonic effects of things are "in aesthetic experience apprehended to some extent *as if* they were hedonic properties of the external thing," the fact is that "they belong, analytically and abstractly regarded, to the side of the subject and not of the object." In Reid's opinion, "most philosophers would be ready to admit that."[21]

---

[17] In Max Black, ed., *Philosophical Analysis* (Cornell University, Ithaca, New York, 1950), p. 100.

[18] Compare Carroll C. Pratt, *The Meaning of Music*, p. 162.

[19] C. J. Ducasse, *The Philosophy of Art* (The Dial Press, New York, 1929), p. 177.

[20] Ralph Barton Perry, *General Theory of Value* (Longmans, Green and Co., New York, 1926), p. 31.

[21] *A Study in Aesthetics*, p. 79.

Hence, if music expresses sadness to a listener, what is happening is that his listening to the music causes the listener to be sad, and he erroneously interprets the sadness affecting him to be a characteristic not of himself but of the music. Again we have the problem of explaining "how a feeling can be got into an object." It gets there, it is variously said, by being incorporated or objectified (Santayana), empathized (Lee and Lipps), distanced (Bullough), imagined (Reid), or in some other way "projected" from the subject into the object. In these versions of the two terms theory, contemplative perception of the sad music is dual. It consists in part in our *taking* the first term for what it really is, and in part in our mistaking the second term, or feeling import, for what it really is not.

The *prima facie* plausibility of these versions largely vanishes, I think, when we notice their tacit shifts in the meaning of the word "object," or, better, the way they shuttle back and forth between the use of "object" in the sense of aesthetic, i.e., phenomenological object, and its use in the sense of ontological, i.e., "real" object.[22] When these shifts or shuttlings are made explicit, what these versions all contend is that while feeling import admittedly *does* characterize the aesthetic object, in precisely the way sense qualities do, there are reasons for believing that it does *not* characterize the ontological object. Feeling import is not "literally in" ontological objects in the sense that it is, after all, an affect in, and therefore existentially dependent on, the contemplator; if there were no contemplators, there would be no feeling import, even though there were ontological objects. At the same time, these versions take it for granted (else why do they protest so much the objectivity of feeling?) that the first term characterizes not only the aesthetic object but *also* the ontological object. The qualities constituting it are presumed to be "literally in" the ontological object in the sense that they would characterize it even if no contemplators existed. We may well ask, therefore, What, exactly, according to these versions, constitutes the first term? What qualities of aesthetic objects are "objective" in the sense that, unlike feeling import, they are also qualities of ontological objects?

The most likely candidate is the sterilized aesthetic surface—the pattern of sense qualities devoid of feeling import. The difficulty here is that if we hold that this surface is objective in the sense required, i.e., that colors, sounds, and other sense qualities are "literally in" the ontological object, whereas feeling import never is, we are accepting some sort of naive

[22] Cf. C. D. Broad, *The Mind and its Place in Nature* (Kegan Paul, Trench, Trubner and Co., Ltd., London, 1925), pp. 141-43.

realism with respect to the former, at the same time that we are arbitrarily denying it with respect to the latter. This is what Reid does most of the time that he discusses aesthetic expression. Reid never notices that the same sort of reasons that are given for believing that feeling import does not characterize ontological objects may also be given for believing that sense qualities do not characterize ontological objects. Reid says, "When our blood is stirred and we feel martial, we call the trumpet's note martial. From the queer shivers it gives us, we say that the flute 'complains.' "[23] When we apprehend phenomenologically objective feeling, that is, the feel of bodily processes is being "imputed" to an external thing. Yet the very same thing may be said about sense qualities. "What is the color of the sky," Prall asks, "but the way it strikes our eye, the way it feels through vision?"[24] Hartshorne suggests that when we see a red book, "what we intuit as red is the state of our own nerves. . . ."[25]

Santayana, in spite of his adherence to the two terms doctrine, is consistent on this point. When he proposes its phenomenological objectivity as the differentia of aesthetic pleasure, he writes: "If we say that other men should see the beauties we see, it is because we think those beauties are *in the object,* like its color, proportion, or size. . . . But this notion is radically absurd and contradictory. . . . A beauty not perceived is a pleasure not felt, and a contradiction. But modern philosophy has taught us to say the same thing of every element of the perceived world; all are sensations; and their grouping into objects imagined to be permanent and external is the work of certain habits of our intelligence." For Santayana, in this place at least, the status of phenomenologically objective feeling is no different from that of phenomenologically objective color or sound quality. The one is no more or no less "literally in" the ontological object than the other: "Convenience and economy of thought alone determine what combination of our sensations we shall continue to objectify and treat as the cause of the rest."[26]

So far, to avoid complicating our argument, we have made no mention of representation. But a theory of expression must account for the expressiveness of aesthetic objects which are represented, as well as presented, entities. The expressive thing need not be a sensuous pattern; it may be something represented by such a pattern. And it need not be something sensed or perceived; it might be something conceived or imagined. As Ducasse says, "the realm of possible objects of aesthetic contemplation includes every entity

[23] *A Study in Aesthetics,* p. 79.

[24] D. W. Prall, *Aesthetic Analysis* (Thomas Y. Crowell Co., New York, 1936), p. 148.

[25] Charles Hartshorne, *The Philosophy and Psychology of Sensation* (The University of Chicago Press, Chicago, 1934), p. 247.

[26] *The Sense of Beauty,* pp. 35-37.

which in any way whatever can become a content of attention."[27] Now, in no matter what way an entity becomes a content of contemplative attention, it is, *qua* such a content, "the thing presented ... the expressive thing," with its characteristic feeling import. It is doubtful that anyone who feels obliged to insist that feeling import is not literally in the object would want to insist, when the aesthetic object is a non-existent, imagined object, that any other quality is. But then by what criterion would he distinguish between the two terms?

5. *The aesthetically expressive object is one thing, not a fusion of two.* If the preceding contentions are sound, and none of the three criteria usually put forward for distinguishing two terms in aesthetic expression is satisfactory, to save the two terms theory we must find some other criterion which is satisfactory. One possible alternative, that of the alleged independent variability of the two terms, is reserved for consideration below. Meanwhile, in view of the difficulties in the two terms theory so far considered, it seems worthwhile entertaining the hypothesis, defended by Pratt, Hartshorne, and Langer, that the aesthetically expressive object really is but one thing, and not a distinguishable fusion of two.

All three of these writers hold fast to the phenomenological distinction between subjective and objective feelings. The sadness evoked by bereavement is in us, but the sadness expressed by music is not in us but in the object. If the relation between subjective and objective sadness were one of identity, this would raise the question how a feeling can be got into an object in an insoluble form. But, according to Pratt and Langer, the relation is one of analogy of structure. Pratt, reserving the word "emotion" for subjective feelings exclusively, holds that "visual and especially auditory processes intrinsically contain certain properties which, because of their close resemblance to certain characteristics in the subjective realm, are frequently confused with emotions proper."[28] On his view, sad music *sounds* the way (subjective) sadness *feels*.[29] According to Langer, "there are certain aspects of the so-called 'inner life'—physical or mental—which have formal properties similar to those of music—patterns of motion and rest, of tension and release, of agreement and disagreement, preparation, fulfillment, excitation, sudden change, etc."[30] What the sad music reflects to the contemplator is "the morphology" of subjective or "real" sadness.[31] In sum, according to Pratt and

[27] *The Philosophy of Art*, p. 224.
[28] *The Meaning of Music*, p. 191.
[29] *Ibid.*, p. 203.
[30] Susanne K. Langer, *Philosophy in a New Key* (Penguin Books, New York, 1948), pp. 184-185.
[31] *Ibid.*, p. 193.

Langer the sad music is like subjective sadness in its structure, and, when
savored in aesthetic contemplation, it feels like it. Of course, since its quality
is "distanced," "embodied," "not our own," etc., it does not feel *exactly*
like it.

Charles Hartshorne's view is more radical. In his fascinating but apparently strangely neglected *The Philosophy and Psychology of Sensation*,[32]
he presents "the contradictory of the doctrine of the irreducible distinctness
of sensory qualities and affective tones."[33] He contends that sensory qualities
constitute a subclass of feeling tones, as do subjective emotions. "Indeed,
a maximum of attention upon sensations themselves shows them to be
feelings, to possess emotional qualities as their intrinsic essence."[34] "The
'affective' tonality, the aesthetic or tertiary quality, usually supposed to be
merely 'associated with' a given sensory quality is, in part at least, identical
with that quality, one with its nature or essence. Thus, the 'gaiety' of yellow
(the peculiar highly specific gaiety) is the yellowness of the yellow. The two
are identical in that the 'yellowness' is the unanalyzed and but denotatively
identified x of which the 'gaiety' is the essential description or analysis."[35]
On Hartshorne's view, when music expresses sadness to a listener, his experience of the music is a species of the same genus as his experience of subjective sadness. The two experiences qualitatively are not merely analogous;
they are generically identical. Hartshorne also contends, rightly, I believe,
that quality as well as structure is expressive.

The three views agree that in aesthetic expression, the feeling import
apprehended is not something numerically identical with subjective feeling,
though there are resemblances between them. It is because of the resemblances
that the two are called by the same name. They all agree that feeling import
is emphatically not a characteristic erroneously imputed to the aesthetic
object, but veridically so. And, on all three views, taking the aesthetic
attitude is not a way of shifting gears which makes it possible for us to
interpret "even our 'subjective' affections not as modes of *our* being but
rather as characteristics of the phenomenon."[36] Rather, it is a way of making
ourselves receptive to the ordinarily disregarded feeling import of the phe-

---

[32] See note 25. In leafing through a random selection of books dealing with our subject, and
published later than Hartshorne's work, I found not a single reference to this book; and this
seems odd. Those who accept the two terms theory will find it contains arguments worth refut-
ing. Those who reject that theory might welcome its powerful support.

[33] *The Philosophy and Psychology of Sensation*, pp. 6-7.

[34] *Ibid.*, p. 133.

[35] *Ibid.*, p. 7.

[36] Edward Bullough, " 'Psychical Distance' as a Factor in Art and an Aesthetic Principle,"
in Melvin Rader, ed., *A Modern Book of Esthetics* (Henry Holt and Co., New York, 1952),
pp. 403-4.

nomenon. The concept of aesthetic expression remains mysterious, I think, except on a theory in which these assertions, all of which the two terms theory denies, are incorporated.

6. *On the alleged independent variability of the two terms*. It seems widely accepted that any theory that acquiesces in the deliverances of aesthetic observation by asserting that feeling import is in the aesthetic object, in whatever sense aesthetic surface is, cannot account for the independent variability of "the expressive thing" and "the thing expressed"; that this fact, if such it be, can be accounted for only by some version of the two terms theory, reinforced by the laws of association. A typical formulation of this point of view is one by Henry D. Aiken:

> Unless the emotional effect of a work of art is located *in us* rather than in the object itself, we fall at once into aesthetic paradoxes which have continually beplagued the theorist. If, as Prall suggests, we *identify* the solemnity or gaiety of a work of music with its specifications of tempo, loudness, timbre, pitch, and so on; if, as he says, a "quick solemnity is a contradiction in terms," then, I think, it becomes unintelligible why it is that the same specifications of tempo, loudness, and so on, do *not* express the same specifications of feeling to all people, or even to all discriminating observers. In point of fact, the different values which different qualified observers attribute to the same work are, in part, due precisely to the fact that while they perceive the same, or closely similar, sensory surfaces, these do not succeed in evoking in each of them the same degree or even the same kind of emotional feeling. Indeed, the variability in the "expressiveness" which the same work of art has for different observers largely explains why there exists such a wide discrepancy between the descriptions of the quality of the impact which the same works of art produce upon different observers.[37]

Bearing in mind the distinctions we found to be needful above, we may observe with respect to the first sentence in Aiken's passage that if by "work of art" and "object itself" is meant "physical," or, more generally, "ontological" object, not only is its emotional effect "in us," but so is its sensory effect. The "work of music with its specifications of tempo, loudness, timbre, pitch, and so on," if it is to function as the expressive thing, must be an aesthetic object, i.e., a content of attention aesthetically contemplated. There is a possible ambiguity in the phrase "and so on." The sensory surface experienced by two contemplators, who are listening to the same orchestra, might be the same, or closely similar, when what the

[37] Henry D. Aiken, "Art as Expression and Surface," *The Journal of Aesthetics and Art Criticism*, IV, 2 (December 1945), p. 91.

surface suggests to them is very different. In such a case, if the listeners are attending not only to the surface but to what it suggests, they are not attending to the same aesthetic object; and a difference in the feeling import they experience can be attributed to a difference between the objects being attended to.

Aiken, no doubt, means to exclude this and similar possibilities. His view seems to be that, as a matter of fact, two contemplators, listening to the same orchestra, and attending *only* to a sensuous surface, can (a) both be apprehending the same surface and (b) can one of them apprehend the surface as solemn and the other apprehend it as gay.

The first thing to be said about this possibility is that, far from its being a "point of fact," whether it ever occurs is still a subject of controversy. Hartshorne analyzed what he describes, in what might very well be an understatement, as "a considerable quantity of experimental data (chaps. ii, iv, vii) which hitherto has lain scattered through the psychological literature, largely unknown to philosophers, and apparently not yet correlated and seen as a whole even by psychologists."[38] One of his conclusions is that "The assumption that persons whose sense of the meaning of a piece of music differs can yet have the very same sense perception of sounds is, so far as I know, devoid of all evidence."[39] Gestalt theorists not only deny the assertion Aiken begins with the words, "In point of fact"; they seem also to regard "the variability in the 'expressiveness' which the same (physical) work of art has for different obervers" as evidence of divergence in the phenomenal object apprehended.[40]

If we left the matter here, we could conclude the case against the two terms theory by saying that of four criteria for distinguishing between the two terms, three of them are useless for this purpose, while the fourth assumes something to be a well-known fact which is in truth a matter of controversy, yet to be resolved. But the case becomes stronger when we determine what the root of the controversy is.

Experimental results which seem to bear on the question whether sensory surface and feeling import can vary independently are not facts which speak for themselves. Suppose that when two subjects listened to an orchestra playing a tune with a brisk tempo, one of them reported that the music he heard was solemn, and the other reported that the music he heard

[38] *The Philosophy and Psychology of Sensation,* p. vii.

[39] *Ibid.,* p. 186.

[40] Cf. Kurt Koffka, "Problems in the Psychology of Art," *Bryn Mawr Notes and Monographs,* IX (1940).

was gay. How shall we interpret this fact? Possibly the subjects heard "the same music," but each experienced a different feeling import. But possibly the difference in feeling import is due to the fact that they did not hear "the same music." To decide between these possibilities, we need first to apply some criterion which tells us when the music two people hear is "the same."[41] I have no idea of what that criterion might be. Obviously, the criterion of identity of stimulus will not do. Possibly the interpretation one makes of results like our hypothetical one is determined, in large measure, by the theory one espouses concerning the nature of sensation, affection, and aesthetic expression. Thus, if one's theory implied that "quick solemnity" is *not* a contradiction in terms, one might be inclined to attach considerable weight to reports of disagreement in the feeling import experienced by different subjects in the presence of the same physical stimulus. Reports of such disagreement would count as "evidence" in favor of the independent variability of the two terms. On the other hand, if one's theory implied that "quick solemnity" *is* a contradiction, one might be inclined to sift such reports; and one might even emerge with the conclusion that the assumption of independent variability is, despite the reports, "devoid of all evidence."

If this is what the state of affairs is, the decision between the two terms theory and its rival cannot be made by a mere appeal to experimental data of the sort Aiken might have had in mind when he wrote that independent variability of aesthetic surface and feeling import is a point of fact. What the data tell us is ambiguous, and to remove the ambiguity we must apply a theory. When we consider which theory can most fruitfully be applied, we must bear in mind the logical difficulties involved in the usual versions of the two terms theory.

7. *Application of the concept of aesthetic expression to artistic expression.* If an account of aesthetic expression on the lines suggested in section 5 is correct, how should artistic expression, which is defined in terms of it, be conceived? What is the artist doing when he is "embodying" or "objectifying" feelings in a sensuous medium?

An enlightening preliminary point is one made earlier. Not all *objectively* expressive objects are products of artistic expression. We may adopt the attitude of aesthetic contemplation toward natural objects, such as sunsets, real landscapes, and driftwood; and, when we do, we find our experiences of them have their feeling import. Yet no one embodied his feelings in them. This fact suggests that artistic expression of feeling is not a process

41 Compare Arnold Isenberg, *Analytical Philosophy and the Study of Art* (A Report to the Rockefeller Foundation, 1950), p. 36.

by means of which an artist endows a sensuous material with a feeling quality it does not have, but one in which he is working with materials *already* charged with their specific feeling import. Reid says, "Expression, we shall argue, implies 'embodiment' of some sort in a 'body.' . . . And in some sense something *other* than the 'body' must be 'embodied.' "[42] On this view, it would seem, there is the feeling of the artist, and there is something *other* than his feeling, say a red patch devoid of feeling quality, and artistic expression or embodiment is the mysterious act which fuses the feeling with the patch. When the artist objectifies cheerfulness by painting a rosy apple, he is, so to speak, welding cheerfulness to a red, round patch. But the artist could not fuse a cheerful feeling with a depressing gray or a somber black. And when he does objectify cheerfulness by using cheerful colors, he is not fusing a feeling to anything.

Rather, in large measure, the task of the artist who is objectifying, embodying, or expressing feeling is one of *selecting*, from among a variety of materials each item of which is *already* charged with specific feeling import, that one or combination of them which, when contemplated by him, feels like the feeling he wishes to express.[43]

---

[42] *A Study in Aesthetics,* p. 47. See also p. 60.

[43] I do not want to imply that prior to the act of expression, the artist is fully aware of what he is trying to express.

Bibliography

Specific criticism of Tomas's paper (printed here) appears in a companion piece by Douglas Morgan, in the original Symposium, "The Concept of Expression in Art." Other of the best-known of recent discussions of the concept of expression include:

> O. K. Bouwsma, "The Expression Theory of Art," reprinted in William Elton (ed.), *Aesthetics and Language* (Oxford, 1954);
>
> John Hospers, "The Concept of Artistic Expression," reprinted (revised) in Morris Weitz (ed.), *Problems in Aesthetics* (New York, 1959).

The classic target of most contemporary discussions is found in:

> Benedetto Croce, *Aesthetic,* translated by Douglas Ainslie (2nd edition, London, 1922), Part I.

Also of interest in this regard are:

> R. G. Collingwood, *The Principles of Art* (Oxford, 1938), Chapters VI, VII, XII;
>
> John Hospers, "The Croce-Collingwood Theory of Art," *Philosophy,* Volume XXXI (1956), 3-20.

For other versions of the expression theory, see:

> John Dewey, *Art as Experience* (New York, 1934), Chapters IV-V;
>
> C. J. Ducasse, *The Philosophy of Art* (New York, 1929), Chapter VIII;
>
> Susanne Langer, *Feeling and Form* (New York, 1953), Chapter III;
>
> George Santayana, *The Sense of Beauty* (New York, 1896), Part IV;
>
> Leo Tolstoy, *What is Art?,* translated by Aylmer Maude (1905).

III

THE WORK OF ART

ESTHETICIANS are perennially trying to define what a work of art is. The variety of answers advanced is itself worth noticing, because it suggests that the question may be irregular in some way. Still, there is perhaps no quicker introduction to classical discussions of art than to summarize the master definitions that have been provided, say, from Plato to Clive Bell.

It should be noticed that 'work of art' is used in two entirely different ways, at the very least. For one, it is a value-laden term applied to things in virtue of certain alleged excellences. And for a second, it is one of the most basic category-terms in aesthetics, designating objects that are to be examined from a certain point of view—objects possibly, though not necessarily, entitled to be characterized as "works of art" on the first use of the phrase. This distinction is generally overlooked, though it would appear to affect decisively the nature of any effort to define 'work of art.'

The trouble with any effort to fix the basic category-term, 'work of art,' is that it will depend on what counts as an aesthetic point of view. But what counts as an aesthetic point of view cannot itself be decided by some simple inspection of actual usage. Philosophers seem to decide, more than

46

to find, what the boundaries of aesthetic interest are. And the definition of 'work of art' may vary according to the varying boundaries assigned to the aesthetic. This means that at least some apparent incompatibilities in definition may reflect the shifting decisions of philosophers regarding the definition of the aesthetic.

In recent years, the question has been raised whether (following the lead of Wittgenstein, who did not however discuss the concept) it is at all possible to isolate the essential and distinctive properties of works of art. It has been argued, for instance, that works of art exhibit only "family resemblances" or "strands of similarities" but not essential and distinctive properties common to all admitted instances. The question is a vexed one, because it is not entirely clear what sort of initial restrictions may properly be placed on the collection of things for which this claim, or the counterclaim, could be confirmed. Hence, if no restriction is allowed, it would seem trivially true that no definition of the required sort could be put forward, since an expression like 'work of art' is probably used in a great variety of somewhat unrelated ways (Is a sunset a work of art, for instance? Is life a work of art? Is driftwood art?). And if an initial restriction is allowed, will it be a logical or an empirical matter that a definition of the required sort cannot be found? The question at stake is not, specifically, *the* definition of art but the eligibility of the effort to define art.

Still, if 'work of art' is a basic category-term, its importance probably is to be located elsewhere than in the presumed effort to discover its essential conditions (which may, nevertheless, remain legitimate). Because to identify such essential conditions is to summarize the findings of other primary investigations—for instance, the nature and orientation of criticism upon the fine arts. That is, the definition probably serves to indicate the focus of a systematic account of other questions of aesthetics more directly concerned with the professional and amateur examination of works of art themselves.

Morris Weitz's Matchette Prize essay (1955) has undoubtedly been responsible for a lively reconsideration of what are perhaps the best-known theories in aesthetics, which have regularly been advanced in the form of definitions of art.

The Role of Theory in Aesthetics

MORRIS WEITZ

THEORY has been central in aesthetics and is still the preoccupation of the philosophy of art. Its main avowed concern remains the determination of the nature of art which can be formulated into a definition of it. It construes definition as the statement of the necessary and sufficient properties of what is being defined, where the statement purports to be a true or false claim about the essence of art, what characterizes and distinguishes it from everything else. Each of the great theories of art—Formalism, Voluntarism, Emotionalism, Intellectualism, Intuitionism, Organicism—converges on the attempt to state the defining properties of art. Each claims that it is the true theory because it has formulated correctly into a real definition the nature of art; and that the others are false because they have left out some necessary or sufficient property. Many theorists contend that their enterprise is no mere intellectual exercise but an absolute necessity for any understanding of art and our proper evaluation of it. Unless we know what art is, they say, what are its necessary and sufficient properties, we cannot begin to respond to it adequately or to say why one work is good or better than

From *The Journal of Aesthetics and Art Criticism*, Volume XV (September, 1956), 27-35. Reprinted by permission of the author and the editor of *The Journal of Aesthetics and Art Criticism*.

another. Aesthetic theory, thus, is important not only in itself but for the foundations of both appreciation and criticism. Philosophers, critics, and even artists who have written on art, agree that what is primary in aesthetics is a theory about the nature of art.

Is aesthetic theory, in the sense of a true definition or set of necessary and sufficient properties of art, possible? If nothing else does, the history of aesthetics itself should give one enormous pause here. For, in spite of the many theories, we seem no nearer our goal today than we were in Plato's time. Each age, each art-movement, each philosophy of art, tries over and over again to establish the stated ideal only to be succeeded by a new or revised theory, rooted, at least in part, in the repudiation of preceding ones. Even today, almost everyone interested in aesthetic matters is still deeply wedded to the hope that the correct theory of art is forthcoming. We need only examine the numerous new books on art in which new definitions are proffered; or, in our own country especially, the basic textbooks and anthologies to recognize how strong the priority of a theory of art is.

In this essay I want to plead for the rejection of this problem. I want to show that theory—in the requisite classical sense—is *never* forthcoming in aesthetics, and that we would do much better as philosophers to supplant the question, "What is the nature of art?," by other questions, the answers to which will provide us with all the understanding of the arts there can be. I want to show that the inadequacies of the theories are not primarily occasioned by any legitimate difficulty such, e.g., as the vast complexity of art, which might be corrected by further probing and research. Their basic inadequacies reside instead in a fundamental misconception of art. Aesthetic theory—all of it—is wrong in principle in thinking that a correct theory is possible because it radically misconstrues the logic of the concept of art. Its main contention that "art" is amenable to real or any kind of true definition is false. Its attempt to discover the necessary and sufficient properties of art is logically misbegotten for the very simple reason that such a set and, consequently, such a formula about it, is never forthcoming. Art, as the logic of the concept shows, has no set of necessary and sufficient properties, hence a theory of it is logically impossible and not merely factually difficult. Aesthetic theory tries to define what cannot be defined in its requisite sense. But in recommending the repudiation of aesthetic theory I shall not argue from this, as too many others have done, that its logical confusions render it meaningless or worthless. On the contrary, I wish to reassess its role and its contribution primarily in order to show that it is of the greatest importance to our understanding of the arts.

Let us now survey briefly some of the more famous extant aesthetic theories in order to see if they do incorporate correct and adequate statements about the nature of art. In each of these there is the assumption that it is the true enumeration of the defining properties of art, with the implication that previous theories have stressed wrong definitions. Thus, to begin with, consider a famous version of Formalist theory, that propounded by Bell and Fry. It is true that they speak mostly of painting in their writings but both assert that what they find in that art can be generalized for what is "art" in the others as well. The essence of painting, they maintain, are the plastic elements in relation. Its defining property is significant form, i.e., certain combinations of lines, colors, shapes, volumes—everything on the canvas except the representational elements—which evoke a unique response to such combinations. Painting is definable as plastic organization. The nature of art, what it *really* is, so their theory goes, is a unique combination of certain elements (the specifiable plastic ones) in their relations. Anything which is art is an instance of significant form; and anything which is not art has no such form.

To this the Emotionalist replies that the truly essential property of art has been left out. Tolstoy, Ducasse, or any of the advocates of this theory, find that the requisite defining property is not significant form but rather the expression of emotion in some sensuous public medium. Without projection of emotion into some piece of stone or words or sounds, etc., there can be no art. Art is really such embodiment. It is this that uniquely characterizes art, and any true, real definition of it, contained in some adequate theory of art, must so state it.

The Intuitionist disclaims both emotion and form as defining properties. In Croce's version, for example, art is identified not with some physical, public object but with a specific creative, cognitive and spiritual act. Art is really a first stage of knowledge in which certain human beings (artists) bring their images and intuitions into lyrical clarification or expression. As such, it is an awareness, non-conceptual in character, of the unique individuality of things; and since it exists below the level of conceptualization or action, it is without scientific or moral content. Croce singles out as the defining essence of art this first stage of spiritual life and advances its identification with art as a philosophically true theory or definition.

The Organicist says to all of this that art is really a class of organic wholes consisting of distinguishable, albeit inseparable, elements in their causally efficacious relations which are presented in some sensuous medium. In A. C. Bradley, in piece-meal versions of it in literary criticism, or in my own generalized adaptation of it in my *Philosophy of the Arts,* what is claimed is that anything which is a work of art is in its nature a unique complex of interrelated parts—in painting, for example, lines, colors, volumes, subjects, etc., all interacting upon one another on a paint surface of some sort. Certainly, at one time at least it seemed to me that this organic theory constituted the one true and real definition of art.

My final example is the most interesting of all, logically speaking. This is the Voluntarist theory of Parker. In his writings on art, Parker persistently calls into question the traditional simple-minded definitions of aesthetics. "The assumption underlying every philosophy of art is the existence of some common nature present in all the arts."[1] "All the so popular brief definitions of art—'significant form,' 'expression,' 'intuition,' 'objectified pleasure' —are fallacious, either because, while true of art, they are also true of much that is not art, and hence fail to differentiate art from other things; or else because they neglect some essential aspect of art."[2] But instead of inveighing against the attempt at definition of art itself, Parker insists that what is needed is a complex definition rather than a simple one. "The definition of art must therefore be in terms of a complex of characteristics. Failure to recognize this has been the fault of all the well-known definitions."[3] His own version of Voluntarism is the theory that art is essentially three things: embodiment of wishes and desires imaginatively satisfied, language, which characterizes the public medium of art, and harmony, which unifies the language with the layers of imaginative projections. Thus, for Parker, it is a true definition to say of art that it is ". . . the provision of satisfaction through the imagination, social significance, and harmony. I am claiming that nothing except works of art possesses all three of these marks."[4]

Now, all of these sample theories are inadequate in many different ways. Each purports to be a complete statement about the defining features of all works of art and yet each of them leaves out something which the others take to be central. Some are circular, e.g., the Bell-Fry theory of art as significant form which is defined in part in terms of our response to significant form. Some of them, in their search for necessary and sufficient properties, emphasize too few properties, like (again) the Bell-Fry definition which leaves out subject-representation in painting, or the Croce theory which omits inclusion of the very important feature of the public, physical character, say, of architecture. Others are too general and cover objects

---

[1] D. Parker, "The Nature of Art," reprinted in E. Vivas and M. Krieger, *The Problems of Aesthetics* (N.Y., 1953), p. 90.
[2] *Ibid.*, pp. 93-94.
[3] *Ibid.*, p. 94.
[4] *Ibid.*, p. 104.

that are not art as well as works of art. Organicism is surely such a view since it can be applied to *any* causal unity in the natural world as well as to art.[5] Still others rest on dubious principles, e.g., Parker's claim that art embodies imaginative satisfactions, rather than real ones; or Croce's assertion that there is nonconceptual knowledge. Consequently, even if art has one set of necessary and sufficient properties, none of the theories we have noted or, for that matter, no aesthetic theory yet proposed, has enumerated that set to the satisfaction of all concerned.

Then there is a different sort of difficulty. As real definitions, these theories are supposed to be factual reports on art. If they are, may we not ask, Are they empirical and open to verification or falsification? For example, what would confirm or disconfirm the theory that art is significant form or embodiment of emotion or creative synthesis of images? There does not even seem to be a hint of the kind of evidence which might be forthcoming to test these theories; and indeed one wonders if they are perhaps honorific definitions of "art," that is, proposed redefinitions in terms of some *chosen* conditions for applying the concept of art, and not true or false reports on the essential properties of art at all.

But all these criticisms of traditional aesthetic theories—that they are circular, incomplete, untestable, pseudo-factual, disguised proposals to change the meaning of concepts—have been made before. My intention is to go beyond these to make a much more fundamental criticism, namely, that aesthetic theory is a logically vain attempt to define what cannot be defined, to state the necessary and sufficient properties of that which has no necessary and sufficient properties, to conceive the concept of art as closed when its very use reveals and demands its openness.

The problem with which we must begin is not "What is art?," but "What sort of concept is 'art'?" Indeed, the root problem of philosophy itself is to explain the relation between the employment of certain kinds of concepts and the conditions under which they can be correctly applied. If I may paraphrase Wittgenstein, we must not ask, What is the nature of any philosophical x?, or even, according to the semanticist, What does "x" mean?, a transformation that leads to the disastrous interpretation of "art" as a name for some specifiable class of objects; but rather, What is the use or employment of "x"? What does "x" do in the language? This, I take it, is the initial question, the begin-all if not the end-all of any philosophical

[5] See M. Macdonald's review of my *Philosophy of the Arts, Mind,* Oct., 1951, pp. 561-564, for a brilliant discussion of this objection to the Organic theory.

problem and solution. Thus, in aesthetics, our first problem is the elucidation of the actual employment of the concept of art, to give a logical description of the actual functioning of the concept, including a description of the conditions under which we correctly use it or its correlates.

My model in this type of logical description or philosophy derives from Wittgenstein. It is also he who, in his refutation of philosophical theorizing in the sense of constructing definitions of philosophical entities, has furnished contemporary aesthetics with a starting point for any future progress. In his new work, *Philosophical Investigations*,[6] Wittgenstein raises as an illustrative question, What is a game? The traditional philosophical, theoretical answer would be in terms of some exhaustive set of properties common to all games. To this Wittgenstein says, let us consider what we call "games": "I mean board-games, card-games, ball-games, Olympic games, and so on. What is common to them all?—Don't say: 'there *must* be something common, or they would not be called "games"' but *look and see* whether there is anything common to all.—For if you look at them you will not see something that is common to *all*, but similarities, relationships, and a whole series of them at that . . ."

Card games are like board games in some respects but not in others. Not all games are amusing, nor is there always winning or losing or competition. Some games resemble others in some respects—that is all. What we find are no necessary and sufficient properties, only "a complicated network of similarities overlapping and crisscrossing," such that we can say of games that they form a family with family resemblances and no common trait. If one asks what a game is, we pick out sample games, describe these, and add, "This and *similar things* are called 'games.'" This is all we need to say and indeed all any of us knows about games. Knowing what a game is is not knowing some real definition or theory but being able to recognize and explain games and to decide which among imaginary and new examples would or would not be called "games."

The problem of the nature of art is like that of the nature of games, at least in these respects: If we actually look and see what it is that we call "art," we will also find no common properties—only strands of similarities. Knowing what art is is not apprehending some manifest or latent essence but being able to recognize, describe, and explain those things we call "art" in virtue of these similarities.

But the basic resemblance between these concepts is their open texture. In elucidating them, certain (paradigm) cases can be given, about which there

---

[6] L. Wittgenstein, *Philosophical Investigations* (Oxford, 1953), tr. by E. Anscombe; see esp. Part I, Sections 65-75. All quotations are from these sections.

can be no question as to their being correctly described as "art" or "game," but no exhaustive set of cases can be given. I can list some cases and some conditions under which I can apply correctly the concept of art but I cannot list all of them, for the all-important reason that unforeseeable or novel conditions are always forthcoming or envisageable.

A concept is open if its conditions of application are emendable and corrigible; i.e., if a situation or case can be imagined or secured which would call for some sort of *decision* on our part to extend the use of the concept to cover this, or to close the concept and invent a new one to deal with the new case and its new property. If necessary and sufficient conditions for the application of a concept can be stated, the concept is a closed one. But this can happen only in logic or mathematics where concepts are constructed and completely defined. It cannot occur with empirically-descriptive and normative concepts unless we arbitrarily close them by stipulating the ranges of their uses.

I can illustrate this open character of "art" best by examples drawn from its sub-concepts. Consider questions like "Is Dos Passos' *U. S. A.* a novel?," "Is V. Woolf's *To the Lighthouse* a novel?," "Is Joyce's *Finnegan's Wake* a novel?" On the traditional view, these are construed as factual problems to be answered yes or no in accordance with the presence or absence of defining properties. But certainly this is not how any of these questions is answered. Once it arises, as it has many times in the development of the novel from Richardson to Joyce (e.g., "Is Gide's *The School for Wives* a novel or a diary?"), what is at stake is no factual analysis concerning necessary and sufficient properties but a decision as to whether the work under examination is similar in certain respects to other works, already called "novels," and consequently warrants the extension of the concept to cover the new case. The new work is narrative, fictional, contains character delineation and dialogue but (say) it has no regular time-sequence in the plot or is interspersed with actual newspaper reports. It is like recognized novels, A, B, C . . . , in some respects but not like them in others. But then neither were B and C like A in some respects when it was decided to extend the concept applied to A to B and C. Because work N + 1 (the brand new work) is like A, B, C . . . N in certain respects—has strands of similarity to them—the concept is extended and a new phase of the novel engendered. "Is N+1 a novel?," then, is no factual, but rather a decision problem, where the verdict turns on whether or not we enlarge our set of conditions for applying the concept.

What is true of the novel is, I think, true of every sub-concept of art: "tragedy," "comedy," "painting," "opera," etc., of "art" itself. No "Is X a novel, painting, opera, work of art, etc.?" question allows of a definitive answer in the sense of a factual yes or no report. "Is this *collage* a painting or not?" does not rest on any set of necessary and sufficient properties of painting but on whether we decide—as we did!—to extend "painting" to cover this case.

"Art," itself, is an open concept. New conditions (cases) have constantly arisen and will undoubtedly constantly arise; new art forms, new movements will emerge, which will demand decisions on the part of those interested, usually professional critics, as to whether the concept should be extended or not. Aestheticians may lay down similarity conditions but never necessary and sufficient ones for the correct application of the concept. With "art" its conditions of application can never be exhaustively enumerated since new cases can always be envisaged or created by artists, or even nature, which would call for a decision on someone's part to extend or to close the old or to invent a new concept. (E.g., "It's not a sculpture, it's a mobile.")

What I am arguing, then, is that the very expansive, adventurous character of art, its ever-present changes and novel creations, makes it logically impossible to ensure any set of defining properties. We can, of course, choose to close the concept. But to do this with "art" or "tragedy" or "portraiture," etc., is ludicrous since it forecloses on the very conditions of creativity in the arts.

Of course there are legitimate and serviceable closed concepts in art. But these are always those whose boundaries of conditions have been drawn for a *special* purpose. Consider the difference, for example, between "tragedy" and "(extant) Greek tragedy." The first is open and must remain so to allow for the possibility of new conditions, e.g., a play in which the hero is not noble or fallen or in which there is no hero but other elements that are like those of plays we already call "tragedy." The second is closed. The plays it can be applied to, the conditions under which it can be correctly used are all in, once the boundary, "Greek," is drawn. Here the critic can work out a theory or real definition in which he lists the common properties at least of the extant Greek tragedies. Aristotle's definition, false as it is as a theory of all the plays of Aeschylus, Sophocles, and Euripides, since it does not cover some of them,[7] properly called "tragedies," can be interpreted as a real (albeit incorrect) definition of this closed concept; although it can also be, as it unfortunately has been, conceived as a purported real definition of "tragedy," in which case it suffers from the logical mistake of trying to define what cannot be defined—of trying to squeeze what is an open concept into an honorific formula for a closed concept.

[7] See H. D. F. Kitto, *Greek Tragedy* (London, 1939), on this point.

What is supremely important, if the critic is not to become muddled, is to get absolutely clear about the way in which he conceives his concepts; otherwise he goes from the problem of trying to define "tragedy," etc., to an arbitrary closing of the concept in terms of certain preferred conditions or characteristics which he sums up in some linguistic recommendation that he mistakenly thinks is a real definition of the open concept. Thus, many critics and aestheticians ask, "What is tragedy?," choose a class of samples for which they may give a true account of its common properties, and then go on to construe this account of the chosen closed class as a true definition or theory of the whole open class of tragedy. This, I think, is the logical mechanism of most of the so-called theories of the sub-concepts of art: "tragedy," "comedy," "novel," etc. In effect, this whole procedure, subtly deceptive as it is, amounts to a transformation of correct criteria for *recognizing* members of certain legitimately closed classes of works of art into recommended criteria for *evaluating* any putative member of the class.

The primary task of aesthetics is not to seek a theory but to elucidate the concept of art. Specifically, it is to describe the conditions under which we employ the concept correctly. Definition, reconstruction, patterns of analysis are out of place here since they distort and add nothing to our understanding of art. What, then, is the logic of "X is a work of art"?

As we actually use the concept, "Art" is both descriptive (like "chair") and evaluative (like "good"); i.e., we sometimes say, "This is a work of art," to describe something and we sometimes say it to evaluate something. Neither use surprises anyone.

What, first, is the logic of "X is a work of art," when it is a descriptive utterance? What are the conditions under which we would be making such an utterance correctly? There are no necessary and sufficient conditions but there are the strands of similarity conditions, i.e., bundles of properties, none of which need be present but most of which are, when we describe things as works of art. I shall call these the "criteria of recognition" of works of art. All of these have served as the defining criteria of the individual traditional theories of art; so we are already familiar with them. Thus, mostly, when we describe something as a work of art, we do so under the conditions of there being present some sort of artifact, made by human skill, ingenuity, and imagination, which embodies in its sensuous, public medium—stone, wood, sounds, words, etc.—certain distinguishable elements and relations. Special theorists would add conditions like satisfaction of wishes, objectification or expression of emotion, some act of empathy, and so on; but these latter conditions seem to be quite adventitious, present to some but not to other spectators when things are described as works of art. "X is a work of art and contains *no* emotion, expression, act of empathy, satisfaction, etc.," is perfectly good sense and may frequently be true. "X is a work of art and . . . was made by no one," or . . . "exists only in the mind and not in any publicly observable thing," or . . . "was made by accident when he spilled the paint on the canvas," in each case of which a normal condition is denied, are also sensible and capable of being true in certain circumstances. None of the criteria of recognition is a defining one, either necessary or sufficient, because we can sometimes assert of something that it is a work of art and go on to deny any one of these conditions, even the one which has traditionally been taken to be basic, namely, that of being an artifact: Consider, "This piece of driftwood is a lovely piece of sculpture." Thus, to say of anything that it is a work of art is to commit oneself to the presence of *some* of these conditions. One would scarcely describe X as a work of art if X were not an artifact, or a collection of elements sensuously presented in a medium, or a product of human skill, and so on. If none of the conditions were present, if there were no criteria present for recognizing something as a work of art, we would not describe it as one. But, even so, no one of these or any collection of them is either necessary or sufficient.

The elucidation of the descriptive use of "Art" creates little difficulty. But the elucidation of the evaluative use does. For many, especially theorists, "This is a work of art" does more than describe; it also praises. Its conditions of utterance, therefore, include certain preferred properties or characteristics of art. I shall call these "criteria of evaluation." Consider a typical example of this evaluative use, the view according to which to say of something that it is a work of art is to imply that it is a *successful* harmonization of elements. Many of the honorific definitions of art and its sub-concepts are of this form. What is at stake here is that "Art" is construed as an evaluative term which is either identified with its criterion or justified in terms of it. "Art" is defined in terms of its evaluative property, e.g., successful harmonization. On such a view, to say "X is a work of art" is (1) to say something which is taken *to mean* "X is a successful harmonization" (e.g., "Art *is* significant form") or (2) to say something praiseworthy *on the basis* of its successful harmonization. Theorists are never clear whether it is (1) or (2) which is being put forward. Most of them, concerned as they are with this evaluative use, formulate (2), i.e., that feature of art that *makes* it art in the praise-sense, and then go on to state (1), i.e., the definition of "Art" in terms of its art-making feature. And this is clearly to confuse the conditions under which we say something evaluatively with the meaning of what we say. "This is a work of art," said evaluatively, cannot mean "This is a successful harmonization of elements"—except by stipulation—but at most is said in virtue of the art-making property, which is taken as a (the) criterion of "Art," when "Art" is employed to assess. "This is a work of art," used evaluatively, serves to praise and not to affirm the reason why it is said.

The evaluative use of "Art," although distinct from the conditions of its use, relates in a very intimate way to these conditions. For, in every instance of "This is a work of art" (used to praise), what happens is that the criterion of evaluation (e.g., successful harmonization) for the employment of the concept of art is converted into a criterion of recognition. This is why, on its evaluative use, "This is a work of art" implies "This has P," where "P" is some chosen art-making property. Thus, if one chooses to employ "Art" evaluatively, as many do, so that "This is a work of art and not (aesthetically) good" makes no sense, he uses "Art" in such a way that he refuses to *call* anything a work of art unless it embodies his criterion of excellence.

There is nothing wrong with the evaluative use; in fact, there is good reason for using "Art" to praise. But what cannot be maintained is that theories of the evaluative use of "Art" are true and real definitions of the necessary and sufficient properties of art. Instead they are honorific definitions, pure and simple, in which "Art" has been redefined in terms of chosen criteria.

But what makes them—these honorific definitions—so supremely valuable is not their disguised linguistic recommendations; rather it is the *debates* over the reasons for changing the criteria of the concept of art which are built into the definitions. In each of the great theories of art, whether correctly understood as honorific definitions or incorrectly accepted as real definitions, what is of the utmost importance are the reasons proffered in the argument for the respective theory, that is, the reasons given for the chosen or preferred criterion of excellence and evaluation. It is this perennial debate over these criteria of evaluation which makes the history of aesthetic theory the important study it is. The value of each of the theories resides in its attempt to state and to justify certain criteria which are either neglected or distorted by previous theories. Look at the Bell-Fry theory again. Of course, "Art is significant form" cannot be accepted as a true, real definition of art; and most certainly it actually functions in their aesthetics as a re-definition of art in terms of the chosen condition of significant form. But what gives it its aesthetic importance is what lies behind the formula: In an age in which literary and representational elements have become paramount in painting, *return* to the plastic ones since these are indigenous to painting. Thus, the role of the theory is not to define anything but to use the definitional form, almost epigrammatically, to pin-point a crucial recommendation to turn our attention once again to the plastic elements in painting.

Once we, as philosophers, understand this distinction between the formula and what lies behind it, it behooves us to deal generously with the traditional theories of art; because incorporated in every one of them is a debate over and argument for emphasizing or centering upon some particular feature of art which has been neglected or perverted. If we take the aesthetic theories literally, as we have seen, they all fail; but if we reconstrue them, in terms of their function and point, as serious and argued-for recommendations to concentrate on certain criteria of excellence in art, we shall see that aesthetic theory is far from worthless. Indeed, it becomes as central as anything in aesthetics, in our understanding of art, for it teaches us what to look for and how to look at it in art. What is central and must be articulated in all the theories are their debates over the reasons for excellence in art—debates over emotional depth, profound truths, natural beauty, exactitude, freshness of treatment, and so on, as criteria of evaluation—the whole of which converges on the perennial problem of what makes a work of art good. To understand the role of aesthetic theory is not to conceive it as definition, logically doomed to failure, but to read it as summaries of seriously made recommendations to attend in certain ways to certain features of art.

Bibliography

The most recent discussions of the definition of a work of art include:

Monroe C. Beardsley, "The Definition of the Arts," *Journal of Aesthetics and Art Criticism,* Volume XX (1961), 175-187;

Margaret Macdonald, "Art and Imagination," *Proceedings of the Aristotelian Society,* Volume LIII (1952-1953);

Joseph Margolis, "Mr. Weitz and the Definition of Art," *Philosophical Studies,* Volume IX (1958), 88-94;

Douglas N. Morgan, "Art Pure and Simple," *Journal of Aesthetics and Art Criticism,* Volume XX (1961), 187-195;

Mary Mothersill, "Critical Comments," *Journal of Aesthetics and Art Criticism,* Volume XX (1961), 195-198; Comments on Beardsley and Morgan (above) in a joint symposium;

C. L. Stevenson, "On 'What is a Poem?,'" *Philosophical Review,* Volume LXVI (1957), 329-362;

Paul Ziff, "The Task of Defining a Work of Art," *Philosophical Review,* Volume LXIII (1953), 68-78.

Reference may also be made, for the general philosophical setting for all of these papers (including Weitz's), to:

Ludwig Wittgenstein, *Philosophical Investigations,* trans. by G. E. M. Anscombe (New York, 1953), I, pars. 65-67.

Related papers, concerned with the individuation of works of art, include:

Monroe Beardsley, *Aesthetics* (New York, 1958), Chapter I;

Donald Henze, "Is the Work of Art a Construct?," *Journal of Philosophy,* Volume LII (1955), 433-439;

Margaret Macdonald, "Some Distinctive Features of Arguments Used in Criticism of the Arts," reprinted (revised) in William Elton (ed.), *Aesthetics and Language* (Oxford, 1954);

Joseph Margolis, "The Identity of a Work of Art," *Mind,* Volume LXVII (1959), 34-50;

Stephen Pepper, "Further Considerations on the Aesthetic Work of Art," *Journal of Philosophy,* Volume XLIX (1952), 274-279;

Jeanne Wacker, "Particular Works of Art," *Mind,* Volume LIX (1960), 223-233;

Paul Ziff, "Art and the 'Object of Art,' " reprinted in Elton, *loc. cit.*

IV

AESTHETIC QUALITIES

CONTEMPORARY linguistic analysis has benefited aesthetics, in a very notice-able way, by subjecting to detailed scrutiny large lists of the familiar terms we use to characterize works of art. The truth is that this examination has never been attempted before in a fully systematic way and with the advantage of a powerful and well-developed philosophical method. The result has been some discoveries of considerable importance.

The pivotal question for all such analysis is, what are the conditions on which we correctly apply a characterizing term to a given work of art? The finding has been that these vary strikingly with different sets of terms. The question is obviously important, since only by means of the analysis indicated could we hope to describe the logical nature of disputes about works of art. Is, for example, this Rembrandt *somber?* Are those colors *garish?* Would you say she has a *regal* manner? Clearly, the issue spreads far beyond the narrow confines of art to the appreciative remarks we make in general conversation.

There is, of course, an extraordinarily large number of respects in which all of our characterizing terms may be classified. Can we state necessary conditions for their use? sufficient conditions? necessary and sufficient conditions? Are there terms for which we can supply neither necessary nor sufficient conditions? If there are, how is their use supported? Are there purely descriptive terms? purely evaluative terms? terms which are mixed in this regard? Are there descriptive and evaluative terms whose proper use depends on affective responses on our part? on dispositions to respond? Are there terms for which one can provide paradigm cases? terms for which one cannot? And if the latter (think of epithets like "He's the Michelangelo of poetry"), can and how can they be supported?

From the vantage of a large perspective, one can see that the sort of analysis indicated is simply the application of a widespread method of working to a range of terms having a somewhat local interest for specialists in aesthetics and the arts. The main force of this way of working has already been marked out very clearly in the philosophical contributions of such authors as Wittgenstein and John Wisdom. But what is fascinating to observe is the correspondence among findings made in the most disparate fields of philosophical analysis.

The point can be made in either of two ways. We have been made to notice that a large number of expressions central to talk in different domains are readily but informally associated with paradigm instances, without, however, permitting us to formulate either necessary or sufficient conditions for their use. Otherwise stated, we have been made to notice that arguments supporting certain sorts of judgment central in different domains cannot be classified as deductive or inductive but depend on some "intermediate" logic in accord with which we may specify only "characteristically" favorable or unfavorable evidence. There are cases, that is, in which we argue more from instance to instance than from principle or rule to application. And this, it turns out, is particularly worth emphasizing in the domain of aesthetics.

Frank Sibley's discussion of qualities prominent in aesthetic discourse is probably the most thoroughgoing effort made to date to fix the "intermediate" logic of the bulk of the expressions employed there.

Aesthetic Concepts

FRANK SIBLEY

THE remarks we make about works of art are of many kinds. For the
purpose of this paper I wish to indicate two broad groups. I shall do
this by examples. We say that a novel has a great number of characters
and deals with life in a manufacturing town; that a painting uses pale
colors, predominantly blues and greens, and has kneeling figures in the
foreground; that the theme in a fugue is inverted at such a point and that
there is a stretto at the close; that the action of a play takes place in the
span of one day and that there is a reconciliation scene in the fifth act.
Such remarks may be made by, and such features pointed out to, anyone
with normal eyes, ears, and intelligence. On the other hand, we also say
that a poem is tightly-knit or deeply moving; that a picture lacks balance,
or has a certain serenity and repose, or that the grouping of the figures sets
up an exciting tension; that the characters in a novel never really come to
life, or that a certain episode strikes a false note. It would be neutral enough
to say that the making of such judgments as these requires the exercise of
taste, perceptiveness, or sensitivity, of aesthetic discrimination or apprecia-

From *The Philosophical Review,* Volume LXVIII (October, 1959), 421-450 (now, with
extensive minor revisions). Reprinted with the permission of the author and *The
Philosophical Review.*

tion; one would not say this of my first group. Accordingly, when a word or expression is such that taste or perceptiveness is required in order to apply it, I shall call it an *aesthetic* term or expression, and I shall, correspondingly, speak of *aesthetic* concepts or *taste* concepts.[1]

Aesthetic terms span a great range of types and could be grouped into various kinds and sub-species. But it is not my present purpose to attempt any such grouping; I am interested in what they all have in common. Their almost endless variety is adequately displayed in the following list: *unified, balanced, integrated, lifeless, serene, somber, dynamic, powerful, vivid, delicate, moving, trite, sentimental, tragic.* The list of course is not limited to adjectives; expressions in artistic contexts like *telling contrast, sets up a tension, conveys a sense of,* or *holds it together* are equally good illustrations. It includes terms used by both layman and critic alike, as well as some which are mainly the property of professional critics and specialists.

I have gone for my examples of aesthetic expressions in the first place to critical and evaluative discourse about works of art because it is there particularly that they abound. But now I wish to widen the topic; we employ terms the use of which requires an exercise of taste not only when discussing the arts but quite liberally throughout discourse in everyday life. The examples given above are expressions which, appearing in critical contexts, most usually, if not invariably, have an aesthetic use; outside critical discourse the majority of them more frequently have some other use unconnected with taste. But many expressions do double duty even in everyday discourse, sometimes being used as aesthetic expressions and sometimes not. Other words again, whether in artistic or daily discourse, function only or predominantly as aesthetic terms; of this kind are *graceful, delicate, dainty, handsome, comely, elegant, garish.* Finally, to make the contrast with all the preceding examples, there are many words which are seldom used as aesthetic terms at all: *red, noisy, brackish, clammy, square, docile, curved, evanescent, intelligent, faithful, derelict, tardy, freakish.*

Clearly, when we employ words as aesthetic terms we are often making and using metaphors, pressing into service words which do not primarily function in this manner. Certainly also, many words *have come* to be aesthetic terms by some kind of metaphorical transference. This is so with those like "dynamic," "melancholy," "balanced," "tightly-knit" which, except in artistic and critical writings, are not normally aesthetic terms. But

[1] I shall speak loosely of an "aesthetic term," even when, because the word sometimes has other uses, it would be more correct to speak of its *use* as an aesthetic term. I shall also speak of "nonaesthetic" words, concepts, features, and so on. None of the terms other writers use, "natural," "observable," "perceptual," "physical," "objective" (qualities), "neutral," "descriptive" (language), when they approach the distinction I am making, is really apt for my purpose.

the aesthetic vocabulary must not be thought wholly metaphorical. Many words, including the most common (*lovely, pretty, beautiful, dainty, graceful, elegant*), are certainly not being used metaphorically when employed as aesthetic terms, the very good reason being that this is their primary or only use, some of them having no current non-aesthetic use. And though expressions like "dynamic," "balanced," and so forth *have come* by a metaphorical shift to be aesthetic terms, their employment in criticism can scarcely be said to be more than quasi-metaphorical. Having entered the language of art description and criticism as metaphors they are now standard vocabulary in that language.[2]

The expressions I am calling aesthetic terms form no small segment of our discourse. Often, it is true, people with normal intelligence and good eyesight and hearing lack, at least in some measure, the sensitivity required to apply them; a man need not be stupid or have poor eyesight to fail to see that something is graceful. Thus taste or sensitivity is somewhat more rare than certain other human capacities; people who exhibit a sensitivity both wide-ranging and refined are a minority. It is over the application of aesthetic terms too that, notoriously, disputes and differences sometimes go helplessly unsettled. But almost everybody is able to exercise taste to some degree and in some matters. It is surprising therefore that aesthetic terms have been so largely neglected. They have received glancing treatment in the course of other aesthetic discussions; but as a broad category they have not received the direct attention they merit.

The foregoing has marked out the area I wish to discuss. One warning should perhaps be given. When I speak of taste in this paper, I shall not be dealing with questions which center upon expressions like "a matter of taste" (meaning, roughly, a matter of personal preference or liking). It is with an ability to *notice* or *see* or *tell* that things have certain qualities that I am concerned.

I

In order to support our application of an aesthetic term, we often refer to features the mention of which involves other aesthetic terms: "it has an extraordinary vitality because of its free and vigorous style of drawing," "graceful in the smooth flow of its lines," "dainty because of the delicacy

---

[2] A contrast will reinforce this. If a critic were to describe a passage of music as chattering, carbonated, or gritty, a painter's coloring as vitreous, farinaceous, or effervescent, or a writer's style as glutinous, or abrasive, he *would* be using live metaphors rather than drawing on the more normal language of criticism. Words like "athletic," "vertiginous," "silken" may fall somewhere between.

and harmony of its coloring." It is as normal to do this as it is to justify
one mental epithet by other epithets of the same general type, *intelligent*
by *ingenious, inventive, acute,* and so on. But often when we apply aesthetic
terms, we explain why by referring to features which do *not* depend for
their recognition upon an exercise of taste: "delicate because of its pastel
shades and curving lines," or "it lacks balance because one group of figures
is so far off to the left and is so brightly illuminated." When no explanation of this latter kind is offered, it is legitimate to ask or search for one.
Finding a satisfactory answer may sometimes be difficult, but one cannot
ordinarily reject the question. When we cannot ourselves quite say what
non-aesthetic features make something delicate or unbalanced or powerful
or moving, the good critic often puts his finger on something which strikes
us as the right explanation. In short, aesthetic terms always ultimately apply
because of, and aesthetic qualities always ultimately depend upon, the
presence of features which, like curving or angular lines, color contrasts,
placing of masses, or speed of movement, are visible, audible, or otherwise
discernible without any exercise of taste or sensibility. Whatever kind of
dependence this is, and there are various relationships between aesthetic
qualities and non-aesthetic features, what I want to make clear in this
paper is that there are no non-aesthetic features which serve in *any* circumstances as logically *sufficient conditions* for applying aesthetic terms.
Aesthetic or taste concepts are not in *this* respect condition-governed at all.

There is little temptation to suppose that aesthetic terms resemble words
which, like "square," are applied in accordance with a set of necessary and
sufficient conditions. For whereas each square is square in virtue of the *same*
set of conditions, four equal sides and four right angles, aesthetic terms
apply to widely varied objects; one thing is graceful because of these features,
another because of those, and so on almost endlessly. In recent times philosophers have broken the spell of the strict necessary-and-sufficient model
by showing that many everyday concepts are not of that type. Instead, they
have described various other types of concepts which are governed only in
a much looser way by conditions. However, since these newer models
provide satisfactory accounts of many familiar concepts, it might plausibly
be thought that aesthetic concepts are of some such kind and that they
similarly are governed in some looser way by conditions. I want to argue
that aesthetic concepts differ radically from any of these other concepts.

Amongst these concepts to which attention has recently been paid are
those for which no *necessary-and-sufficient* conditions can be provided, but
for which there are a number of relevant features, A, B, C, D, E, such that
the presence of some groups or combinations of these features is *sufficient*

for the application of the concept. The list of relevant features may be an open one; that is, given A, B, C, D, E, we may not wish to close off the possible relevance of other unlisted features beyond E. Examples of such concepts might be "dilatory," "discourteous," "possessive," "capricious," "prosperous," "intelligent" (but see below p. 71). If we begin a list of features relevant to "intelligent" with, for example, ability to grasp and follow various kinds of instructions, ability to master facts and marshall evidence, ability to solve mathematical or chess problems, we might go on adding to this list almost indefinitely.

However, with concepts of this sort, although decisions may have to be made and judgment exercised, it is always possible to extract and state, from cases which have *already* clearly been decided, the sets of features or conditions which were regarded as sufficient in those cases. These relevant features which I am calling conditions are, it should be noted, features which, though not sufficient *alone* and needing to be combined with other similar features, nevertheless carry some weight and can count only in one direction. Being a good chess player can count only *towards* and not *against* intelligence. Whereas mention of it may enter sensibly along with other remarks in expressions like "I say he is intelligent because . . ." or "the reason I call him intelligent is that . . . ;" it cannot be used to complete such negative expressions as "I say he is *un*intelligent because. . . ." But what I want particularly to emphasize about features which function as conditions for a term is that *some* group or set of them *is* sufficient fully to ensure or warrant the application of that term. An individual characterized by some of these features may not yet qualify to be called lazy or intelligent, and so on, beyond all question, but all that is needed is to add some further (indefinite) number of such characterizations and a point is reached where we have enough. There are individuals possessing a number of such features of whom one cannot deny, cannot but admit, that they are intelligent. We have left necessary-and-sufficient conditions behind, but we are still in the realm of sufficient conditions.

But aesthetic concepts are not condition-governed even in this way. There are no sufficient conditions, no non-aesthetic features such that the presence of some set or numbers of them will beyond question logically justify or warrant the application of an aesthetic term. It is impossible (barring certain limited exceptions, see below pp. 73-74) to make any statements corresponding to those we can make for condition-governed words. We are able to say "If it is true he can do this, and that, and the other, then one just cannot deny that he is intelligent," or "if he does A, B, and C, I don't see how it can be denied that he is lazy," but we cannot make *any* general statement of the form "If the vase is pale pink, somewhat curving, lightly mottled, and so forth, it will be delicate, cannot but be delicate." Nor again can one say *any* such things here as "Being tall and thin is not enough *alone* to ensure that a vase is delicate, but if it is, for example, slightly curving and pale colored (and so forth) as well, it cannot be denied that it is." Things may be described to us in non-aesthetic terms as fully as we please but we are not thereby put in the position of having to admit (or being unable to deny) that they are delicate or graceful or garish or exquisitely balanced.[3]

No doubt there are some respects in which aesthetic terms *are* governed by conditions or rules. For instance, it may be impossible that a thing should be garish if all its colors are pale pastels, or flamboyant if all its lines are straight. There may be, that is, descriptions using only non-aesthetic terms which are incompatible with descriptions employing certain aesthetic terms. If I am told that a painting in the next room consists solely of one or two bars of very pale blue and very pale grey set at right angles on a pale fawn ground, I can be sure that it cannot be fiery or garish or gaudy or flamboyant. A description of this sort may make certain aesthetic terms *in*applicable or *in*appropriate; and if from this description I inferred that the picture was, or even might be, fiery or gaudy or flamboyant, this might be taken as showing a failure to understand these words. I do not wish to deny therefore that taste concepts may be governed *negatively* by conditions.[4] What I am emphasizing is that they quite lack governing conditions of a sort many other concepts possess. Though on *seeing* the picture we might say, and rightly, that it is delicate or serene or restful or sickly or insipid, no *description* in non-aesthetic terms permits us to claim that these or any other aesthetic terms must undeniably apply to it.

I have said that if an object is characterized *solely* by certain sorts of features this may count decisively against the possibility of applying to it certain aesthetic terms. But of course the presence of *some* such features need not count decisively; other features may be enough to outweigh those

---

[3] In a paper reprinted in *Aesthetics and Language,* ed. by W. Elton (Oxford, 1954), pp. 131-146, Arnold Isenberg discusses certain problems about aesthetic concepts and qualities. Like others who approach these problems, he does not isolate them, as I do, from questions about verdicts on the *merits* of works of art, or from questions about *likings* and *preferences.* He says something parallel to my remarks above: "There is not in all the world's criticism a single purely descriptive statement concerning which one is prepared to say beforehand, 'if it is true, I shall *like* that work so much the better'" (p. 139, my italics). I should think *this* is highly questionable.

[4] Isenberg (*op. cit.* p. 132) makes a somewhat similar but mistaken point: "If we had been told that the colors of a certain painting are garish, it would be *astonishing* to find that they are all, very pale and unsaturated" (my italics). But if we say "all" rather than "predominantly," then "astonishing" is the wrong word. The word that goes with "all" is "impossible"; "astonishing" might go with "predominantly."

which, on their own, would render the aesthetic term inapplicable. A painting might be garish even though much of its color is pale. These facts call attention to a further feature of taste concepts. One *can* find general features or descriptions which in some sense count in one direction only, only *for* or only *against* the application of certain aesthetic terms. Angularity, fatness, brightness, or intensity of color are typically *not* associated with delicacy or grace. Slimness, lightness, gentle curves, lack of intensity of color are associated with delicacy, but not with flamboyance, majesty, grandeur, splendor or garishness. This is shown by the naturalness of saying, for example, that someone is graceful *because* she's so light, but *in spite of* being quite angular or heavily built; and by the corresponding oddity of saying that something is graceful *because* it is so heavy or angular, or delicate *because* of its bright and intense coloring. This may therefore sound quite similar to what I have said already about conditions in discussing terms like "intelligent." There are nevertheless very significant differences. Although there is this sense in which slimness, lightness, lack of intensity of color, and so on, count only towards, not against, delicacy, these features, I shall say, at best count only *typically* or *characteristically* towards delicacy; they do not count towards in the same sense as condition-features count towards laziness or intelligence; that is, no group of them is ever logically sufficient.

One way of reinforcing this is to notice how features which are characteristically associated with one aesthetic term may also be similarly associated with other and rather different aesthetic terms. "Graceful" and "delicate" may be on the one hand sharply contrasted with terms like "violent," "grand," "fiery," "garish," or "massive" which have characteristic non-aesthetic features quite unlike those for "delicate" and "graceful." But on the other hand "graceful" and "delicate" may also be contrasted with aesthetic terms which stand much closer to them, like "flaccid," "weakly," "washed out," "lanky," "anaemic," "wan," "insipid"; and the range of features characteristic of *these* qualities, pale color, slimness, lightness, lack of angularity and sharp contrast, is virtually identical with the range for "delicate" and "graceful." Similarly many of the features typically associated with "joyous," "fiery," "robust," or "dynamic" are identical with those associated with "garish," "strident," "turbulent," "gaudy," or "chaotic." Thus an object which is described very fully, but exclusively in terms of qualities characteristic of delicacy, may turn out on inspection to be not delicate at all, but anaemic or insipid. The failures of novices and the artistically inept prove that quite close similarity in point of line, color, or technique gives no assurance of gracefulness or delicacy. A failure and a success in the manner of Degas may be generally more alike, so far as their non-aesthetic features go, than either is like a successful Fragonard. But it is not necessary to go even this far to make my main point. A painting which has only the kind of features one would associate with vigor and energy but which even so fails to be vigorous and energetic *need* not have some other character, need not be instead, say, strident or chaotic. It may fail to have any particular character whatever. It may employ bright colors, and the like, without being particularly lively and vigorous at all; but one may feel unable to describe it as chaotic or strident or garish either. It is, rather, simply lacking in character (though of course this too is an aesthetic judgment; taste is exercised also in seeing that the painting has no character).

There are of course many features which do not in these ways characteristically count for (or against) particular aesthetic qualities. One poem has strength and power because of the regularity of its meter and rhyme; another is monotonous and lacks drive and strength because of its regular meter and rhyme. We do not feel the need to switch from "because of" to "in spite of." However, I have concentrated upon features which are characteristically associated with aesthetic qualities because, if a case could be made for the view that taste concepts are in any way governed by sufficient conditions, these would seem to be the most promising candidates for governing conditions. But to say that features are associated only *characteristically* with an aesthetic term *is* to say that they can never amount to sufficient conditions; no description however full, even in terms characteristic of gracefulness, puts it beyond question that something is graceful in the way a description may put it beyond question that someone is lazy or intelligent.

It is important to observe, however, that in this paper I am not merely claiming that no sufficient conditions can be stated for taste concepts. For if this were all, taste concepts might not be after all really different from one kind of concept recently discussed. They could be accommodated perhaps with those concepts which Professor H. L. A. Hart has called "defeasible"; it is a characteristic of defeasible concepts that we cannot state sufficient conditions for them because, for any sets we offer, there is always an (open) list of defeating conditions any of which might rule out the application of the concept. The most we can say schematically for a defeasible concept is that, for example, A, B, and C together are sufficient for the concept to apply *unless* some feature is present which overrides or voids them. But, I want to emphasize, the very fact that we *can* say this sort of thing shows that we are still to that extent in the realm of conditions.[5] The features governing defeasible concepts can ordinarily count only one way, *either* for *or* against. To take Hart's example, "offer" and "acceptance" can count only towards the existence of a valid contract, and fraudulent misrepresentation, duress, and lunacy can count only against. And even with defeasible concepts, if we are told that there are no voiding features present, we can know that some set of conditions or features, A, B, C, . . ., is enough, in this absence of voiding features, to ensure, for example, that there is a contract. The very notion of a defeasible concept seems to require that some group of features *would* be sufficient *in certain circumstances,* that is, in the absence of overriding or voiding features. In a certain way defeasible concepts lack sufficient conditions then, but they are still, in the sense described, condition-governed. My claim about taste concepts is stronger; that they are not, except negatively, governed by conditions at all. We could not conclude even in certain circumstances, e.g., if we were told of the absence of all "voiding" or uncharacteristic features (no angularities, and the like), that an object *must* certainly be graceful, no matter how fully it was described to us as possessing features characteristic of gracefulness.

My arguments and illustrations so far have been rather simply schematic. Many concepts, including most of the examples I have used (*intelligent,* and so on, p. 67), are much more thoroughly open and complex than my illustrations suggest. Not only may there be an open list of relevant conditions; it may be impossible to give precise rules telling how many features from the list are needed for a sufficient set or in which combinations; impossible similarly to give precise rules covering the extent or degree to which such features need to be present in those combinations. Indeed, we may have to abandon as futile any attempt to describe or formulate anything like a complete set of precise conditions or rules, and content ourselves with giving only some general account of the concept, making reference to samples or cases or precedents. We cannot fully master or employ these concepts therefore *simply* by being equipped with lists of conditions, readily applicable procedures or sets of rules, however complex. For to exhibit a mastery of one of these concepts we must be able to go ahead and apply the word correctly to new individual cases, at least to central ones; and each new case may be a uniquely different object, just as each intelligent child or student may differ from others in relevant features and exhibit a unique combination of kinds and degrees of achievement and ability. In

---

[5] H. L. A. Hart, "The Ascription of Responsibility and Rights" in *Logic and Language,* First Series, ed. by A. G. N. Flew (Oxford, 1951). Hart indeed speaks of "conditions" throughout, see p. 148.

dealing with these new cases mechanical rules and procedures would be useless; we have to exercise our judgment, guided by a complex set of examples and precedents. Here then there is a marked *superficial* similarity to aesthetic concepts. For in using aesthetic terms too we learn from samples and examples, not rules, and we have to apply them, likewise, without guidance by rules or readily applicable procedures, to new and unique instances. Neither kind of concept admits of a simply "mechanical" employment.

But this is *only* a superficial similarity. It is at least noteworthy that in applying words like "lazy" or "intelligent" to new and unique instances we say that we are required to exercise *judgment;* it would be indeed odd to say that we are exercising *taste.* In exercising judgment we are called upon to weigh the pros and cons against each other, and perhaps sometimes to decide whether a quite new feature is to be counted as weighing on one side or on the other. But this goes to show that, though we may learn from and rely upon samples and precedents rather than a set of stated conditions, we are not out of the realm of general conditions and guiding principles. These precedents necessarily embody, and are used by us to illustrate, a complex web of governing and relevant conditions which it is impossible to formulate completely. To profit by precedents we have to understand them; and we must argue consistently from case to case. This is the very function of precedents. Thus it is possible, even with these very loosely condition-governed concepts, to take clear or paradigm cases of X and to say "this is X because . . .," and follow it up with an account of features which logically clinch the matter.

Nothing like this is possible with aesthetic terms. Examples undoubtedly play a crucial role in giving us a grasp of these concepts; but we do not and cannot derive from these examples conditions and principles, however complex, which will enable us, if we are consistent, to apply the terms even to some new cases. When, with a clear case of something which is in fact graceful or balanced or tightly-knit, someone tells me why it is, what features make it so, it is always possible for me to wonder whether, in spite of these features, it really is graceful, balanced, and so on. No such features logically clinch the matter.

The point I have argued may be reinforced in the following way. A man who failed to realize the nature of aesthetic concepts, or someone who, knowing he lacked sensitivity in aesthetic matters, did not want to reveal this lack might by assiduous application and shrewd observation provide himself with some rules and generalizations; and by inductive procedures and intelligent guessing, he might frequently say the right things. But he could have no great confidence or certainty; a slight change in an object might at any time unpredictably ruin his calculations, and he might as easily have been wrong as right. No matter how careful he has been about working out a set of consistent principles and conditions, he is only in a position to think that the object is very possibly delicate. With concepts like *lazy, intelligent,* or *contract,* someone who intelligently formulated rules that led him aright appreciably often *would* thereby show the beginning of a grasp of those concepts; but the person we are considering is not even beginning to show an awareness of what delicacy is. Though he sometimes says the right thing, he has not seen, but guessed, that the object is delicate. However intelligent he might be, we could easily tell him wrongly that something was delicate and "explain" why without his being able to detect the deception. (I am ignoring complications now about negative conditions.) But if we did the same with, say, "intelligent" he could at least often uncover some incompatibility or other which would need explaining. In a world of beings like himself he would have no use for concepts like delicacy. As it is, these concepts would play a quite different role in his life. He would, for himself, have no more reason to choose tasteful objects, pictures, and so on, than a deaf man would to avoid noisy places. He could not be praised for exercising taste; at best his ingenuity and intelligence might come in for mention. In "appraising" pictures, statuettes, poems, he would be doing something quite different from what other people do when they exercise taste.

At this point I want to notice in passing that there are times when it may look as if an aesthetic word could be applied according to a rule. These cases vary in type; I shall mention only one. One might say, in using "delicate" of glassware perhaps, that the thinner the glass, other things being equal, the more delicate it is. Similarly, with fabrics, furniture, and so on, there are perhaps times when the thinner or more smoothly finished or more highly polished something is, the more certainly some aesthetic term or other applies. On such occasions someone might formulate a rule and follow it in applying the word to a given range of articles. Now it may be that sometimes when this is so, the word being used is not really an aesthetic term at all; "delicate" applied to glass in this way may at times really mean no more than "thin" or "fragile." But this is certainly not always the case; people often *are* exercising taste even when they say that glass is very delicate because it is so thin, and know that it would be less so if thicker and more so if thinner. These instances where there appear to be rules are peripheral cases of the use of aesthetic terms. If someone did merely follow a rule we should not say he was exercising taste, and we should hesitate to admit that he had any real notion of delicacy until he satisfied us that he could discern it in other instances where no rule was available. In any event, these occasions when aesthetic words can be applied by rule are exceptional, not central or typical, and there is still no reason to think we are dealing with a logical entailment.[6]

It must not be thought that the impossibility of stating any conditions (other than negative) for the application of aesthetic terms results from an accidental poverty or lack of precision in language, or that it is simply a question of extreme complexity. It is true that words like "pink," "bluish," "curving," "mottled" do not permit of anything like a specific naming of each and every varied shade, curve, mottling, and blending. But if we were to give special names much more liberally than either we or even the specialists do (and no doubt there are limits beyond which we could not go), or even if, instead of names, we were to use vast numbers of specimens and samples of particular shades, shapes, mottlings, lines, and configurations, it would still be impossible, and for the same reasons, to supply any conditions.

We do indeed, in talking about a work of art, concern ourselves with its individual and specific features. We say that it is delicate not simply because it is in pale colors but because of *those* pale colors, that it is graceful not because its outline curves slightly but because of *that* particular curve. We use expressions like "because of *its* pale coloring," "because of *the* flecks of bright blue," "because of *the* way the lines converge" where it is clear we are referring not to the presence of general features but to very specific and particular ones. But it is obvious that even with the help of precise

[6] I cannot in the compass of this paper discuss the other types of apparent exceptions to my thesis. Cases where a man *lacking* in sensitivity might learn and follow a rule, as above, ought to be distinguished from cases where someone who *possesses* sensitivity might know, from a non-aesthetic description, that an aesthetic term applies. I have stated my thesis as though this latter kind of case never occurs because I have had my eye on the logical features of *typical* aesthetic judgments and have preferred to over- rather than understate my view. But with certain aesthetic terms, especially negative ones, there may perhaps be some rare genuine exceptions when a description enables us to visualize very fully, and when what is described belongs to certain restricted classes of things, say human faces or animal forms. Perhaps a description like "One eye red and rheumy, the other missing, a wart-covered nose, a twisted mouth, a greenish pallor" may justify in a strong sense ("must be," "cannot but be,") the judgments "ugly" or "hideous." If so, such cases are marginal, form a very small minority, and are uncharacteristic or atypical of aesthetic judgments in general. Usually when, on hearing a description, we say "it *must* be very beautiful (graceful, or the like)," we mean no more than "it surely must be, it's only remotely possible that it isn't." Different again are situations, and these are very numerous, where we can move quite simply from "bright colors" to "gay," or from "reds and yellows" to "warm," but where we are as yet only on the borderline of anything that could be called an expression of taste or aesthetic sensibility. I have stressed the importance of this transitional and border area between non-aesthetic and obviously aesthetic judgments below (p. 85).

names, or even samples and illustrations, of particular shades of color, contours and lines, any attempt to state conditions would be futile. After all, the very same feature, say a color or shape or line of a particular sort, which helps make one work may quite spoil another. "It would be quite delicate if it were not for that pale color there" may be said about the very color which is singled out in another picture as being largely responsible for its delicate quality. No doubt one way of putting this is to say that the features which make something delicate or graceful, and so on, are combined in a peculiar and unique way; that the aesthetic quality depends upon exactly this individual or unique combination of just these specific colors and shapes so that even a slight change might make all the difference. Nothing is to be achieved by trying to single out or separate features and generalizing about them.

I have now argued that in certain ways aesthetic concepts are not and cannot be condition- or rule-governed.[7] Not to be so governed is one of their essential characteristics. In arguing this I first claimed in a general way that no non-aesthetic features are possible candidates for conditions, and then considered more particularly both the "characteristic" *general* features associated with aesthetic terms and the individual or *specific* features found in particular objects. I have not attempted to examine what relationship these specific features of a work do bear to its aesthetic qualities. An examination of the locutions we use when we refer to them in the course of explaining or supporting our application of an aesthetic term reinforces with linguistic evidence the fact that we are certainly not offering them as explanatory or justifying *conditions*. When we are asked why we say a certain person is lazy or intelligent or courageous, we are being asked in virtue of what do we *call* him this; we reply with "because of the way he regularly leaves his work unfinished," or "because of the ease with which he handles such and such problems," and so on. But when we are asked to say why, in our opinion, a picture lacks balance or is somber in tone, or why a poem is moving or tightly organized, we are doing a different kind

---

[7] Helen Knight says (Elton, *op. cit.*, p. 152) that "piquant" (one of my "aesthetic" terms) "depends on" various features (a *retroussé* nose, a pointed chin, and the like) and that these features are *criteria* for it; this is what I am denying. She also maintains that "good," when applied to works of art, depends on *criteria* like balance, solidity, depth, profundity (my aesthetic terms again; I should place piquancy in this list). I would deny this too, though I regard it as a different question and do not consider it in this paper. The two questions need separating: the relation of non-aesthetic features (*retroussé*, pointed) to aesthetic qualities, and the relation of aesthetic qualities to "aesthetically good" (verdicts). Most writings which touch on the nature of aesthetic concepts have this other (verdict) question mainly in mind. Mrs. Knight blurs this difference when she says, for example, " 'piquant' is the same kind of word as 'good.' "

of thing. We may use similar locutions: "his verse has strength and variety *because of the way* he handles the meter and employs the caesura," or "it is nobly austere *because of* the lack of detail and the restricted palette." But we can also express what we want to by using quite other expressions: "it is the handling of meter and caesura which is *responsible for* its strength and variety," "its nobly austere quality is *due to* the lack of detail and the use of a restricted palette," "its lack of balance *results from* the high-lighting of the figures on the left," "those minor chords *make it* extremely moving," "those converging lines *give it* an extraordinary unity." These are locutions we cannot switch to with "lazy" or "intelligent"; to say what *makes* him lazy, what is *responsible for* his laziness, what it is *due to,* is to broach another question entirely.

One after another, in recent discussions, writers have insisted that aesthetic judgments are not "mechanical": "Critics do not formulate general standards and apply these mechanically to all, or to classes of, works of art." "Technical points can be settled rapidly, by the application of rules," but aesthetic questions "cannot be settled by any mechanical method." Instead, these writers on aesthetics have emphasized that there is no "substitute for individual judgment" with its "spontaneity and speculation" and that "The final standard . . . [is] the judgment of personal taste."[8] What is surprising is that, though such things have been repeated again and again, no one seems to have said what is meant by "taste" or by the word "mechanical." There are many judgments besides those requiring taste which demand "spontaneity" and "individual judgment" and are not "mechanical." Without a detailed comparison we cannot see in what particular way *aesthetic* judgments are not "mechanical," or how they differ from those other judgments, nor can we begin to specify what taste is. This I have attempted. It is a characteristic and essential feature of judgments which employ an aesthetic term that they cannot be made by appealing, in the sense explained, to non-aesthetic conditions.[9] This, I believe, is a logical feature of aesthetic or taste judgments in general, though I have argued it here only as regards the more restricted range of judgments which employ aesthetic terms. It is part of what "taste" means.

[8] See articles by Margaret Macdonald and J. A. Passmore in Elton, *op. cit.,* pp. 118, 41, 40, 119.

[9] As I indicated, p. 66 above, I have dealt only with the relation of *non-aesthetic* to aesthetic features. Perhaps a description in *aesthetic* terms may occasionally suffice for applying another aesthetic term. Johnson's Dictionary gives "handsome" as "beautiful with dignity"; Shorter O. E. D. gives "pretty" as "beautiful in a slight, dainty, or diminutive way."

II

A great deal of work remains to be done on aesthetic concepts. In the remainder of this paper I shall offer some further suggestions which may help towards an understanding of them.

The realization that aesthetic concepts are governed only negatively by conditions is likely to give rise to puzzlement over how we manage to apply the words in our aesthetic vocabulary. If we are not following rules and there are no conditions to appeal to, how are we to know when they are applicable? One very natural way to counter this question is to point out that some other sorts of concepts also are not condition-governed. We do not apply simple color words by following rules or in accordance with principles. We see that the book is red by looking, just as we tell that the tea is sweet by tasting it. So too, it might be said, we just see (or fail to see) that things are delicate, balanced, and the like. This kind of comparison between the exercise of taste and the use of the five senses is indeed familiar; our use of the word "taste" itself shows that the comparison is age-old and very natural. Yet whatever the similarities, there are great dissimilarities too. A careful comparison cannot be attempted here though it would be valuable; but certain differences stand out, and writers who have emphasized that aesthetic judgments are not "mechanical" have sometimes dwelt on and been puzzled by them.

In the first place, while our ability to discern aesthetic features is dependent upon our possession of good eyesight, hearing, and so on, people normally endowed with senses and understanding may nevertheless fail to discern them. "Those who listen to a concert, walk round a gallery, read a poem may have roughly similar sense perceptions, but some get a great deal more than others," Miss Macdonald says; but she adds that she is "puzzled by this feature 'in the object' which can be seen only by a specially qualified observer" and asks, "What is this 'something more'?"[10]

It is this difference between aesthetic and perceptual qualities which in part leads to the view that "works of art are esoteric objects . . . not simple objects of sense perception."[11] But there is no good reason for calling an object esoteric simply because we discern aesthetic qualities in it. The *objects* to which we apply aesthetic words are of the most diverse kinds and by no means esoteric: people and buildings, flowers and gardens, vases and furni-

[10] Macdonald in Elton, *op. cit.*, pp. 114, 119. See also pp. 120, 122.
[11] Macdonald, *ibid.*, pp. 114, 120-123. She speaks of non-aesthetic properties here as "physical" or "observable" qualities, and distinguishes between "physical object" and "work of art."

ture, as well as poems and music. Nor does there seem any good reason for
calling the *qualities* themselves esoteric. It is true that someone with perfect
eyes or ears might miss them, but we do after all say we *observe* or *notice*
them ("Did you notice how very graceful she was?," "Did you observe the
exquisite balance in all his pictures?"). In fact, they are very familiar indeed.
We learn while quite young to use many aesthetic words, though they are,
as one might expect from their dependence upon our ability to see, hear,
distinguish colors, and the like, not the earliest words we learn; and our
mastery and sophistication in using them develop along with the rest of our
vocabulary. They are not rarities; some ranges of them are in regular use
in everyday discourse.

The second notable difference between the exercise of taste and the use
of the five senses lies in the way we support those judgments in which
aesthetic concepts are employed. Although we use these concepts without
rules or conditions, we do defend or support our judgments, and convince
others of their rightness, by talking; "disputation about art is not futile,"
as Miss Macdonald says, for critics do "attempt a certain kind of explanation
of works of art with the object of establishing correct judgments."[12] Thus
even though this disputation does not consist in "deductive or inductive
inference" or "reasoning," its occurrence is enough to show how very different these judgments are from those of a simple perceptual sort.

Now the critic's talk, it is clear, frequently consists in mentioning or
pointing out the features, including easily discernible non-aesthetic ones,
upon which the aesthetic qualities depend. But the puzzling question remains how, by mentioning these features, the critic is thereby justifying or
supporting his judgments. To this question a number of recent writers have
given an answer. Stuart Hampshire, for example, says that "One engages
in aesthetic discussion for the sake of what one might see on the way . . . if
one has been brought to see what there is to be seen in the object, the
purpose of discussion is achieved . . . The point is to bring people to see
these features."[13] The critic's talk, that is, often serves to support his judgments in a special way; it helps us to *see* what he has seen, namely, the
aesthetic qualities of the object. But even when it is agreed that this is one
of the main things that critics do, puzzlement tends to break out again
over *how* they do it. How is it that by talking about features of the work

---

[12] *Ibid.,* pp. 115-116; cf. also John Holloway, *Proceedings of the Aristotelian Society,* Supplementary Vol. XXIII (1949), pp. 175-176.

[13] Stuart Hampshire in Elton, *op. cit.,* p. 165. Cf. also remarks in Elton by Isenberg (pp. 142,
145), Passmore (p. 38), in *Philosophy and Psycho-analysis* by John Wisdom (Oxford, 1953),
pp. 223-224, and in Holloway, *op. cit.,* p. 175.

(largely non-aesthetic ones) we can manage to bring others to see what they had not seen? "What sort of endowment is this which *talking* can modify? . . . Discussion does not improve eyesight and hearing" (my italics).[14]

Yet of course we do succeed in applying aesthetic terms, and we frequently do succeed by talking (and pointing and gesturing in certain ways) in bringing others to see what we see. One begins to suspect that puzzlement over how we can possibly do this, and puzzlement over the "esoteric" character of aesthetic qualities too, arises from bearing in mind inappropriate philosophical models. When someone is unable to see that the book on the table is brown, we cannot get him to see that it is by talking; consequently it seems puzzling that we might get someone to see that the vase is graceful by talking. If we are to dispel this puzzlement and recognize aesthetic concepts and qualities for what they are, we must abandon unsuitable models and investigate how we actually employ these concepts. With so much interest in and agreement about *what* the critic does, one might expect descriptions of *how* he does it to have been given. But little has been said about this, and what has been said is unsatisfactory.

Miss Macdonald,[15] for example, subscribes to this view of the critic's task as presenting "what is not obvious to casual or uninstructed inspection," and she does ask the question "What sort of considerations are involved, *and how,* to justify a critical verdict?" (my italics). But she does not in fact go on to answer it. She addresses herself instead to the different, though related, question of the interpretation of art works. In complex works different critics claim, often justifiably, to discern different features; hence Miss Macdonald suggests that in critical discourse the critic is bringing us to see what he sees by offering new interpretations. But if the question is "what (the critic) does and how he does it," he cannot be represented either wholly or even mainly as providing new interpretations. His task quite as often is simply to help us appreciate qualities which other critics have regularly found in the works he discusses. To put the stress upon *new* interpretations is to leave untouched the question how, by talking, he can help us to see *either* the newly appreciated aesthetic qualities *or* the old. In any case, besides complex poems or plays which may bear many interpretations, there are also relatively simple ones. There are also vases, buildings, and furniture, not to mention faces, sunsets, and scenery, about which no questions of "interpretation" arise but about which we talk in similar ways and make similar judgments. So the "puzzling" questions remain: how do

---

[14] Macdonald, *op. cit.*, pp. 119-120.

[15] *Ibid.*, see pp. 127, 122, 125, 115. Other writers also place the stress on interpretation, cf. Holloway, *op. cit.*, p. 173 ff.

we support these judgments and how do we bring others to see what we see?

Hampshire,[16] who likewise believes that the critic brings us "to see what there is to be seen in the object," does give some account of how the critic does this. "The greatest service of the critic" is to point out, isolate, and place in a frame of attention the "particular features of the particular object which *make* it ugly or beautiful"; for it is "difficult to see and hear all that there is to see and hear," and simply a prejudice to suppose that while "things really do have colors and shapes . . . there do not exist literally and objectively, concordances of colors and perceived rhythms and balances of shapes." However, these "extraordinary qualities" which the critic "may have seen (in the wider sense of 'see')" are "qualities which are of no direct practical interest." Consequently, to bring us to see them the critic employs "an unnatural use of words in description"; "the common vocabulary, being created for practical purposes, obstructs any disinterested perception of things"; and so these qualities "are normally described metaphorically by some transference of terms from the common vocabulary."

Much of what Hampshire says is right. But there is also something quite wrong in the view that the "common" vocabulary "obstructs" our aesthetic purposes, that it is "unnatural" to take it over and use it metaphorically, and that the critic "is under the necessity of building . . . a vocabulary *in opposition to the main tendency of his language*" (my italics). First, while we do often coin new metaphors in order to describe aesthetic qualities, we are by no means always under the necessity of wresting the "common vocabulary" from its "natural" uses to serve our purposes. There does exist, as I observed earlier, a large and accepted vocabulary of aesthetic terms some of which, whatever their metaphorical origins, are now not metaphors at all, others of which are at most quasi-metaphorical. Second, this view that our use of metaphor and quasi-metaphor for aesthetic purposes is unnatural or a makeshift into which we are forced by a language designed for other purposes misrepresents fundamentally the character of aesthetic qualities and aesthetic language. There is nothing unnatural about using words like "forceful," "dynamic," or "tightly-knit" in criticism; they do their work perfectly and are exactly the words needed for the purposes they serve. We do not want or need to replace them by words which lack the metaphorical element. In using them to describe works of art, the very point is that we are noticing aesthetic qualities related to their literal or common meanings. If we possessed a quite different word from "dynamic," one we could use to point out an aesthetic quality unrelated to the common meaning of

[16] *Op. cit.*, pp. 165-168.

"dynamic," it could not be used to describe that quality which "dynamic" does serve to point out. Hampshire pictures "a colony of aesthetes, disengaged from practical needs and manipulations" and says that "descriptions of aesthetic qualities, which for us are metaphorical, might seem to them to have an altogether literal and familiar sense"; they might use "a more directly descriptive vocabulary." But if they had a new and "directly descriptive" vocabulary lacking the links with non-aesthetic properties and interests which our vocabulary possesses, they would have to remain silent about many of the aesthetic qualities we can describe; further, if they were more completely "disengaged from practical needs" and other non-aesthetic awarenesses and interests, they would perforce be blind to many aesthetic qualities we can appreciate. The links between aesthetic qualities and non-aesthetic ones are both obvious and vital. Aesthetic concepts, all of them, carry with them attachments and in one way or another are tethered to or parasitic upon non-aesthetic features. The fact that many aesthetic terms are metaphorical or quasi-metaphorical in no way means that common language is an ill-adapted tool with which we have to struggle. When someone writes as Hampshire does, one suspects again that critical language is being judged against other models. To use language which is frequently metaphorical might be strange for some *other* purpose or from the standpoint of doing something else, but for the purpose and from the standpoint of making aesthetic observations it is not. To say it is an unnatural use of language for doing *this* is to imply there is or could be for this purpose some other and "natural" use. But these *are* natural ways of talking about aesthetic matters.

To help understand what the critic does, then, how he supports his judgments and gets his audience to see what he sees, I shall attempt a brief description of the methods we use as critics.[17]

(1) We may simply mention or point out non-aesthetic features: "Notice these flecks of color, that dark mass there, those lines." By merely drawing attention to those easily discernible features which make the painting luminous or warm or dynamic, we often succeed in bringing someone to see these aesthetic qualities. We get him to see B by mentioning something different, A. Sometimes in doing this we are drawing attention to features which may have gone unnoticed by an untrained or insufficiently attentive eye or ear: "Just listen for the repeated figure in the left hand," "Did you notice the figure of Icarus in the Breughel? It is very small." Sometimes they are features which have been seen or heard but of which the

---

[17] Holloway, *op. cit.*, pp. 173-174, lists some of these very briefly.

significance or purpose has been missed in any of a variety of ways: "Notice how much darker he has made the central figure, how much brighter these colors are than the adjacent ones," "Of course, you've observed the ploughman in the foreground; but had you considered how he, like everyone else in the picture, is going about his business without noticing the fall of Icarus?" In mentioning features which may be discerned by anyone with normal eyes, ears, and intelligence, we are singling out what may serve as a kind of key to grasping or seeing something else (and the key may not be the same for each person).

(2) On the other hand we often simply mention the very qualities we want people to see. We point to a painting and say, "Notice how nervous and delicate the drawing is," or "See what energy and vitality it has." The use of the aesthetic term itself may do the trick; we say what the quality or character is, and people who had not seen it before see it.

(3) Most often, there is a linking of remarks about aesthetic and non-aesthetic features: "Have you noticed this line and that, and the points of bright color here and there . . . don't they give it vitality, energy?"

(4) We do, in addition, often make extensive and helpful use of similes and genuine metaphors: "It's as if there were small points of light burning," "as though he had thrown on the paint violently and in anger," "the light shimmers, the lines dance, everything is air, lightness and gaiety," "his canvasses are fires, they crackle, burn, and blaze, even at their most subdued always restlessly flickering, but often bursting into flame, great pyrotechnic displays," and so on.

(5) We make use of contrasts, comparisons, and reminiscences: "Suppose he had made that a lighter yellow, moved it to the right, how flat it would have been," "Don't you think it has something of the quality of a Rembrandt?", "Hasn't it the same serenity, peace, and quality of light of those summer evenings in Norfolk?" We use what keys we have to the known sensitivity, susceptibilities, and experience of our audience.

Critics and commentators may range, in their methods, from one extreme to the other, from painstaking concentration on points of detail, line and color, vowels and rhymes, to more or less flowery and luxuriant metaphor. Even the enthusiastic biographical sketch decorated with suitable epithet and metaphor may serve. What is best depends on both the audience and the work under discussion. But this would not be a complete sketch unless certain other notes were added.

(6) Repetition and reiteration often play an important role. When we are in front of a canvas we may come back time and again to the same points, drawing attention to the same lines and shapes, repeating the same words, "swirling," "balance," "luminosity," or the same similes and metaphors, as if time and familiarity, looking harder, listening more carefully, paying closer attention may help. So again with variation; it often helps to talk round what we have said, to build up, supplement with more talk *of the same kind*. When someone misses the swirling quality, when one epithet or one metaphor does not work, we throw in related ones; we speak of its wild movement, how it twists and turns, writhes and whirls, as though, failing to score a direct hit, we may succeed with a barrage of near-synonyms.

(7) Finally, besides our verbal performances, the rest of our behavior is important. We accompany our talk with appropriate tones of voice, expression, nods, looks, and gestures. A critic may sometimes do more with a sweep of the arm than by talking. An appropriate gesture may make us see the violence in a painting or the character of a melodic line.

These ways of acting and talking are not significantly different whether we are dealing with a particular work, paragraph, or line, or speaking of an artist's work as a whole, or even drawing attention to a sunset or scenery. But even with the speaker doing all this, we may fail to see what he sees. There may be a point, though there need be no limit except that imposed by time and patience, at which he gives up and sets us (or himself) down as lacking in some way, defective in sensitivity. He may tell us to look or read again, or to read or look at other things and then come back again to this; he may suspect there are experiences in life we have missed. But these are the things he does. This is what succeeds if anything does; indeed it is all that can be done.

By realizing clearly that, whether we are dealing with art or scenery or people or natural objects, this is how we operate with aesthetic concepts, we may recognize this sphere of human activity for what it is. We operate with different kinds of concepts in different ways. If we want someone to agree that a color is red we may take it into a good light and ask him to look; if it is viridian we may fetch a color chart and make him compare; if we want him to agree that a figure is fourteen-sided we get him to count; and to bring him to agree that something is dilapidated or that someone is intelligent or lazy we may do other things, citing figures, reasoning and arguing about them, weighing and balancing. These are the methods appropriate to these various concepts. But the ways we get someone to see aesthetic qualities are different; they are of the kind I have described. With each kind of concept we can describe what we do and how we do it. But the methods suited to these other concepts will not do for aesthetic ones, or vice versa. We cannot prove by argument or by assembling a sufficiency of conditions that something is graceful; but this is no more puzzling than our inability to prove, by using the methods, metaphors, and gestures of the art critic, that it will be mate in ten moves. The questions raised admit of no answer beyond the sort of description I have given. To go on to ask, with puzzlement, how it is that *when* we do these things people come to see, is like asking how is it that, when we take the book into a good light, our companion agrees with us that it is red. There is no place for this kind of question or puzzlement. Aesthetic concepts are as natural, as little esoteric, as any others. It is against the background of different and philosophically more familiar models that they seem queer or puzzling.

I have described how people justify aesthetic judgments and bring others to see aesthetic qualities in things. I shall end by showing that the methods I have outlined are the ones natural for and characteristic of taste concepts from the start. When someone tries to make me see that a painting is delicate or balanced, I have some understanding of these terms already and know in a sense what I am looking for. But if there is puzzlement over how, by talking, he can bring me to see these qualities in this picture, there should be a corresponding puzzlement over how I learned to use aesthetic terms and discern aesthetic qualities in the first place. We may ask, therefore, how we learn to do these things; and this is to inquire (1) what natural potentialities and tendencies people have and (2) how we develop and take advantage of these capacities in training and teaching. Now for the second of these, there is no doubt that our ability to notice and respond to aesthetic qualities is cultivated and developed by our contacts with parents and teachers from quite an early age. What is interesting for my present purpose is that, while we are being taught in the presence of examples what grace, delicacy, and so on are, the methods used, the language and behavior, are of a piece with those of the critic as I have already described them.

To pursue these two questions, consider first those words like "dynamic," "melancholy," "balanced," "taut," or "gay" the aesthetic use of which is quasi-metaphorical. It has already been emphasized that we could not use them thus without some experience of situations where they are used literally. The present inquiry is how we shift from literal to aesthetic uses of them. For this it is required that there be certain abilities and tendencies to link experiences, to regard certain things as similar, and to see, explore, and be interested in these similarities. It is a feature of human intelligence and sensitivity that we do spontaneously do these things and that the tendency can be encouraged and developed. It is no more baffling that we should employ aesthetic terms of this sort than that we should make metaphors at all. Easy and smooth transitions by which we shift to the use of these aesthetic terms are not hard to find. We suggest to children that simple pieces of music are hurrying or running or skipping or dawdling, from there we move to lively, gay, jolly, happy, smiling, or sad, and, as their experiences and vocabulary broaden, to solemn, dynamic, or melancholy. But the child also discovers for himself many of these parallels and takes interest or delight in them. He is likely on his own to skip, march, clap, or laugh with the music, and without this natural tendency our training would get nowhere. Insofar, however, as we do take advantage of this tendency and help him by training, *we do just what the critic does*. We may merely need to persuade the child to pay attention, to look or listen; or we may simply *call* the music jolly. But we are also likely to use, as the critic does, reiteration, synonyms, parallels, contrasts, similes, metaphors, gestures, and other expressive behavior.

Of course the recognition of similarities and simple metaphorical extensions are not the only transitions to the aesthetic use of language. Others are made in different ways; for instance, by the kind of peripheral cases I mentioned earlier. When our admiration is for something as simple as the thinness of a glass or the smoothness of a fabric, it is not difficult to call attention to such things, evoke a similar delight, and introduce suitable aesthetic terms. These transitions are only the beginnings; it may often be questionable whether a term is yet being used aesthetically or not. Many of the terms I have mentioned may be used in ways which are not straightforwardly literal but of which we should hesitate to say that they demanded much yet by way of aesthetic sensitivity. We speak of warm and cool colors, and we may say of a brightly colored picture that at least it is gay and lively. When we have brought someone to make this sort of metaphorical extension of terms, he has made one of the transitional steps from which he may move on to uses which more obviously deserve to be called aesthetic and demand more aesthetic appreciation. When I said at the outset that aesthetic sensitivity was rarer than some other natural endowments, I was not denying that it varies in degree from the rudimentary to the refined. Most people learn easily to make the kinds of remarks I am now considering. But when someone can call bright canvasses gay and lively without being able to spot the one which is really vibrant, or can recognize the obvious outward vigor and energy of a student composition played *con fuoco* while failing to see that it lacks inner fire and drive, we do not regard his aesthetic sensitivity in these areas as particularly developed. However, once these transitions from common to aesthetic uses are begun in the more obvious cases, the domain of aesthetic concepts may broaden out, and they may become more subtle and even partly autonomous. The initial steps, however varied the metaphorical shifts and however varied the experiences upon which they are parasitic, are natural and easy.

Much the same is true when we turn to those words which have no standard non-aesthetic use, "lovely," "pretty," "dainty," "graceful," "elegant." We cannot say that these are learned by a metaphorical shift. But they still are linked to non-aesthetic features in many ways and the learning of them also is made possible by certain kinds of natural response, reaction, and ability. We learn them not so much by noticing similarities, but by our attention being caught and focussed in other ways. Certain phenomena which are outstanding or remarkable or unusual catch the eye or ear, seize our attention and interest, and move us to surprise, admiration, delight, fear, or distaste. Children begin by reacting in these ways to spectacular sunsets, woods in autumn, roses, dandelions, and other striking and colorful objects, and it is in these circumstances that we find ourselves introducing general aesthetic words to them, like "lovely," "pretty," and "ugly." It is not an accident that the first lessons in aesthetic appreciation consist in drawing the child's attention to roses rather than to grass; nor is it surprising that we remark to him on the autumn colors rather than on the subdued tints of winter. We all of us, not only children, pay aesthetic attention more readily and easily to such outstanding and easily noticeable things. We notice with pleasure early spring grass or the first snow, hills of notably marked and varied contours, scenery flecked with a great variety of color or dappled variously with sun and shadow. We are struck and impressed by great size or mass, as with mountains or cathedrals. We are similarly responsive to unusual precision or minuteness or remarkable feats of skill, as with complex and elaborate filigree, or intricate wood carving and fan-vaulting. It is at these times, taking advantage of these natural interests and admirations, that we first teach the simpler aesthetic words. People of moderate aesthetic sensitivity and sophistication continue to exhibit aesthetic interest mainly on such occasions and to use only the more general words ("pretty," "lovely," and the like). But these situations may serve as a beginning from which we extend our aesthetic interests to wider and less obvious fields, mastering as we go the more subtle and specific vocabulary of taste. The principles do not change; the basis for learning more specific terms like "graceful," "delicate," and "elegant" is also our interest in and admiration for various non-aesthetic natural properties ("She seems to move *effortlessly, as if floating*," "So very *thin* and *fragile, as if a breeze might destroy it*," "So *small* and yet so *intricate*," "So *economical* and *perfectly adapted*").[18] And even with these aesthetic terms which are not metaphorical themselves ("graceful," "delicate," "elegant"), we rely in the same way upon the critic's methods, including comparison, illustration, and metaphor, to teach or make clear what they mean.

I have wished to emphasize in the latter part of this paper the natural basis of responses of various kinds without which aesthetic terms could not be learned. I have also outlined what some of the features are to which we naturally respond: similarities of various sorts, notable colors, shapes, scents, size, intricacy, and much else besides. Even the non-metaphorical aesthetic terms have significant links with all kinds of natural features by which our interest, wonder, admiration, delight, or distaste is aroused. But in particular I have wanted to urge that it should not strike us as puzzling that the critic supports his judgments and brings us to see aesthetic qualities by pointing out key features and talking about them in the way he does. It is by the very same methods that people helped us develop our aesthetic sense and master its vocabulary from the beginning. If we responded to those methods then, it is not surprising that we respond to the critic's discourse now. It would be surprising if, by using this language and behavior, people could *not* sometimes bring us to see the aesthetic qualities of things; for this would prove us lacking in one characteristically human kind of awareness and activity.

---

[18] It is worth noticing that most of the words which in current usage are primarily or exclusively aesthetic terms had earlier non-aesthetic uses and gained their present use by some kind of metaphorical shift. Without reposing too great weight on these etymological facts, it can be seen that their history reflects connections with the responses, interests, and natural features I have mentioned as underlying the learning and use of aesthetic terms. These transitions suggest both the dependence of aesthetic upon other interests, and what some of these interests are. Connected with liking, delight, affection, regard, estimation, or choice—*beautiful, graceful, delicate, lovely, exquisite, elegant, dainty*; with fear or repulsion—*ugly*; with what notably catches the eye or attention—*garish, splendid, gaudy*; with what attracts by notable rarity, precision, skill, ingenuity, elaboration—*dainty, nice, pretty, exquisite*; with adaptation to function, suitability to ease of handling—*handsome*.

Bibliography

The prevailing philosophical orientation in recent views of aesthetic qualities (actually, the general orientation in recent views of descriptive and characterizing expressions) may be found in:

P. H. Nowell-Smith, *Ethics* (London, 1954), Chapters V, VI;

John Wisdom, "Gods," reprinted in his *Philosophy and Psycho-analysis* (Oxford, 1953);

Ludwig Wittgenstein, *The Blue and Brown Books* (Oxford, 1958).

None of these is narrowly concerned with aesthetics.

There are relatively few sustained discussions of aesthetic qualities, but the following has some comments of relevance and interest:

John Hospers, "The Concept of Artistic Expression," reprinted (revised) in Morris Weitz (ed.), *Problems in Aesthetics* (New York, 1959).

For a flavor of somewhat older discussions, see:

C. J. Ducasse, *The Philosophy of Art* (New York, 1929), Chapter XII;

Stephen Pepper, *Aesthetic Quality* (New York, 1937), Chapter IV;

David Prall, *Aesthetic Judgment* (New York, 1929), Chapter V.

V

THE ARTIST'S INTENTION

THE ISSUE of the Intentional Fallacy is a special, but rather heavily debated, version of more general puzzles regarding what may be critically
eligible or relevant (that is, short of true or false, or correct or incorrect)
in interpreting works of art and performing particular works. Characteristically, we ask whether, say, James Joyce intended *Finnegan's Wake* to
be construed this way or that, or whether Stanislavski's production of *The
Cherry Orchard* accords with Chekhov's intentions. The questions are quite
familiar. But one may puzzle over the critical eligibility of these very
questions. Is it "aesthetically" relevant to inquire regarding the artist's intention? As soon as the question is put in this form, we see that the issue
depends on the ease with which we may decide what the aesthetic point of
view in criticism is. Are we faced with a finding or a ruling? If a finding,
how are we to judge conflicting opinions here? If a ruling, what is the
force of the term 'fallacy'? We notice that critics, in their practice, sometimes
appeal to the artist's intention. What then is the logical status of a judgment
that such appeals are inadmissible? And how may the artist's intention
be determined: through autobiographical materials? through psychoanalysis?

89

through the work of art itself? And will the answer be quite general for all the arts? For example, will adjustments be advisable when we possess a composer's musical notation?

The issue of the Fallacy is tangentially related to that of the artist's expression, since it is one variant of the view that the artist expresses himself to hold that to understand a work one must know the artist's intention. Sometimes the relationship is reversed and one insists that the merit of a work is to be judged solely or chiefly on whether the artist's intention has been fulfilled. But more directly, the issue of the Fallacy presupposes some fairly clean-cut conception of what "the work of art" is. Otherwise, we should have difficulty determining the relevance or irrelevance of critical comments—whether intentionally oriented, psychoanalytically oriented, oriented in terms of cultural history, or oriented in accord with frankly partisan convictions (e.g., Marxist, Roman Catholic). So the issue of the Fallacy spreads inevitably to that of the general relationship of critical interpretations to the work of art. And if we ask ourselves how we define the boundaries of a poem, what are the implications of a changing tradition of dramatic and musical performance, we are at once placed at the center of the difficulties. If a psychoanalytically oriented interpretation of *Hamlet* be eligible, why not one that accords with Shakespeare's autobiographical remains? And if we may at times restrict dramatic and musical performances in terms of period style, why not in terms of the artist's intention? May we perhaps judge, with equal ease in the context of appreciation, that some particular performance is both ingenious and not in accord with the artist's original conception? And what are the differences, with regard to appreciation itself, between two such remarks as these?

All of these questions have been revived by the appearance of Wimsatt and Beardsley's "The Intentional Fallacy." The essay has attracted considerable attention and a very large portion of the professionally relevant literature since its appearance is explicitly concerned to defend or criticize its views.

The Intentional Fallacy

WILLIAM K. WIMSATT, JR.
  and
MONROE BEARDSLEY

"He owns with toil he wrote the following scenes;
But, if they're naught, ne'er sparc him for his pains:
Damn him the more; have no commiseration
For dullness on mature deliberation."

William Congreve
Prologue to *The Way of the World*

I

THE CLAIM of the author's "intention" upon the critic's judgment has been challenged in a number of recent discussions, notably in the debate entitled *The Personal Heresy,* between Professors Lewis and Tillyard. But it seems doubtful if this claim and most of its romantic corollaries are as yet subject to any widespread questioning. The present writers, in a short article entitled "Intention" for a *Dictionary*[1] of literary criticism,

From *The Verbal Icon,* by W. K. Wimsatt, Jr. (Lexington: University of Kentucky Press, 1954), Chapter I. Reprinted by permission of the authors and the University of Kentucky Press.

[1] *Dictionary of World Literature,* Joseph T. Shipley, ed. (New York, 1942), 326-29.

raised the issue but were unable to pursue its implications at any length. We argued that the design or intention of the author is neither available nor desirable as a standard for judging the success of a work of literary art, and it seems to us that this is a principle which goes deep into some differences in the history of critical attitudes. It is a principle which accepted or rejected points to the polar opposites of classical "imitation" and romantic expression. It entails many specific truths about inspiration, authenticity, biography, literary history and scholarship, and about some trends of contemporary poetry, especially its allusiveness. There is hardly a problem of literary criticism in which the critic's approach will not be qualified by his view of "intention."

"Intention," as we shall use the term, corresponds to *what he intended* in a formula which more or less explicitly has had wide acceptance. "In order to judge the poet's performance, we must know *what he intended*." Intention is design or plan in the author's mind. Intention has obvious affinities for the author's attitude toward his work, the way he felt, what made him write.

We begin our discussion with a series of propositions summarized and abstracted to a degree where they seem to us axiomatic.

1. A poem does not come into existence by accident. The words of a poem, as Professor Stoll has remarked, come out of a head, not out of a hat. Yet to insist on the designing intellect as a *cause* of a poem is not to grant the design or intention as a *standard* by which the critic is to judge the worth of the poet's performance.

2. One must ask how a critic expects to get an answer to the question about intention. How is he to find out what the poet tried to do? If the poet succeeded in doing it, then the poem itself shows what he was trying to do. And if the poet did not succeed, then the poem is not adequate evidence, and the critic must go outside the poem—for evidence of an intention that did not become effective in the poem. "Only one *caveat* must be borne in mind," says an eminent intentionalist[2] in a moment when his theory repudiates itself; "the poet's aim must be judged at the moment of the creative act, that is to say, by the art of the poem itself."

3. Judging a poem is like judging a pudding or a machine. One demands that it work. It is only because an artifact works that we infer the intention of an artificer. "A poem should not mean but be." A poem can *be* only through its *meaning*—since its medium is words—yet it *is,* simply *is,* in the sense that we have no excuse for inquiring what part is intended or meant.

[2] J. E. Spingarn, "The New Criticism," in *Criticism in America* (New York, 1924), 24-25.

Poetry is a feat of style by which a complex of meaning is handled all at once. Poetry succeeds because all or most of what is said or implied is relevant; what is irrelevant has been excluded, like lumps from pudding and "bugs" from machinery. In this respect poetry differs from practical messages, which are successful if and only if we correctly infer the intention. They are more abstract than poetry.

4. The meaning of a poem may certainly be a personal one, in the sense that a poem expresses a personality or state of soul rather than a physical object like an apple. But even a short lyric poem is dramatic, the response of a speaker (no matter how abstractly conceived) to a situation (no matter how universalized). We ought to impute the thoughts and attitudes of the poem immediately to the dramatic *speaker,* and if to the author at all, only by an act of biographical inference.

5. There is a sense in which an author, by revision, may better achieve his original intention. But it is a very abstract sense. He intended to write a better work, or a better work of a certain kind, and now has done it. But it follows that his former concrete intention was not his intention. "He's the man we were in search of, that's true," says Hardy's rustic constable, "and yet he's not the man we were in search of. For the man we were in search of was not the man we wanted."

"Is not a critic," asks Professor Stoll, "a judge, who does not explore his own consciousness, but determines the author's meaning or intention, as if the poem were a will, a contract, or the constitution? The poem is not the critic's own." He has accurately diagnosed two forms of irresponsibility, one of which he prefers. Our view is yet different. The poem is not the critic's own and not the author's (it is detached from the author at birth and goes about the world beyond his power to intend about it or control it). The poem belongs to the public. It is embodied in language, the peculiar possession of the public, and it is about the human being, an object of public knowledge. What is said about the poem is subject to the same scrutiny as any statement in linguistics or in the general science of psychology.

A critic of our *Dictionary* article, Ananda K. Coomaraswamy, has argued[3] that there are two kinds of inquiry about a work of art: (1) whether the artist achieved his intentions; (2) whether the work of art "ought ever to have been undertaken at all" and so "whether it is worth preserving." Number (2), Coomaraswamy maintains, is not "criticism of any work of art *qua* work of art," but is rather moral criticism; number (1) is artistic criticism. But we maintain that (2) need not be moral criticism: that there is

---

[3] Ananda K. Coomaraswamy, "Intention," in *American Bookman,* I (1944), 41-48.

another way of deciding whether works of art are worth preserving and whether, in a sense, they "ought" to have been undertaken, and this is the way of objective criticism of works of art as such, the way which enables us to distinguish between a skillful murder and a skillful poem. A skillful murder is an example which Coomaraswamy uses, and in his system the difference between the murder and the poem is simply a "moral" one, not an "artistic" one, since each if carried out according to plan is "artistically" successful. We maintain that (2) is an inquiry of more worth than (1), and since (2) and not (1) is capable of distinguishing poetry from murder, the name "artistic criticism" is properly given to (2).

II

It is not so much a historical statement as a definition to say that the intentional fallacy is a romantic one. When a rhetorician of the first century A.D. writes: "Sublimity is the echo of a great soul," or when he tells us that "Homer enters into the sublime actions of his heroes" and "shares the full inspiration of the combat," we shall not be surprised to find this rhetorician considered as a distant harbinger of romanticism and greeted in the warmest terms by Saintsbury. One may wish to argue whether Longinus should be called romantic, but there can hardly be a doubt that in one important way he is.

Goethe's three questions for "constructive criticism" are "What did the author set out to do? Was his plan reasonable and sensible, and how far did he succeed in carrying it out?" If one leaves out the middle question, one has in effect the system of Croce—the culmination and crowning philosophic expression of romanticism. The beautiful is the successful intuition-expression, and the ugly is the unsuccessful; the intuition or private part of art is *the* aesthetic fact, and the medium or public part is not the subject of aesthetic at all.

> The Madonna of Cimabue is still in the Church of Santa Maria Novella; but does she speak to the visitor of to-day as to the Florentines of the thirteenth century?
>
> *Historical interpretation* labors . . . to reintegrate in us the psychological conditions which have changed in the course of history. It . . . enables us to see a work of art (a physical object) as its *author saw* it in the moment of production.[4]

[4] It is true that Croce himself in his *Ariosto, Shakespeare and Corneille* (London, 1920), Chap. VII, "The Practical Personality and the Poetical Personality," and in his *Defence of Poetry* (Oxford, 1934), 24, and elsewhere, early and late, has delivered telling attacks on emotive geneticism, but the main drive of the *Aesthetic* is surely toward a kind of cognitive intentionalism.

The first italics are Croce's, the second ours. The upshot of Croce's system is an ambiguous emphasis on history. With such passages as a point of departure a critic may write a nice analysis of the meaning or "spirit" of a play by Shakespeare or Corneille—a process that involves close historical study but remains aesthetic criticism—or he may, with equal plausibility, produce an essay in sociology, biography, or other kinds of non-aesthetic history.

III

> I went to the poets; tragic, dithyrambic, and all sorts. . . . I took them some of the most elaborate passages in their own writings, and asked what was the meaning of them. . . . Will you believe me? . . . there is hardly a person present who would not have talked better about their poetry than they did themselves. Then I knew that not by wisdom do poets write poetry, but by a sort of genius and inspiration.

That reiterated mistrust of the poets which we hear from Socrates may have been part of a rigorously ascetic view in which we hardly wish to participate, yet Plato's Socrates saw a truth about the poetic mind which the world no longer commonly sees—so much criticism, and that the most inspirational and most affectionately remembered, has proceeded from the poets themselves.

Certainly the poets have had something to say that the critic and professor could not say; their message has been more exciting: that poetry should come as naturally as leaves to a tree, that poetry is the lava of the imagination, or that it is emotion recollected in tranquillity. But it is necessary that we realize the character and authority of such testimony. There is only a fine shade of difference between such expressions and a kind of earnest advice that authors often give. Thus Edward Young, Carlyle, Walter Pater:

> I know two golden rules from *ethics,* which are no less golden in *Composition,* than in life. 1. *Know thyself;* 2dly, *Reverence thyself.*

> This is the grand secret for finding readers and retaining them: let him who would move and convince others, be first moved and convinced himself. Horace's rule, *Si vis me flere,* is applicable in a wider sense than the literal one. To every poet, to every writer, we might say: Be true, if you would be believed.

> Truth! there can be no merit, no craft at all, without that. And further, all beauty is in the long run only *fineness* of truth, or what we call expression, the finer accommodation of speech to that vision within.

And Housman's little handbook to the poetic mind yields this illustration:

Having drunk a pint of beer at luncheon—beer is a sedative to the brain,
and my afternoons are the least intellectual portion of my life—I would go
out for a walk of two or three hours. As I went along, thinking of nothing
in particular, only looking at things around me and following the progress
of the seasons, there would flow into my mind, with sudden and unaccount-
able emotion, sometimes a line or two of verse, sometimes a whole stanza
at once.

This is the logical terminus of the series already quoted. Here is a confession
of how poems were written which would do as a definition of poetry just as
well as "emotion recollected in tranquillity"—and which the young poet
might equally well take to heart as a practical rule. Drink a pint of beer,
relax, go walking, think on nothing in particular, look at things, surrender
yourself to yourself, search for the truth in your own soul, listen to the sound
of your own inside voice, discover and express the *vraie vérité*.

It is probably true that all this is excellent advice for poets. The young
imagination fired by Wordsworth and Carlyle is probably closer to the
verge of producing a poem than the mind of the student who has been
sobered by Aristotle or Richards. The art of inspiring poets, or at least of
inciting something like poetry in young persons, has probably gone further
in our day than ever before. Books of creative writing such as those issued
from the Lincoln School are interesting evidence of what a child can do.[5]
All this, however, would appear to belong to an art separate from criticism
—to a psychological discipline, a system of self-development, a yoga, which
the young poet perhaps does well to notice, but which is something different from the public art of evaluating poems.

Coleridge and Arnold were better critics than most poets have been,
and if the critical tendency dried up the poetry in Arnold and perhaps in
Coleridge, it is not inconsistent with our argument, which is that judgment of poems is different from the art of producing them. Coleridge has
given us the classic "anodyne" story, and tells what he can about the
genesis of a poem which he calls a "psychological curiosity," but his
definitions of poetry and of the poetic quality "imagination" are to be
found elsewhere and in quite other terms.

It would be convenient if the passwords of the intentional school, "sin-

---

[5] See Hughes Mearns, *Creative Youth* (Garden City, 1925), esp. 10, 27-29. The technique of
inspiring poems has apparently been outdone more recently by the study of inspiration in successful poets and other artists. See, for instance, Rosamond E. M. Harding, *An Anatomy of Inspiration* (Cambridge, 1940); Julius Portnoy, *A Psychology of Art Creation* (Philadelphia, 1942);
Rudolf Arnheim and others, *Poets at Work* (New York, 1947); Phyllis Bartlett, *Poems in Process*
(New York, 1951); Brewster Ghiselin (ed.), *The Creative Process: A Symposium* (Berkeley and
Los Angeles, 1952).

cerity," "fidelity," "spontaneity," "authenticity," "genuineness," "origin-
ality," could be equated with terms such as "integrity," "relevance," "unity,"
"function," "maturity," "subtlety," "adequacy," and other more precise terms
of evaluation—in short, if "expression" always meant aesthetic achievement.
But this is not so.

"Aesthetic" art, says Professor Curt Ducasse, an ingenious theorist of
expression, is the conscious objectification of feelings, in which an intrinsic part is the critical moment. The artist corrects the objectification
when it is not adequate. But this may mean that the earlier attempt was not
successful in objectifying the self, or "it may also mean that it was a
successful objectification of a self which, when it confronted us clearly,
we disowned and repudiated in favor of another."[6] What is the standard
by which we disown or accept the self? Professor Ducasse does not say.
Whatever it may be, however, this standard is an element in the definition
of art which will not reduce to terms of objectification. The evaluation
of the work of art remains public; the work is measured against something
outside the author.

IV

There is criticism of poetry and there is author psychology, which when
applied to the present or future takes the form of inspirational promotion;
but author psychology can be historical too, and then we have literary
biography, a legitimate and attractive study in itself, one approach, as
Professor Tillyard would argue, to personality, the poem being only a
parallel approach. Certainly it need not be with a derogatory purpose that
one points out personal studies, as distinct from poetic studies, in the realm
of literary scholarship. Yet there is danger of confusing personal and poetic
studies; and there is the fault of writing the personal as if it were poetic.

There is a difference between internal and external evidence for the
meaning of a poem. And the paradox is only verbal and superficial that
what is (1) internal is also public: it is discovered through the semantics
and syntax of a poem, through our habitual knowledge of the language,
through grammars, dictionaries, and all the literature which is the source
of dictionaries, in general through all that makes a language and culture;
while what is (2) external is private or idiosyncratic; not a part of the
work as a linguistic fact: it consists of revelations (in journals, for example,
or letters or reported conversations) about how or why the poet wrote the

---

[6] Curt Ducasse, *The Philosophy of Art* (New York, 1929), 116.

poem—to what lady, while sitting on what lawn, or at the death of what friend or brother. There is (3) an intermediate kind of evidence about the character of the author or about private or semiprivate meanings attached to words or topics by the author or by a coterie of which he is a member. The meaning of words is the history of words, and the biography of an author, his use of a word, and the associations which the word had for *him,* are part of the word's history and meaning.[7] But the three types of evidence, especially (2) and (3), shade into one another so subtly that it is not always easy to draw a line between examples, and hence arises the difficulty for criticism. The use of biographical evidence need not involve intentionalism, because while it may be evidence of what the author intended, it may also be evidence of the meaning of his words and the dramatic character of his utterance. On the other hand, it may not be all this. And a critic who is concerned with evidence of type (1) and moderately with that of type (3) will in the long run produce a different sort of comment from that of the critic who is concerned with (2) and with (3) where it shades into (2).

The whole glittering parade of Professor Lowes' *Road to Xanadu,* for instance, runs along the border between types (2) and (3) or boldly traverses the romantic region of (2). " 'Kubla Khan' " says Professor Lowes, "is the fabric of a vision, but every image that rose up in its weaving had passed that way before. And it would seem that there is nothing haphazard or fortuitous in their return." This is not quite clear—not even when Professor Lowes explains that there were clusters of associations, like hooked atoms, which were drawn into complex relation with other clusters in the deep well of Coleridge's memory, and which then coalesced and issued forth as poems. If there was nothing "haphazard or fortuitous" in the way the images returned to the surface, that may mean (1) that Coleridge could not produce what he did not have, that he was limited in his creation by what he had read or otherwise experienced, or (2) that having received certain clusters of associations, he was bound to return them in just the way he did, and that the value of the poem may be described in terms of the experiences on which he had to draw. The latter pair of propositions (a sort of Hartleyan associationism which Coleridge himself repudiated in the *Biographia*) may not be assented to. There were certainly other combinations, other poems, worse or better, that might have been written by men who had read Bartram and Purchas and Bruce and Milton. And this will be true no matter how many times we are able to add to the brilliant

---

[7] And the history of words *after* a poem is written may contribute meanings which if relevant to the original pattern should not be ruled out by a scruple about intention.

complex of Coleridge's reading. In certain flourishes (such as the sentence we have quoted) and in chapter headings like "The Shaping Spirit," "The Magical Synthesis," "Imagination Creatrix," it may be that Professor Lowes pretends to say more about the actual poems than he does. There is a certain deceptive variation in these fancy chapter titles; one expects to pass on to a new stage in the argument, and one finds—more and more sources, more and more about "the streamy nature of association."[8]

"Wohin der Weg?" quotes Professor Lowes for the motto of his book. "Kein Weg! Ins Unbretretene." Precisely because the way is *unbetreten,* we should say, it leads away from the poem. Bartram's *Travels* contains a good deal of the history of certain words and of certain romantic Floridian conceptions that appear in "Kubla Khan." And a good deal of that history has passed and was then passing into the very stuff of our language. Perhaps a person who has read Bartram appreciates the poem more than one who has not. Or, by looking up the vocabulary of "Kubla Khan" in the *Oxford English Dictionary,* or by reading some of the other books there quoted, a person may know the poem better. But it would seem to pertain little to the poem to know that *Coleridge* had read Bartram. There is a gross body of life, of sensory and mental experience, which lies behind and in some sense causes every poem, but can never be and need not be known in the verbal and hence intellectual composition which is the poem. For all the objects of our manifold experience, for every unity, there is an action of the mind which cuts off roots, melts away context—or indeed we should never have objects or ideas or anything to talk about.

It is probable that there is nothing in Professor Lowes' vast book which could detract from anyone's appreciation of either *The Ancient Mariner* or "Kubla Khan." We next present a case where preoccupation with evidence of type (3) has gone so far as to distort a critic's view of a poem (yet a case not so obvious as those that abound in our critical journals).

In a well-known poem by John Donne appears this quatrain:

> Moving of th'earth brings harmes and feares,
> Men reckon what it did and meant,
> But trepidation of the spheares,
> Though greater farre, is innocent.

A recent critic in an elaborate treatment of Donne's learning has written of this quatrain as follows:

[8] Chaps. VIII, "The Pattern," and XVI, "The Known and Familiar Landscape," will be found of most help to the student of the poem.

He touches the emotional pulse of the situation by a skillful allusion to the
new and the old astronomy. . . . Of the new astronomy, the "moving of
the earth" is the most radical principle; of the old, the "trepidation of the
spheares" is the motion of the greatest complexity. . . . The poet must
exhort his love to quietness and calm upon his departure; and for this
purpose the figure based upon the latter motion (trepidation), long ab-
sorbed into the traditional astronomy, fittingly suggests the tension of the
moment without arousing the "harmes and feares" implicit in the figure
of the moving earth.[9]

The argument is plausible and rests on a well substantiated thesis that
Donne was deeply interested in the new astronomy and its repercussions
in the theological realm. In various works Donne shows his familiarity
with Kepler's *De Stella Nova,* with Galileo's *Siderius Nuncius,* with
William Gilbert's *De Magnete,* and with Clavius' commentary on the *De
Sphaera* of Scarobosco. He refers to the new science in his Sermon at
Paul's Cross and in a letter to Sir Henry Goodyer. In *The First Anni-
versary* he says the "new philosophy calls all in doubt." In the *Elegy on
Prince Henry* he says that the "least moving of the center" makes "the
world to shake."

It is difficult to answer argument like this, and impossible to answer it
with evidence of like nature. There is no reason why Donne might not
have written a stanza in which the two kinds of celestial motion stood for
two sorts of emotion at parting. And if we become full of astronomical
ideas and see Donne only against the background of the new science, we
may believe that he did. But the text itself remains to be dealt with,
the analyzable vehicle of a complicated metaphor. And one may observe:
(1) that the movement of the earth according to the Copernician theory
is a celestial motion, smooth and regular, and while it might cause religious or philosophic fears, it could not be associated with the crudity
and earthiness of the kind of commotion which the speaker in the poem
wishes to discourage; (2) that there is another moving of the earth, an
earthquake, which has just these qualities and is to be associated with
the tear-floods and sigh-tempests of the second stanza of the poem; (3)
that "trepidation" is an appropriate opposite of earthquake, because each
is a shaking or vibratory motion; and "trepidation of the spheares" is
"greater farre" than an earthquake, but not much greater (if two such motions
can be compared as to greatness) than the annual motion of the earth;
(4) that reckoning what it "did and meant" shows that the event has

[9] Charles M. Coffin, *John Donne and the New Philosophy* (New York, 1927), 97-98.

passed, like an earthquake, not like the incessant celestial movement of the earth. Perhaps a knowledge of Donne's interest in the new science may add another shade of meaning, an overtone to the stanza in question, though to say even this runs against the words. To make the geocentric and heliocentric antithesis the core of the metaphor is to disregard the English language, to prefer private evidence to public, external to internal.

V

If the distinction between kinds of evidence has implications for the historical critic, it has them no less for the contemporary poet and his critic. Or, since every rule for a poet is but another side of a judgment by a critic, and since the past is the realm of the scholar and critic, and the future and present that of the poet and the critical leaders of taste, we may say that the problems arising in literary scholarship from the intentional fallacy are matched by others which arise in the world of progressive experiment.

The question of "allusiveness," for example, as acutely posed by the poetry of Eliot, is certainly one where a false judgment is likely to involve the intentional fallacy. The frequency and depth of literary allusion in the poetry of Eliot and others has driven so many in pursuit of full meanings to the *Golden Bough* and the Elizabethan drama that it has become a kind of commonplace to suppose that we do not know what a poet means unless we have traced him in his reading—a supposition redolent with intentional implications. The stand taken by F. O. Matthiessen is a sound one and partially forestalls the difficulty.

> If one reads these lines with an attentive ear and is sensitive to their sudden shifts in movement, the contrast between the actual Thames and the idealized vision of it during an age before it flowed through a megalopolis is sharply conveyed by that movement itself, whether or not one recognizes the refrain to be from Spenser.

Eliot's allusions work when we know them—and to a great extent when we do not know them, through their suggestive power.

But sometimes we find allusions supported by notes, and it is a nice question whether the notes function more as guides to send us where we may be educated, or more as indications in themselves about the character of the allusions. "Nearly everything of importance . . . that is apposite to an appreciation of 'The Waste Land,'" writes Matthiessen of Miss Weston's book, "has been incorporated into the structure of the poem itself, or into Eliot's Notes." And with such an admission it may begin

to appear that it would not much matter if Eliot invented his sources (as
Sir Walter Scott invented chapter epigraphs from "old plays" and "anonymous" authors, or as Coleridge wrote marginal glosses for *The Ancient
Mariner*). Allusions to Dante, Webster, Marvell, or Baudelaire doubtless
gain something because these writers existed, but it is doubtful whether
the same can be said for an allusion to an obscure Elizabethan:

> The sound of horns and motors, which shall bring Sweeney to Mrs. Porter in
> the spring.

"Cf. Day, *Parliament of Bees*": says Eliot,

> When of a sudden, listening, you shall hear,
> A noise of horns and hunting, which shall bring
> Actaeon to Diana in the spring,
> Where all shall see her naked skin.

The irony is completed by the quotation itself; had Eliot, as is quite
conceivable, composed these lines to furnish his own background, there
would be no loss of validity. The conviction may grow as one reads Eliot's
next note: "I do not know the origin of the ballad from which these lines
are taken: it was reported to me from Sydney, Australia." The important
word in this note—on Mrs. Porter and her daughter who washed their
feet in soda water—is "ballad." And if one should feel from the lines themselves their "ballad" quality, there would be little need for the note.
Ultimately, the inquiry must focus on the integrity of such notes as parts of
the poem, for where they constitute special information about the meaning
of phrases in the poem, they ought to be subject to the same scrutiny as
any of the other words in which it is written. Matthiessen believes the notes
were the price Eliot "had to pay in order to avoid what he would have
considered muffling the energy of his poem by extended connecting links
in the text itself." But it may be questioned whether the notes and the
need for them are not equally muffling. F. W. Bateson has plausibly argued
that Tennyson's "The Sailor Boy" would be better if half the stanzas were
omitted, and the best versions of ballads like "Sir Patrick Spens" owe their
power to the very audacity with which the minstrel has taken for granted
the story upon which he comments. What then if a poet finds he cannot
take so much for granted in a more recondite context and rather than
write informatively, supplies notes? It can be said in favor of this plan
that at least the notes do not pretend to be dramatic, as they would
if written in verse. On the other hand, the notes may look like un-
assimilated material lying loose beside the poem, necessary for the mean-

ing of the verbal symbol, but not integrated, so that the symbol stands incomplete.

We mean to suggest by the above analysis that whereas notes tend to seem to justify themselves as external indexes to the author's *intention,* yet they ought to be judged like any other parts of a composition (verbal arrangement special to a particular context), and when so judged their reality as parts of the poem, or their imaginative integration with the rest of the poem, may come into question. Matthiessen, for instance, sees that Eliot's titles for poems and his epigraphs are informative apparatus, like the notes. But while he is worried by some of the notes and thinks that Eliot "appears to be mocking himself for writing the note at the same time that he wants to convey something by it," Matthiessen believes that the "device" of epigraphs "is not at all open to the objection of not being sufficiently structural." "The *intention,*" he says, "is to enable the poet to secure a condensed expression in the poem itself." "In each case the epigraph *is designed* to form an integral part of the effect of the poem." And Eliot himself, in his notes, has justified his poetic practice in terms of intention.

> The Hanged Man, a member of the traditional pack, fits my purpose in two ways: because he is associated in my mind with the Hanged God of Frazer, and because I associate him with the hooded figure in the passage of the disciples to Emmaus in Part V. . . . The man with Three Staves (an authentic member of the Tarot pack) I associate, quite arbitrarily, with the Fisher King himself.

And perhaps he is to be taken more seriously here, when off guard in a note, than when in his Norton Lectures he comments on the difficulty of saying what a poem means and adds playfully that he thinks of prefixing to a second edition of *Ash Wednesday* some lines from *Don Juan:*

> I don't pretend that I quite understand
> My own meaning when I would be *very* fine;
> But the fact is that I have nothing planned
> Unless it were to be a moment merry.

If Eliot and other contemporary poets have any characteristic fault, it may be in *planning* too much.

Allusiveness in poetry is one of several critical issues by which we have illustrated the more abstract issue of intentionalism, but it may be for today the most important illustration. As a poetic practice allusiveness would appear to be in some recent poems an extreme corollary of the romantic intentionalist assumption, and as a critical issue it challenges and brings to light in a special way the basic premise of intentionalism. The following instance from the poetry of Eliot may serve to epitomize the practical implications of what we have been saying. In Eliot's "Love Song of J. Alfred Prufrock," toward the end, occurs the line: "I have heard the mermaids singing, each to each," and this bears a certain resemblance to a line in a Song by John Donne, "Teach me to heare Mermaides singing," so that for the reader acquainted to a certain degree with Donne's poetry, the critical question arises: Is Eliot's line an allusion to Donne's? Is Prufrock thinking about Donne? Is Eliot thinking about Donne? We suggest that there are two radically different ways of looking for an answer to this question. There is (1) the way of poetic analysis and exegesis, which inquires whether it makes any sense if Eliot-Prufrock *is* thinking about Donne. In an earlier part of the poem, when Prufrock asks, "Would it have been worth while, . . . To have squeezed the universe into a ball," his words take half their sadness and irony from certain energetic and passionate lines of Marvell's "To His Coy Mistress." But the exegetical inquirer may wonder whether mermaids considered as "strange sights" (to hear them is in Donne's poem analogous to getting with child a mandrake root) have much to do with Prufrock's mermaids, which seem to be symbols of romance and dynamism, and which incidentally have literary authentication, if they need it, in a line of a sonnet by Gérard de Nerval. This method of inquiry may lead to the conclusion that the given resemblance between Eliot and Donne is without significance and is better not thought of, or the method may have the disadvantage of providing no certain conclusion. Nevertheless, we submit that this is the true and objective way of criticism, as contrasted to what the very uncertainty of exegesis might tempt a second kind of critic to undertake: (2) the way of biographical or genetic inquiry, in which, taking advantage of the fact that Eliot is still alive, and in the spirit of a man who would settle a bet, the critic writes to Eliot and asks him what he meant, or if he had Donne in mind. We shall not here weigh the probabilities—whether Eliot would answer that he meant nothing at all, had nothing at all in mind—a sufficiently good answer to such a question—or in an unguarded moment might furnish a clear and, within its limit, irrefutable answer. Our point is that such an answer to such an inquiry would have nothing to do with the poem "Prufrock"; it would not be a critical inquiry. Critical inquiries, unlike bets, are not settled in this way. Critical inquiries are not settled by consulting the oracle.

Bibliography

Most current discussions of the artist's intentions are critically focussed on Wimsatt and Beardsley's paper (printed here). Among the more interesting are:

Henry Aiken, "The Aesthetic Relevance of Artists' Intentions," *Journal of Philosophy*, Volume LII (1955), 742-753;

Leslie Fiedler, "Archetype and Signature: A Study of the Relationship Between Biography and Poetry," *Sewanee Review*, Volume LX (1952), 253-273;

Isabel Hungerland, "The Concept of Intention in Art Criticism," *Journal of Philosophy*, Volume LII (1955), 733-742;

Richard Kuhns, "Criticism and the Problem of Intention," *Journal of Philosophy*, Volume LVII (1960), 5-23;

Erwin Panofsky, "The History of Art as a Humanistic Discipline," in T. M. Greene (ed.), *The Meaning of the Humanities* (Princeton, 1940);

Theodore Redpath, "Some Problems of Modern Aesthetics," in C. A. Mace (ed.), *British Philosophy in the Mid-Century* (London, 1957);

Eliseo Vivas, "Mr. Wimsatt on the Theory of Literature," *Comparative Literature*, Volume VII (1955), 344-361.

The general question of intention, outside the narrow domain of aesthetics, has been most fully canvassed in:

G. E. M. Anscombe, *Intention* (Oxford, 1957).

VI

THE CRITIC'S
INTERPRETATION

IN PRINCIPLE, it would seem that one could not evaluate a work of art unless it were possible to describe it first in a value-neutral way. Otherwise, one supposes, we could not fix its identity for purposes of disputing its merit. Nevertheless, it is difficult to individuate works of art and it is difficult to hold that the accounts we give of particular works of art (in any of the arts) are always merely descriptive.

At times, we provide interpretations of the works before us. Think, for example, of our efforts to interpret Schönberg's music, or Picasso's *Guernica*, or Joyce's *Finnegan's Wake*, or Eliot's *Four Quartets*, or Martha Graham's *Oedipus*. The striking fact is that, often, we cannot say with precision where description ends and interpretation begins. The boundaries of works of art are not easily set. Consequently, logical questions arise about whether our accounts, at times clearly descriptive, at times clearly interpretive, may be said merely to be true or false, accurate or inaccurate; or whether we must provide for the admissibility of plural interpretations possibly incompatible one with another (think of the performing arts) and, consequently, provide for models of plausibility and reasonableness that may at times displace those of truth and accuracy.

Interpretations, clearly, must be compatible with those elements of a work of art that are, without dispute, open to description. This is the lower limit of interpretation. But a question arises about the upper limit. How are we to sort out acceptable and unacceptable interpretations of given works that manage to meet the lower condition? Part of the difficulty is that critics are inevitably partisans of this or that way of interpreting. There is evidence of converging professional standards, not, however, formally agreed upon, that would be tolerant of interpretations advanced from a variety of unrelated, even incompatible, points of view. But there is also evidence that disputes about interpretations advanced quite frequently reflect the appreciative bias of a commentator rather than his effort to measure such hypotheses by what are admittedly loose professional criteria of competence.

It was, not long ago, interesting to debate whether the artist or the critic was the more creative. The issue was more important to set than to resolve, because it pointed to the virtuoso aspect of interpretive criticism. One cannot say in advance what the limits will be on the plausibility of new interpretations. The cultural setting changes and new perspectives become convincing. Ingenious critics then set about reinterpreting the tradition: thus, Marxist and Freudian criticism, to mention the more prominent. But the new frames of imagination within which criticism is attempted need not be always as large-scale as these; a hint may even be provided by the private vision of the artist (think of Blake and Breughel) or by the special and personal focus of the critic. One sees, therefore, important analogies between the interpreting critic and the performing artist —and, inevitably, consequences for the logic of criticism.

Joseph Margolis attempts to formulate a model for interpretive criticism that would accommodate its distinctive features.

The Logic of Interpretation

JOSEPH MARGOLIS

IT IS difficult to decide what is admissible in interpretations of works of art. We surely do not wish to admit every reverie or outburst. But antecedent restrictions are very nearly impossible to agree upon. Suppose, for example, I attempt to interpret Voltaire's *Candide* by relating the action of the tale not merely to the superficial and obviously intended correspondences with Leibniz's philosophy but also to the introspective enterprises of Descartes, of the Reformers, of Hamlet; suppose I claim it to be aesthetically instructive to compare the plan of the tale with *Genesis* and with the *Odyssey;* or suppose I find it helpful to consider its theme in comparison with *Gulliver's Travels* and with the French and American Revolutions, which have not yet occurred. When will my comments be irrelevant, with respect to providing a critical account of the work? Suppose, after having read Wallace Stevens' *Sunday Morning* many times, I happen to read Plotinus just before I pick *Sunday Morning* up again and find the poem considerably illuminated by the specific philosophical imagery of the *Enneads,* though I

This article originally appeared in the *Bucknell Review,* Volume VII (May, 1958), 244-259, under the title, "The Problem of Relevance in Esthetic Criticism" (now, with major revisions). Reprinted with the permission of the *Bucknell Review.*

have not the slightest idea whether or not Stevens had the work in mind. Are my comments that depend on this juxtaposition irrelevant?[1]

Let us be clear about the nature of this question. It is easily confused with that other, concerning perceptual aspects, discussed in the well-known account of Wittgenstein's, of "seeing as," of the "dawning" of an aspect of a thing perceived.[2] I can well imagine that one might be tempted to say that the analysis of Matisse's *The Piano Lesson,* for example, concerns itself with the "dawning" of an aspect of the painting. I should not oppose this way of speaking of discoveries connected with interpretation. Still, 'interpretation,' in the present context, is not taken in the sense Wittgenstein has in mind. "You only 'see the duck and rabbit aspects,' " he says, "if you are already conversant with the shapes of these two animals. There is no analogous condition for seeing the aspects [of the 'double' cross—which may be seen as a white cross on a black ground and as a black cross on a white ground]."[3] I should not deny that Tchelichew's *Hide and Seek* and Picasso's *Three Musicians* exploit both of these kinds of illusions; this is also close to what Heinrich Wölfflin has in mind, discussing painterly and linear styles: for instance, he says that if one paints a turning wheel, "only when the wheel has been made indistinct does it begin to turn."[4] But if we must speak of *interpreting* the branches of a tree, having seen the *solution* of a picture-*puzzle,* as a human shape[5]—Wittgenstein's term is *deuten*[6]— this would still fall short of the problem we have in mind. Again, Wittgenstein says, "It is possible to take the duck-rabbit simply for the picture of a rabbit, the double cross simply for the picture of a black cross, but not to take the bare triangular figure for the picture of an object that has fallen over. To see this aspect of the triangle demands imagination"[7] Imagination is an advance; but the point still remains that, in Wittgenstein's illustration, it is *gratuitous.* It is concerned more with: "Imagine that triangle as . . ." (the case of a child, for instance, imagining a chest to be a house[8]) than with: "Would it be plausible to construe this painting thus?"

Wittgenstein is primarily interested in a certain *clicking-into-place* of per-

[1] W. H. Auden is reported to have found an "ironic commentary on a theory of Kierkegaard in Lear's limerick, 'There was an old man of Whitehaven,' " by David Daiches, in *Critical Approaches to Literature* (Englewood Cliffs, 1956), p. 303.

[2] Ludwig Wittgenstein, *Philosophical Investigations,* translated by G. E. M. Anscombe (New York, 1953), II, xi.

[3] *Ibid.,* p. 207.

[4] *Principles of Art History,* translated by M. D. Hottinger (New York, n.d.), p. 22. Cf. also, Rudolf Arnheim, *Art and Visual Perception* (Berkeley, 1954).

[5] Wittgenstein, *op. cit.,* p. 198.

[6] *Ibid.,* p. 193.

[7] *Ibid.,* p. 207.

[8] *Ibid.,* p. 206.

ception; so the remark becomes relevant: "I can't see it as a . . . *yet*."[9] The question here is rather: "Could you defend this way of seeing it?" Wittgenstein concludes, "Aspect blindness will be *akin* to the lack of a 'musical ear.' "[10] The emphasis, in his account, is always on an ordinary ability to spot aspects of things and on the difficulty for, or incapacity of, someone to spot these aspects. Thus he says the experience rests on "the mastery of a technique,"[11] that one may say, "You are looking at it *wrong*."[12] In a word, Wittgenstein is speaking about getting someone to see something in a certain way; while here, the emphasis is rather on whether a certain way of seeing something is critically admissible. For Wittgenstein, you may be *doing* something wrong if you are not able to see what is required; in our present context, your *account* of a particular work of art may be inadmissible. For him, it is basically a perceptual question; here, it is a question of evidence and justification—applying, by the way, as much to literature as to the visual arts.

Having said this much, I must also add that the decision that a given critical comment about some particular work is defensible belongs to the community of practicing critics; I am not here concerned with it. Also, the question of the relative merit of works of art is logically dependent on just the kind of decision I am taking no notice of here. Similarly, the discussion of the moral, religious, political, medical, and other practical functions of particular works presupposes agreement on the critical account of these works; else, it only pretends to treat the work of art as an aesthetically significant object. I wish to discuss only the sense in which interpretive statements are taken to be relevant, or eligible, and also justifiably included in an effort to clarify the aesthetic design of some particular work of art.

Some of the peculiarities of our critical references may be made clear by the following case in point. William Empson has sketched very skillfully an ingenious and fairly orthodox Freudian interpretation of *Alice in Wonderland*,[13] an account which has been called "probably the most completely successful brief Freudian analysis of literature yet written."[14] The first thing to observe is that, in 1865, Lewis Carroll was not familiar with Freud's theories and could not have used them deliberately. The second is that a really first-rate critic like Empson is not especially bothered by the apparent anachronism (viewing Freudian psychology in a scientifically neutral sense)

---

[9] *Ibid.*, p. 206 (italics mine).
[10] *Ibid.*, p. 214.
[11] *Ibid.*, p. 208.
[12] *Ibid.*, p. 218 (italics mine).
[13] Cf. *Some Versions of Pastoral* (London, 1935).
[14] Stanley Edgar Hyman, *The Armed Vision* (New York, 1948), p. 283.

and, when criticized by his colleagues, is not criticized for this fault.[15] The third thing to observe, in a way the most interesting, is that the scientific validity of Freudian analysis is never really in question and the relevance of Empson's analysis of *Alice* seems to be independent of the scientific issue. That is, bluntly, even if Freudian psychoanalysis were scrapped as false science, it would not lose its possible relevance for the interpretation of works of art.[16] We might, conceivably, devalue a work of art whose design relied on a false theory originally presumed true (though this does not appear to have counted in, say, the evaluation of French pointillism), but we might still be able to give a critical account of some work in terms of that theory (though this could not be properly done with the *kind* of theory to which the pointillists were apparently committed). This tolerance strikes us as odd.

The clue to the puzzle is that, though Freudian psychology claims respectable scientific status, the imagery of psychoanalysis is not at all restricted to the boundaries of its accompanying science; on the contrary, it is so much a part of our general culture that the imagination both of artists and of semi-educated persons is saturated with it. We think, see, and imagine in terms of Freudian symbols, not merely because our subconscious selves employ them for ulterior ends—a debatable thesis in the science of psychology—but because our conscious selves have assimilated the fascinating perspective and fictions that Freud invented.[17]

The force of this defense of a Freudian interpretation of works of art may gain somewhat if we recognize that it relies on an influential "myth," just as does, say, Jacques Maritain's not uninstructive analysis of the poetry of Baudelaire and Rimbaud.[18] Maritain also would insist on the truth of the Catholic vision. Critics may be inspired by the claim, but the truth of the Catholic "myth" need not at all be presupposed in the critical effort to interpret a work of art from the perspective of that "myth." We should otherwise surely have to give up, say, Dante's *Commedia* if we were practicing literary critics and also anti-Catholics in a broader intellectual arena. The very same arguments may be used to support such quasi-

[15] Cf. David Daiches, *op cit.*, pp. 302-312.

[16] This possibility is completely absent, for instance, from Louis Fraiberg, *Psychoanalysis and American Literary Criticism* (Detroit, 1960).

[17] Cf. Jerome S. Bruner, "Freud and the Image of Man," *Partisan Review*, Vol. XXIII (1956), 340-347; also, A. Kazin, "Psychoanalysis and Literary Culture Today," *Partisan Review*, Vol. XXVI (1959), 46-55; Frederick J. Hoffman, *Freudianism and the Literary Mind* (Baton Rouge, 1945); Ernst Kris, "Freudianism and the Literary Mind" (review of Hoffman's book), in *Psychoanalysis Explorations in Art* (New York, 1952); William Phillips (ed.), *Art and Psychoanalysis* (New York, 1957).

[18] Cf. Jacques Maritain, *Creative Intuition in Art and Poetry* (New York, 1953).

scientific doctrines as Marxism and Jungian analytic psychology. These
are powerful systems of ideas which, on the one hand, claim to be true
about some important sector of the world and which, on the other, have
effectively captured a substantial part of society's habits of thinking and
seeing. We should expect someone educated in a Buddhist society to construe the design of Western works of art, wherever promising, in terms
of the "myths" that guide his own imagination. In a way it is inevitable, an
admission that may serve perhaps to soften the quite extraordinary and otherwise perplexingly arrogant comment of Maritain's. I cannot resist quoting it:

> Consider . . . that wherever art, Egyptian, Greek or Chinese, has attained
> a certain degree of grandeur and purity, it is already Christian, Christian
> in hope, because every spiritual splendor is a promise and a symbol of
> the divine harmonies of the Gospel.[19]

Corresponding statements, of course, could be located in the papers of
orthodox Freudians and Marxists.

It must not be supposed that criticism is altogether without rigor, because the practice of professionals is as free-wheeling as I have suggested.
I must insist that I am speaking at this point about the tolerance of criticism
of interpretations initiated from the vantage of the various points of view
mentioned; I am not yet speaking about the testing of such interpretations.
Though I may at least cite Meyer Schapiro's masterful sifting of the defensible and indefensible in Freud's classic study of Leonardo da Vinci.[20]
Schapiro entertains the Freudian proposal as initially eligible and seeks
to test its competence in the light of Leonardo's actual work and the art-
tradition in which it was produced; so it is that he disqualifies particular
interpretations of Freud's, on a critic's grounds, without at all challenging
the appropriateness of approaching paintings from a Freudian point of
view. The point at stake is this: because our habits of seeing, say, paintings
are susceptible of the Freudian perspective—among others—we cannot *a
priori* dismiss a Freudian effort to construe the design of particular paintings in its own characteristic terms; but when we examine, say, Freud's
comments on the *Mona Lisa* or the *Madonna and St. Anne,* the art-critic
Freud can claim no privileges from the psychoanalyst. The first wishes to
exhibit only that one can perceive the design of these paintings through
Freudian habits of thought; the second, that important portions of actual

---

[19] *Art and Scholasticism,* translated by J. F. Scanlan (New York, 1930), p. 54. Maritain
intends his remarks in an interpretive, and not merely an evaluative, sense; cf. *Creative Intuition
in Art and Poetry, passim.*
[20] Leonardo and Freud: an art-historical study," *Journal of the History of Ideas,* Vol. XVII
(April 1956), 147-178.

human behavior—including the activity of making fine art (though not its product, the work of art as such)—may be correctly analyzed by Freudian science.

I submit that, if critical tolerance is such as I have sketched, it is difficult to resist the proposition that in principle plural, non-converging, and even incompatible critical hypotheses may be defended as interpretations of a given work of art. This alone appears to be able to accommodate the arguments advanced; and if it were adopted, it would force us to appraise carefully the truth-status of critical interpretations—interpretations which, on the usual model provided for statements of fact, would in some instances have to be taken as contraries.

I have labelled the Freudian thesis, like the Catholic or the Marxist, a "myth" with respect to its relevance for criticism. This is central to my argument and requires some explanation (though I set no store by the particular term 'myth').[21] I should also say that the atomic theory of matter, even were it in some fair sense scientifically confirmed, could provide a "myth" for criticism. I take it, for instance, that the body of the new Renaissance science generated, in this sense, a "myth" illuminating part of the design of John Donne's *Anniversary* poems. A "myth," in the sense in which I am using the term, is a schema of the imagination which, independent of the scientific status of the propositions it may subtend, is capable of effectively organizing our way of viewing portions of the external world in accord with its distinctions. It goes without saying, therefore, that it can organize our daydreams and reveries—our interior imagination—as well. We know a "myth" to be "objective" for criticism, though it may not be so for science, when the habits of thought and perception and imagination of normal persons are educable in its terms and when their responses to appropriate stimuli are generally predictable.

The Freudian and Marxist and Catholic "myths" pervade our experience in everyday life. Whatever the scientific description of objects and events may be, things appear in the imaginative dimension of our experience to be loaded with emotional associations and symbolic import and even to suffer

[21] There are perhaps a variety of expressions that might have been substituted. A related term in currency is 'archetype'; but though it has been relatively liberated from Jungian psychology, it does nevertheless apply largely to the kind of symbolic image Jung himself originally explored. Cf. Northrop Frye, *Anatomy of Criticism* (Princeton, 1957); also, C. G. Jung, "On the Relation of Analytical Psychology to Poetic Art," *Contributions to Analytical Psychology,* translated by H. G. and C. F. Baynes (London, 1928); also, Maud Bodkin, *Archetypal Patterns in Poetry* (Oxford, 1934); and Joseph Campbell, *The Hero with a Thousand Faces* (New York, 1956). Similarly, the Marxist notion of "ideology" is useful, though restricted. Cf. Christopher Caudwell, *Illusion and Reality* (New York, 1937); also, George Thomson, *Aeschylus and Athens* (London, 1941).

distortions in characteristic ways. Insofar as these "overtones" become clarified and systematic, we may speak of an independent "myth," the power
of which may be seen in its applicability to novel experiences, that is, to experiences beyond those from which it was originally projected. The strength
of these "myths" undoubtedly is fed by the conviction that they subtend
true accounts of human conduct, that is, that they are capable of being
formulated as a science. The "myths" themselves however are merely
persistent habits of imagination capable of being described by an independent science. In themselves, they presume to be accounts of human
conduct; in critical practice, they are merely describable elements of human
conduct.

The imaginative schema (or "myth")[22] that the critic uses need not be as
elaborate and large-scale as the Freudian or Marxist or Catholic visions. It
may merely be a formulable conviction about life that the artist himself
may be supposed to have held, which, considered without regard to its own
truth or falsity, adequacy or inadequacy, may, in the hands of the critic,
enable us to impute a coherent design to a work otherwise defective or
puzzling in this respect. So, for example, Gustav Glück holds that "Brueghel's
habit of concealing the real object of a picture and letting it disappear in the
surrounding masses may be explained by his opinion of the World,
which he considered to be topsy-turvy and wrongheaded, blind to the importance of the most momentous occurrences."[23]

There is a clue here, by the way, concerning the nature of symbolic art.
A symbol need not, as Cleanth Brooks and Robert Penn Warren assert,
be "a metaphor from which the first term has been omitted."[24] A symbol
works by way of association and, quite literally, "stands for" something (however metaphoric the *source* of the symbol); it may appear in any of the arts
(unlike metaphor); also, it is specifically invoked by critics to explain certain
sorts of otherwise defective or puzzling designs of works of art (hence,
characteristically, in an interpretive context). Metaphor, on the other hand,
is a form of figurative speech, a literary device, involving a departure from
"literal" sense—which is not essential to symbols. The difference, then, is
not quantitative, as with Wellek and Austin;[25] it turns rather on a difference in logical use. We think of symbols in terms of what they represent

[22] Compare Rene Wellek and Austen Warren, *Theory of Literature* (2nd ed., New York,
1956), Ch. XV.
[23] *Pieter Brueghel the Elder,* translated by E. B. Shaw (London, 1936), pp. 13f. (cited by
Kenneth C. Lindsay and Bernard Huppe, "Meaning and Method in Brueghel's Painting,"
Journal of Aesthetics and Art Criticism, Vol. XIV [March, 1956]).
[24] *Understanding Poetry* (New York, 1951), p. 688.
[25] *Op. cit.,* p. 178. Their account, moreover, is not entirely self-consistent; compare p. 186.

or what they symbolize; and we think of metaphors in terms of what they mean or how they play with meanings. In the first, we ask what their particular sign function actually is; and in the second, having already conceded words to be signs, we ask only about their particular sense.[26] In a word, we construe symbols more syntactically; metaphor, more semantically.

To return to our illustration, biographical and historical research may make it likely that Brueghel held the view in question; but the adequacy of basing an interpretation of particular paintings upon such a view depends on altogether different considerations. We might conceivably restrict the sources from which eligible interpretations could be drawn, so that a thesis not congruent, say, with the letters of Brueghel be excluded; but having defined the eligible sources, we have not yet succeeded in providing a justifiable interpretation of any painting, based on these very sources. And we may always, of course, as in the unending body of *Hamlet* criticism, invite interpretations as much dependent on current "myths" as on those taken to be prevalent during Shakespeare's own day. Hence, the acceptability of Ernest Jones's Freudian interpretation of *Hamlet,* ignoring altogether the scientific pretensions of psychoanalysis itself (and Jones's application of it to Shakespeare).[27] Also, we shall not be at a loss to prescribe a measure of rigor in confirming such hypotheses, because, for one thing, every interpretation will have to be compatible with the describable properties of the work of art in question and because, for another, the most plausible designs will conform to stable, familiar "myths" or to such, even unfamiliar, as are antecedently rendered eligible on biographical or historical grounds. Isabel Hungerland suggests (having considered the propriety of historically oriented criticism) that

> [i]f my interest centers in aesthetic or artistic excellence[, t]he relevant rule here would be to adopt that interpretation which does the best for the work, i.e., which results in the highest rating in the order of worth.[28]

We need only note that such a selection must be made from among interpretations that are otherwise critically adequate (and possibly mutually incompatible); it depends, then, logically, on a subsidiary but obviously familiar rule, rather like that of restricting interpretations to the artist's intention.

[26] Cf. the illuminating discussion of symbols in Isabel Hungerland, *Poetic Discourse* (Berkeley, 1958), Ch. V, especially pp. 135-144.

[27] Cf. *Hamlet and Oedipus* (New York, 1949).

[28] "The Concept of Intention in Art Criticism," *Journal of Philosophy,* Vol. LII (November 24, 1955), 740.

The characteristic feature of critical interpretation that is philosophically most interesting is its tolerance of alternative and seemingly contrary hypotheses. We should not allow incompatible descriptions of any physical object to stand; at least one would require correction or we should find that the disparities were due to the different purposes the descriptions were to serve or the different circumstances under which they were rendered. But given the goal of interpretation, we do not understand that an admissible account necessarily precludes all others incompatible with itself. Stephen Pepper, we may note, has always insisted that there is some ideal object sto stand; at least one would require correction or we should converge.[29] Monroe Beardsley holds a similar view.[30] But if we simply examine the practice of critics, I think we shall find no warrant at all for the claim.

I should like to suggest that an analogue of this curious tolerance of incompatibles obtains in the physical sciences; and that certain arguments there are based on much the same logical model that is appropriate to interpretive disputes. One sometimes asks, for instance, "How was our solar system created?," "How was the moon formed?," "How did life originate?," "Are all the races of man descended from a common stock?" At the present stage of our researches these questions must be adjusted somewhat. For "How was our solar system created?," we substitute "How could it have been created?" For "Are all the races of man descended from a common stock?," "Is it conceivable both that they originated from different evolutionary lines and from the same evolutionary line?" Questions of this sort do not involve contrary-to-fact conditions. The answers afforded are such that the consequent of our conditional is true (the facts about the present solar system, for example) and the antecedent is meaningful but incapable, under present circumstances, of being verified. We imagine a set of initial conditions, compatible with known laws of nature and operating in accord with selected suitable laws, by means of which we can explain certain of the features of our present world. Some such accounts, say, Buffon's hypothesis or the Kant-Laplace hypothesis, may be demonstrably false, though the correct account be as yet unavailable; and in the absence of such an account, other hypotheses may be entertained that are in accord with preferred causal models and do not violate any relevant facts.[31]

[29] Cf. *The Work of Art* (Bloomington, 1955), pp. 30-31. His view suffers from other difficulties; cf. Donald Henze, "Is the Work of Art a Construct?," *Journal of Philosophy*, Vol. LII (1955), 433-439, and "The Work of Art," *Journal of Philosophy*, Vol. LIV (1957), 429-442.

[30] Cf. *Aesthetics* (New York, 1958), pp. 46-58.

[31] C. S. Peirce has addressed himself to much the same issue, in discussing the concept of "abduction." Cf. "Abduction and Induction," *Philosophical Writings of Peirce*, edited by Justus Buchler (London, 1940).

Now, regardless of the possibility of verifying any given hypothesis about, say, the origin of the solar system at some future time, we are in a position, in the present, to assess the *plausibility* of such an hypothesis; it is even possible to guage to some extent the degree of plausibility of alternative hypotheses. So we have a procedure for determining the plausibility of causal hypotheses that is logically independent of determining their truth. In aesthetic criticism, correspondingly, we have procedures for determining the truth of the statements that enter into our description of a work of art and procedures for determining the plausibility of interpretive statements.[32] And just as an hypothesis about the origin of the solar system must accord with the known laws and facts of the system, would-be interpretations must accord with the description of a given work of art and with admissible "myths" or schemes of imagination.

The following provide the principal distinctions between the "true" and the "plausible." First, we invoke plausibility only when we cannot actually determine truth. Second, no plausible account may be incompatible with an admittedly true statement. Third, neither true nor false statements may be viewed as merely plausible or implausible, and neither plausible nor implausible statements are logically precluded from being judged true or false. Fourth, where the statements "P is true" and "Q is true" are contraries, the statements "P is plausible" and "Q is plausible" are not contraries. Fifth, statements are judged plausible or implausible in virtue of their use of preferred explanatory models in any given domain; and where such models may be weighted for preferability and the features of what is to be accounted for also weighted for priority and importance in explanation, the plausibility of the corresponding statements may also be graded. In science, for example, we may be asked to account plausibly for the origin of the moon without, say, assuming the gravitational activity of any body outside our present solar system, but in accord with the density, size, and composition of the moon itself. Correspondingly, in criticism, we may be asked to interpret a work of art in accord with some well-defined "myth" and in a way that gives due prominence to preferred features of the work itself.

It must be admitted that, though they are always marginal to the main effort of science, considerations of plausibility are more nearly central to aesthetic criticism. In fact, scientific speculations of the sort illustrated are treated in terms of plausibility only because of a technical inability to gain the desired information; critical interpretations, on the other hand, are, in

---

[32] Cf. my "Describing and Interpreting Works of Art," *Philosophy and Phenomenological Research*, Vol. XXII (June, 1961), 537-542.

principle, logically weak. It is this probably that gives the appearance of lack of rigor to critical pronouncements. But it is a prejudice that is unsympathetic to the special interests of criticism and appreciation (which may very well wish to explore the rich possibilities of interpretation of some particular work) and to the special features of works of art (for which causal inquiries are themselves quite marginal).

At any rate, we cannot ask for more precision than the subject will allow.

There is, then, a characteristic rigor to critical interpretations, noticeably weaker than matters of fact ordinarily require. But, more important, the sort of rigor associated with determining matters of fact is flatly inappropriate in the circumstances in which interpretations are provided.

Bibliography

Among recent contributions bearing on the descriptive and interpretive efforts of critics, the following may be noted:

Monroe Beardsley, *Aesthetics* (New York, 1958), Chapter IX;

R. S. Crane et al., *Critics and Criticism* (Chicago, 1952);

T. S. Eliot, "The Frontiers of Criticism," *Sewanee Review,* Volume LXIV (1956), 525-543;

H. S. Eveling, "Composition and Criticism," *Proceedings of the Aristotelian Society,* Volume LIX (1958-1959);

Isabel C. Hungerland, *Poetic Discourse* (Berkeley, 1958), Chapter VI;

Margaret Macdonald, "Some Distinctive Features of Arguments used in Criticism of the Arts," reprinted (revised) in William Elton (ed.), *Aesthetics and Language* (Oxford, 1954);

Joseph Margolis, "Describing and Interpreting Works of Art," *Philosophy and Phenomenological Research,* Volume XXII (1961), 537-542;

Harold Osborne, *Aesthetics and Criticism* (London, 1955), Chapter XI;

C. L. Stevenson, "On the 'Analysis' of a Work of Art," *Philosophical Review,* Volume LXVII (1958), 31-51;

Eliseo Vivas, *Creation and Discovery* (New York, 1955).

Earlier conceptions of criticism are discussed in:

Stephen C. Pepper, *The Basis of Criticism in the Arts* (Cambridge, 1945).

VII

INTERPRETATION
AND EVALUATION

IT IS perhaps too easy to say the critic is performing his professional function when he provides us with interpretations of particular works of art.
This is not to say he is exceeding his right. But, possibly, there are no clearly
formulable criteria by which to gauge the acceptability of his interpretations.
Possibly, to advance an interpretation is, in effect, to direct others to construe
a work this way or that. In short, may it not be that the very activity of
critical interpretation presupposes certain appreciative preferences, that one
could not, in an appreciatively neutral way, appraise the interpretations
advanced by another? May it not be that the "right" interpretation is, ultimately, the interpretation one prefers?

The issue is a subtle one. One supposes that competing descriptions of some
work may be evaluated in a professional way, that to say this or that
analysis is inaccurate need betray no appreciative bias at all. We speak thus
when we are assured that there is some prevailing professional model to
gauge practice by. Because to appeal to such a model is not to deny normative
considerations; on the contrary, it is simply to judge by norms that are not

merely subject to appreciative bias. The question then follows, Are there, at least implicitly, such professional models for interpretation? Or, more loosely, would it be odd in any logical respect to formulate such models for interpretation?

The whole matter is double-edged, however, because the account of what it is an interpretive critic is doing (if one refuses to concede professional standards) may be made to depend on one's general theory of value. Would one, for instance, say that the critic is persuading others to construe a given work of art in his preferred way? or is he telling others to construe it thus? or is he telling others that they ought to construe it thus (supposing that "ought" is not merely persuasive or imperative)? And possibly, even conceding professional standards, the educative role of the critic would lead us to similar value distinctions (though not, of course, in quite the same challenging way).

So the questions resolve themselves into two distinct sets. Are there, or are there emerging, professional norms for critical interpretation, corresponding, however loosely, to the scientist's norms for judging factual claims and competing explanations? Or would it be logically inappropriate to attempt to fit such norms to the actual practice of critics (in a sense that would not merely betray one's own appreciative bias)? On the other hand, in so far as the critic's remarks are appraisals, what will be a suitable description of their logical properties? And will they, or will they not, be similar to the value judgments of other domains of interest?

C. L. Stevenson has, in his discussion of the interpretation of works of art, challengingly adapted his well-known value theory to the domain of aesthetics.

On the Reasons That Can Be Given for the Interpretation of a Poem

CHARLES L. STEVENSON

I

WHEN we are uncertain about what a poem means, wondering whether to interpret it this way or that way, we normally try to make up our minds in the light of reasons. We realize that we may be missing meanings that are "there," or reading in meanings that "aren't there"; and we hope that our reasons, protecting us from such errors, will help us to interpret the poem correctly.

In the present paper I shall try to explain, though only in the most general way, what sort of reasons are available in such cases. Are they the ordinary reasons of deductive or inductive logic, or are they reasons of another sort? My aim will accordingly be *meta*-critical: I shall not be suggesting or de-

Printed here for the first time with the permission of C. L. Stevenson.

fending poetic interpretations of my own, but shall be attempting, merely, to clarify the sort of issue that interpretations are likely to bring with them.

II

An interpretation can be guided, of course, by reasons that appeal to the dictionary. Thus when the sea of faith is described as retreating

> down the vast edges drear
> And naked shingles of the world[1]

an American reader may be temporarily perplexed, feeling that "shingles" obscures the metaphor. He has only to consult the dictionary to find a sense, marked "chiefly British," in which "shingles" refers to gravel-like stones found on the seashore; and his perplexity about the lines will then vanish.

Note, however, that his dictionary reason has only *helped* him to establish his interpretation. For the dictionary, in listing several senses of "shingles," says nothing about which of them is appropriate to Arnold's poem. Our reader has decided that for himself, and in doing so has been tacitly guided by another reason, namely: "The sense I am selecting fits in with the context."

In general, although dictionary reasons, and reasons drawn from the rest of linguistics, manifestly help to establish the foundations of an interpretation, they leave the superstructure to be built by reasons of another sort. Our reader will be encouraged, for instance, to find that his newly discovered sense of "shingles" was current in the nineteenth century; for that frees his interpretation from any suspicion of being anachronistic. The notion of an anachronism, of course, immediately takes him beyond the dictionary. Its connection with the *date of the poem* leads him to take a first step toward relating his interpretation to what he knows about the *poet*.

To find other reasons that can support an interpretation let me turn to a more complicated example—though not without apologies for having to present it so briefly:

In *The Folly of Being Comforted,* by W. B. Yeats, the poet (or imagined speaker) is reminded that his

> well beloved's hair has threads of grey;

but he replies that he will have no comfort for this, insisting that

> Time can but make her beauty over again.

And he concludes with these lines,

[1] From Matthew Arnold's *Dover Beach.*

> O heart! O heart! if she'd but turn her head,
> You'd know the folly of being comforted!

Now these concluding lines, it will be observed, lend themselves to two sharply different interpretations. Perhaps they reiterate the rest of the poem, affirming with renewed confidence that no comfort is needed. But perhaps, instead, they break sharply with the rest of the poem. The poet can no longer pretend that no comfort is needed; his feelings force him, in the end, to see that for such a loss no comfort is *possible*.[2]

Those who have most studied Yeats, I suspect, will favor the second of these interpretations. But reasons of the sort I have previously mentioned—concerned with conventional English, fidelity to context, and freedom from anachronism—will not be very helpful in showing that their interpretation is more defensible than the first one; so let us see what other reasons they might wish to give.

They might begin by pointing out that the second interpretation is far more in the spirit of Yeats, as one can see by examining his other works—a consideration that is both true and relevant, in my opinion, but by no means final. It remains possible that *this* poem *departs* from Yeats's usual spirit.

Or they might call our attention to the fact that the second interpretation is borne out by Yeats's subsequent revisions of the poem. For after its initial publication he altered it in a way that did much to exclude the first, more obvious interpretation—using quotation marks, for instance, to indicate that the last two lines come as the poet's *answer* to his earlier thoughts. This is again a relevant consideration, but it is still less than decisive. For we must remember that a poem, when revised, may be considered as another, related poem. And if there are two poems, our interpretation of the later

---

[2] For the many changes that Yeats made in the poem between 1902 and 1949 see the Variorum Edition of his works, edited by Allt and Alspach (New York, 1957). In *Later Poems* (London, 1929) the complete text reads as follows:

> One that is ever kind said yesterday:
> "Your well-beloved's hair has threads of grey,
> And little shadows come about her eyes;
> Time can but make it easier to be wise
> Though now it seem impossible, and so
> Patience is all that you have need of."
>   No,
> I have not a crumb of comfort, not a grain,
> Time can but make her beauty over again:
> Because of that great nobleness of hers
> The fire that stirs about her, when she stirs
> Burns but more clearly. O she had not these ways,
> When all the wild summer was in her gaze.
> O heart! O heart! if she'd but turn her head,
> You'd know the folly of being comforted.

one does not require us (though it may indeed incline us) to accept the same interpretation for the earlier one.

Again, they might argue that the poem is much *better* when interpreted in the second way. Such a reason is likely to exchange one type of controversy for another. It remains of interest, however; for it reminds us that the interpretation and evaluation of a poem are rarely separable steps in criticism. We do not *first* interpret it and then evaluate it, taking each step with finality. Rather, we test a tentative interpretation by considering the tentative evaluation of the poem to which it leads, progressively altering each in the light of the other.

The reasons that I have been illustrating are very far, of course, from constituting a complete list—nor is it likely that a complete list would be possible. But perhaps they are typical reasons, and will give us a point of departure, at least, for considering how they bear on the interpretive conclusions that they are intended to support.

III

The inconclusiveness of the reasons mentioned (and they remain inconclusive even when used collectively) suggest that they are not premises in an argument that is strictly deductive. So perhaps they are of an inductive character, each giving to an interpretive conclusion this or that sort of partial confirmation. That is an initially plausible view, fully deserving our attention. But it is a view that derives its plausibility, I suspect, from an assumption that normally attends it; so we must be careful to make the assumption explicit.

The assumption has to do with the nature of interpretive *questions*. It takes the questions to be concerned, and exclusively concerned, with what the poet had in mind, or intended, or wished to communicate. Or (more or less equivalently) it takes the question, "Is this what the passage means?" to be a way of asking, "If we understand the passage in this way, will we be understanding it as the poet did?" Now any question of this latter sort, whose hypothetical nature does not prevent it from dealing with a matter of fact,[3] is one to which inductive arguments are applicable; and if it typifies all interpretive questions, then perhaps the reasons I have mentioned simply help, directly or indirectly, to place it in an inductive framework.

---

[3] There are unquestionably other ways of attempting to identify an interpretive question with a factual one. I shall not discuss them explicitly, but let me remark that I suspect them of confusing standards with definitions, in the manner that I shall explain, somewhat implicitly, in Sect. V.

Dictionary reasons are of interest because the poet presumably complied with the dictionary; reasons protesting against anachronisms are of interest because the poet himself couldn't have read his work anachronistically; and so on.

Some of the reasons, to be sure, cannot easily be accounted for in this way—particularly the reason, "It is a better poem when so interpreted." But those who use this reason may think that their sensibilities are akin to those of the poet, and that an interpretation that makes the poem better, *according to their taste,* is more likely than not to be faithful to what the poet had in mind. So even this reason, perhaps, can have its inductive aspects.

And yet there are difficulties about this approach to interpretation. I refer not to the general, epistemological difficulties that bear on the meaning of "had in mind," "wished to communicate," "understood," and so on—though these undoubtedly exist—but rather to some relatively specific difficulties that would remain even if the general ones could be resolved.

In particular, we must remember that the poet's thoughts and feelings change as he writes, his first fragmentary notes having perhaps only a remote connection with his finished work. (As Sapir said of all verbal expression, "The product grows with the instrument."[4]) So on being asked whether an interpretation is faithful to what the poet had in mind, we must ask in return, "Had in mind at which time?" And such a reply as, "Just after he made his first clear copy," is not likely, I think, to spring from any genuine literary interest.

Indeed, when a poet has just finished a work he is too close to it, as he may himself acknowledge, to know whether it says much or says little. He has worked so laboriously over certain lines that he has grown numb to them; or he has deleted certain lines that continue to color his understanding of those that remain. Perhaps that is why he so often puts his work aside, to see what he will make of it at later readings.

And what does he make of it at later readings? Does he understand it in a way that is altogether fixed—a way that remains constant for him in every detail, regardless of his varying recollections, moods, and interests?

I should suppose that he understands his work now in one way and now in another—sometimes wondering, perhaps, whether he isn't interpreting it poorly. And how could it be otherwise? His thoughts and feelings of any one time are not, certainly, thereafter visible to him in some display room of his mind; he can half-renew them, but *only with the help of the lines*

---

[4] *Language,* by Edward Sapir (New York, 1921), p. 14.

that he has written. And the fact that he has written them does not free them from that diversity of possible understandings to which language is heir.

This has its obvious bearing on our problem. We can scarcely suppose that the one, legitimate aim of a critic, in interpreting a poem, is that of reproducing the poet's chameleon-like understanding of it in its true color; nor can we suppose that the critic's reasons must always show, inductively, that he has achieved this aim.

I do not wish to imply, of course, that this observation is *fatal* to an inductive view of interpretation. One might just possibly defend it in a modified form. A poet's understanding of his poem, though it varies, will presumably vary only between certain limits. The task of interpretation, then, might be taken as one of establishing these limits. If a critic finds that certain interpretations lie beyond the limits—and for anachronistic interpretations, for instance, the inductive means of doing so is rather straight forward—he may be expected to reject them as incorrect. And of the *various* interpretations that lie between these limits . . . well, the critic might be expected to say that each has an *equal* claim to being correct, adding that it is no part of his business to choose between them.

One might just possibly, I repeat, defend such a view. Or perhaps one could defend it with still further modifications—making a distinction, say, between the feelings or thoughts that a poet takes to be *expressed* in his poem and the feelings or thoughts that he takes to be *irrelevant* to it, even though the latter happen to come to his mind, occasionally, as he re-reads it. This distinction would help to narrow the limits that I have mentioned. But it would also, let me add, represent the task of interpretive criticism as requiring a curious neutrality, and a curious preoccupation with questions that we should normally classify as belonging to psychology and biography.[5]

In any case, I doubt if anyone will be confident that such a view represents the *sole* aim of interpretation. It doesn't seem faithful to the interpretive interests that a critic invariably has; and if we ask whether it reveals the interests that he ought to have, then we had better delay our answer until we see what alternatives a critic has before him.

I shall accordingly go on to one of these alternatives—an alternative that no longer puts exclusive emphasis on what the poet had in mind, and

[5] My views on this matter are partly borrowed from W. K. Wimsatt and M. C. Beardsley. See their article, "The Intentional Fallacy," [*see also pages 91-104 for the complete text*. J. M.] in *Sewanee Review,* LIV (1946), 468-487. But they are concerned largely with the evaluation of poetry, whereas I am transferring their views, with alterations, to the interpretation of poetry.

accordingly, one that leads us to view the *reasons* for an interpretation in a different light.

IV

I can best proceed by examining a little more closely the type of *question* that a critic's interpretation is expected to answer. It is a question that is often phrased,

What does this passage in the poem mean?

But the sense of "mean" is here more than usually elusive. In addition to those general difficulties about "meaning" that are now so familiar to us in philosophy there is also a *special* difficulty that I must now briefly describe:

It arises from our conviction (and I think virtually all of us will share that conviction) that when we speak of what a passage "means" we are referring to the way it is understood, or would be understood, by a certain group of people. A passage has a meaning *for* this group. And when the passage is from poetry (though the same could be said, to be sure, for certain types of prose) it is often difficult to specify *what group is in question.*

When we ask what such a passage means we are *not* asking, usually, how it would be understood by the average person who speaks the language in which it is written; for we often suspect that this average person would make very little of the passage, or of poetry in general. And we are *not* asking, presumably, how the passage would be understood by those who are greatly interested in poetry, or even by those who have taken special pains to train themselves in reading poetry; for these people may even so understand the passage in various ways, and we cannot easily suppose that these ways are equally defensible. (I am not denying that there may be alternative ways of understanding the passage, all equally defensible; for that impresses me as an interesting and not implausible view. I am only suggesting that the alternative and equally defensible ways, if they exist, need not coincide with the ways found among "those who are greatly interested in poetry," etc.)

So to what group of readers *are* we referring? The conception of interpretation that I have previously mentioned has not, of course, evaded this question. It specifies the group as having the poet himself as its charter member; and it admits others to the group if and only if they read his poetry in the way (or for my amended version, *in one of the ways*) that he did. And if we are to have an alternative to this not wholly satisfactory view, we must specify the group in another manner; for so long as it remains unspecified the very request for an interpretation—the question typified by "What does this passage in the poem mean?"—will have no fixed sense.

Now the alternative that I wish to consider, and to which I can now directly turn, breaks sharply with other views in this respect: it claims that the group of readers, as implicitly mentioned in an interpretive question, cannot be made explicit by means of factual terms alone, but must be indicated, in part, by means of evaluative terms. I shall accordingly refer to it as an "evaluative" or "normative" conception of interpretation; and in explaining it further I shall want to show that in some respects it is very simple, and in other respects highly complex.

It is simple because it does no more than remind us that the readers in question—those whose understanding of the passage is indicative of what the passage means—must initially be specified as the *best* readers, or as those who read the passage *properly,* or *ideally*. Or to put it otherwise, it translates the question, "What does this passage in the poem mean?" into some such question as this: "How would the passage be understood by those who read it as they should—i.e., by those who bring to it a skill and sensibility that is neither too rich nor too poor, but is just right?"

To that extent the view is almost naively simple. Nor does it lose its simplicity when it is confronted by the question, "But what readers *do* read as they should, and what skills and sensibilities *are* just right, etc.?" A normative conception of interpretation, faithful to its meta-critical aims, carefully refrains from answering this question. To those who feel that an answer is mandatory it makes this reply: "If you are asking not for remarks that clarify these evaluative terms, but rather for normative judgments that make use of them—judgments that *predicate* them of certain factually described readers or of certain factually described skills and sensibilities— then your question reduplicates, in good measure, the very question that interpretive critics, whether professionals or amateurs, are themselves trying to answer (though they usually try to answer it only for these or those special cases). For in deciding how a passage would be understood by those who read it as they should, the critics must decide, of course, which readers *do* read it as they should. And it is important to see that such a genuinely normative decision belongs to criticism proper. It belongs to philosophy only when philosophy goes beyond meta-criticism, becoming a kind of generalized criticism that defends a *standard* for *good* interpretations of poetry. It does not belong to the meta-critical part of philosophy, whose business is not to answer questions of literary criticism, but only to clarify them."

But if a normative conception of interpretation is in these ways very simple, it suddenly becomes complicated when it goes on to consider the *meaning* of such terms as "should" and "good." That is a different question, as I see it, from any question about the various factual X's of which the evaluative terms are to be predicated; and it is a question that belongs to meta-criticism beyond any doubt. Indeed, it leads to some of the most familiar problems of contemporary analytical philosophy. Do the value-terms refer to non-natural qualities? Or do they refer, say, to the integration of interests? Or do they function expressively or quasi-imperatively?

Now with regard to these matters I have developed my views elsewhere,[6] and cannot undertake within the scope of the present essay to renew my discussion of them. But even so—even when the evaluative terms are temporarily left with the unanalyzed meanings that they have in every-day discourse—I think that the remarks I have been making deserve atten-tion. For although we know that evaluative terms (i.e., normative terms) will require attention somewhere in aesthetics, we are not so likely to think that they will require attention just here, in connection with interpretation. We tend to make a sharp *contrast* between evaluation and interpretation. But if any form of a normative conception of interpretation is correct, we must make the contrast much less sharp; for interpretation, too, will have its evaluative aspects.

This is not to deny, of course, that the questions, "What does this poem mean?" and "Is it a good poem?" are quite different questions. A normative conception of interpretation can readily distinguish them. The latter is con-cerned with the value *of the poem,* and the former is concerned with the value of something else—namely, with the value of the way in which this or that reader understands the poem, or with the value of the sensibilities, etc., that yield that way of understanding it. Let me explain this by an example:

Suppose that one critic, having interpreted a poem, is told by another critic, "You are reading a meaning into it that simply isn't there." Accord-ing to a normative conception of interpretation, the latter critic is in effect

---

[6] See my *Ethics and Language* (New Haven, 1944), and my paper, "Interpretation and Evalua-tion in Aesthetics," in *Philosophical Analysis,* edited by Max Black (Ithaca, 1950). I there take value-judgments to serve mainly (though not exclusively) to express the speaker's attitude of favor or disfavor, and to do so in a way that invites, as it were, the hearer or hearers to share this attitude. Such a view does not cut off our evaluations from our scientifically established beliefs; for these beliefs, revealing the factual situation that presumably confronts us, normally make a vast difference to the sort of attitude that we express. My remarks about reasons, as developed in the remainder of this paper, are in accordance with this view; but I suspect that much of what I say will be compatible with certain other views as well, and thus will be of interest to some who feel that my general position is open to criticism.

saying, "You are making too much of it; you are bringing to it a sensibility and an ingenuity that is excessive—i.e., one that for this poem goes beyond what is fitting, appropriate, or desirable." And if the first critic replies, "The meaning is there, and you're missing it," he is in effect saying, "My understanding of it is as it should be, and by bringing less to the poem you are making too little of it." Note that neither critic has affirmed or denied that the poem is good, but each—granted the paraphrases, of course—has taken a normative stand on how it is to be understood.

A normative conception of interpretation, let me add, impresses me as akin to a conception that critics themselves often have of their work—though they suggest it, rather than expound it, by saying that criticism is less a science than an art. One might develop this by saying that a critic, as artist, need not be required to make a faithful copy of something in the poet's mind (a highly inaccessible model at best, and one that won't stand still) but can be granted a creative freedom of his own. He recognizes limits to this freedom, of course, not wishing to understand words as Carroll's Humpty Dumpty does; but these limits allow him to put something of his own artistic temperament into his interpretations. He shares this freedom with those other interpretive artists (in a different but related sense) who are actors and virtuosos. And if that much can be granted, we can easily see why evaluative terms have a place in the very formulation of interpretive questions. They lead to the central topic of discussion: a discussion of whether or not a critic is exercising his creative freedom in an acceptable way.

V

I cannot pause to provide a normative conception of interpretation with its many needed qualifications, but must go on to its implications with regard to my chosen topic—the topic of *reasons*. Earlier in the paper I have illustrated reasons of a sort that are commonly used—those that appeal to the dictionary, those that mention the fitness of a word's sense to its context, those that deal with anachronisms, those that refer to the spirit of the poet, those that call attention to the poet's revisions, and those that are concerned with the enhancement of poetic interest or value. What more is to be said about them?

I want to make two points in this connection. The first is that a normative conception of interpretation can readily account for these reasons, showing why critics may be expected to use them. The second is that these reasons cannot, for a normative conception, be taken as typifying all other reasons.

They typify only those that are comparatively simple; and there is always the possibility—the theoretical possibility, at least—of supplementing them by reasons of a much broader and more pervasive sort.

To introduce my first point let me return to my remarks in Section III, where I acknowledged that the reasons might conceivably reveal what the poet intended, or what he had in mind. That is *one* way of attempting to show why the reasons are relevant to an interpretation; so let us consider to what extent a normative conception can accept it.

Quite evidently, a normative conception must qualify any such proposal; but all the same it need not abandon it completely. For it will be remembered that the question, "Just who are the good or ideal readers?" is one that a normative conception carefully leaves unanswered: it lets a critic decide as he sees fit about this central matter. It remains possible, then, that certain critics will decide that the good or ideal readers are those who, to whatever extent is possible, respect what the poet intended or had in mind. And for these critics the reasons in question will become relevant in much the same biographical way, so to speak, that Section III has discussed.

To take the very simplest case: suppose that a critic has an explicit *standard* of interpretation—or in other words, suppose that he accepts a normative generalization comparable to a standard of ethics, for instance, save that it is far smaller in scope, dealing only with good ways of reading poetry, or with the ways that poetry should be understood. And suppose that this small-scale standard is particularly respectful of the poet, so that our critic is prepared to formulate it in these words:

> A poem is understood as it should be if and only if it is understood in one of the ways that the poet himself understood it.

Now, relative to this standard, it will be evident that the reasons I have illustrated have an intelligible place in criticism. The reasons help to establish—and *inductively*—some implicit statement about the poet's own understanding of his work. The standard in question then relates this statement to a "should." With the help of the standard, then, the reasons support an interpretive conclusion.

This manner of accounting for the reasons, however, is possible only when the critic's standard of interpretation is used as a supplementary premiss. And this supplementary premiss, being genuinely normative, presents additional problems. It is presumably *not* true by definition, as even naturalistic theories often imply; for naturalism usually emphasizes some general end in its definition of evaluative terms, and nothing so specific as a respect for the authority of the poet. So the standard will have to be defended in its turn. It too will require reasons—and reasons of a sort presumably different from any that I have yet illustrated.[7]

These remarks are in keeping with both of my central points. They suggest that a normative conception can account for the reason I have illustrated, and that it also envisages reasons of another sort. But I must continue, since my points are still imperfectly established.

A normative conception of interpretation is not committed, of course, to the simple standard I have mentioned. It *permits* this standard but in no way *requires* it; and it is no less interested, for instance, in a standard that runs like this:

> A poem is understood as it should be if and only if: (1) it is understood in a way not altogether foreign to what the poet sometimes had in mind; (2) its words, syntax, and figures of speech are not stretched to such an extent that they couldn't have been so understood by the poet's contemporaries; and (3) within the limits set up by the preceding restrictions, it maximizes the aesthetic value of the poem.

This standard designedly makes less of the authority of the poet, and adds other factors. But it again permits a normative conception to do full justice to the reasons I have illustrated. The reasons help to establish one or more of the numbered points that follow the words "if and only if," and the standard then connects them with a "should." So we have only a complication of the analysis that I gave for the standard previously mentioned. Reasons drawn from linguistics, it will be noted, have as much to do with what the poet's contemporaries made of his work (clause (2) above) as they do with what the poet himself made of it. And the reasons, "That sense of the word fits in with the context," however much it may bear on what the poet had in mind, can also reflect the critic's decision (as in (3) above) about how to maximize the poem's aesthetic value.

---

[7] The standard could be made true by definition, to be sure, provided the definition were of the sort that I have elsewhere called "persuasive." (See my *Ethics and Language*, Ch. IX.) But persuasive definitions are different from any that a neutral, meta-critical study can provide. In their net effect they are tantamount to overt normative judgments: they can be controversial in essentially the same way that overt normative judgments can be controversial, and they have to be supported by essentially the same sorts of reasons.

My objection to the "ideal observer" view of ethics, as developed by Roderick Firth in "Ethical Absolutism and the Ideal Observer" (*Philosophy and Phenomenological Research,* XII, 1952, pp. 317-345) centers on precisely this point. Having introduced the laudatory term, "ideal," he proceeds to define it for his contexts in a highly specific, naturalistic sense; and he assumes that his definition will raise only the usual issues of analytical philosophy. But in my opinion his definition is persuasive—one that, if systematically defended, would introduce in a new terminology all of the genuinely *normative* issues to which ethics is heir. So although I may seem merely to be transferring what he says about ethics to the neighboring field of aesthetics, I am in fact diverging from him quite sharply in my way of handling the word "ideal."

As before, however, the reasons become relevant only with the help of the standard. And since a normative conception conceives of this standard, like any other, as distinct from a statement that is true by definition, it still requires us to consider what reasons could be given for the standard itself.

I could mention other standards of interpretation, of course, but I suspect that they would introduce nothing new in principle. Let me consider, then, the possibility of a critic's interpreting a poem without formulating *any* standard of interpretation—as is presumably the usual case. Suppose, for instance, that he uses no more than thumb-rules, of the "so far so good" variety. If the interpretation is close to what the poet sometimes had in mind (he says) then so far so good. If it is faithful to the spirit of the poet's other work, then again, so far so good. And so on. Our critic may be unable to formulate *all* of his tacitly accepted thumb-rules in advance; and he may not have any formulated principle for summing up the "vectors" of interpretive acceptability that his thumb-rules introduce, but instead may estimate their combined force quite intuitively, and even rather differently for each new case; so he need not have any complete, explicit standard of interpretation at all. Even so, he may repeatedly use the reasons that I have previously illustrated; he may use them in affirming the truth of the purely factual, "if" parts of the thumb-rules, and thus in making inferences by *modus ponens* to the evaluative "then" parts.

But how are the thumb-rules themselves to be justified? Why say "so far so good" in the "then" parts, rather than "so far so bad"? We are again led to envisage supplementary reasons, differing from any that have so far been illustrated.

Of the several qualifications that I should here introduce I shall mention only one—a qualification that is needed with regard to very strange suggestions about standards of interpretation or very strange suggestions about thumb-rules. For suppose (absurdly) that a critic's thumb-rule leads him to divert every word in an English poem into some non-English sense. We should say, no doubt, that such a rule prevents him from interpreting poetry at all. The word "interpret" simply doesn't apply to what he is doing; so *quite apart from any normative considerations,* we may dismiss his proposals as aside from the point. If any normative issue arises it will bear on another question, namely, "Ought he stop doing what he is doing, and interpret poetry instead?"

But if certain proposals about meaning can be excluded in advance, by the very definition of "interpretation," it remains the case that a great many can *not* be so excluded. And of the latter only *some* will comply with standards or thumb-rules that are defensible. So in showing that they are really defensible we shall still need those "other" reasons that I have been mentioning. Just as we cannot, according to a normative conception, eliminate these reasons in favor of linguistic rules governing the common use of such words as "good" and "ideal," so we cannot eliminate them in favor of linguistic rules governing the common use of "interpretation."

VI

It will be well, then, to say a few words about these other and presumably more complicated reasons.

I cannot enter into a full discussion of the matter, but perhaps I can point in the right direction by giving some examples. The examples, let me say in advance, suggest that problems of interpretation are very large problems—so large that it becomes difficult to establish any boundaries within which they can be confined.

Let us consider interpretations that are likely to impress some of us, and perhaps many of us, as "one sided," or "lacking in a sense of proportion." There are literary Fabians, for example, who find Fabian principles underlying the mythology of Wagner's *Ring*. There are extreme Freudians, who take Hamlet's feelings toward Gertrude and Claudius to spring, in essentials, from an incestuous jealousy. And there are also those critics who seem preoccupied not with views about politics or psychology, but rather with views about the complexities of language—as will be evident from the instance that follows:

Mr. F. W. Bateson, in discussing the sonnet of Shakespeare that begins,

> The expense of spirit in a waste of shame

points out that "expense," which sounds so much like "expanse," reminds us of the expanse of a desert, for instance, and thus suggests "waste." So when the word "waste" thereafter appears the line acquires a unity of meaning.[8]

Let us now—though for the sake of argument, and without regard to how we actually feel about the matter—take the position of those who reject these interpretations. We find them "obsessive," urging that a good reader would make far *less* of the points they emphasize. Our position is easily

[8] See *English Poetry and the English Language,* by F. W. Bateson (Oxford, 1934) page 21. Such Joycean touches in interpretation can easily be supplemented by Freudian touches, as when Bateson goes on to say that the word "waste," by suggesting "waist," reinforces the sexual implications of the sonnet.

stated; but it is another matter, of course, to defend it. And what shall we say to those who, disagreeing with us, feel justified in accepting the interpretations?

In essentials, my answer is this: we could argue that the proposed interpretations are indicative of habits of mind that no one *ought* to have. And we could attempt to show this by pointing out the consequences of these habits of mind—consequences that may bear not only on our subsequent understanding of poetry, but may indirectly, by developing distorted perspectives, bear on a vast part of our manner of living.

I say this on the following grounds. What we make of a poem (and there is a familiar adage to this effect) depends not merely on the poetic text itself but also on what we *bring to* it. And what we bring to it includes habits of mind (i.e., sensibilities, interests, skills, convictions, etc.) that can scarcely be taken as causally isolated from our daily life. Their importance extends beyond any purely literary importance; and in evaluating them—in deciding which of them are and which of them are not to be cultivated—we shall want, so far as possible, to consider the full psychological context in which they arise. But whatever we decide about them, in the light of this full psychological context, will remain in part a decision about the habits of mind that we shall bring to a poetic text; it will inevitably make a difference to our decision about how poetry is to be understood. So I venture to draw my conclusion: In judging a proposed interpretation of poetry we can appeal to those varied reasons, often of an ethical or of a prudential character, that help us to evaluate the habits of mind with which the proposed interpretation is correlated.

These remarks readily apply to the interpretations that I have mentioned just above. Having called them "obsessive" we might go on to consider such possibilities as these: A sharply Fabian emphasis in understanding the text of the *Ring* might indicate (say) a political interest of such intensity that it crowds out other interests; and these other interests may include some that are essential not merely to a well-rounded critic but also to a well-rounded *person*. An insistence on Hamlet's incestuous jealousy (and to say this is not to deny that Freud has something new to tell us) may be correlated with a lack of concern with those simpler, less arresting aspects of psychology that we need in handling the problems of practical life. And a tendency to read Shakespeare as though he were Joyce, when it goes beyond certain limits, may manifest a trivial, game-playing mentality, of a sort that blunts our powers of distinguishing between oneupmanship and sensitivity. These are manifestly possibilities; and there would be no irrelevancy, to say the least, in our attempting to find out whether they are actualities. Our inquiries might help us, in keeping with the principles mentioned above, to strengthen our interpretive norms by relating them to much more general norms.

Such is the way in which we might supplement (as distinct from replace) the simpler reasons that I have illustrated at the beginning of my paper. It takes us, of course, well beyond that close reading of the text with which interpretive criticism, by common consent, must always begin. And it takes us well beyond anything that can be called "a dwelling, with aesthetic absorption, on the immediacies of experience"—the latter being essential, according to many writers, to our enjoyment of poetry. But that, so far from being surprising, is only to be expected, for it holds true *whenever* we support an interpretive judgment by reasons. The most commonplace reasons are not exceptions to this rule. We must turn away from the poetic text, and temporarily interrupt our aesthetic absorption, even in the simple act of looking up a word in the dictionary; we must do so again when we enter into historical reflections that bear on anachronisms; and so on. So there can be no heresy, I trust, in saying the same thing about the broader, consequence-regarding reasons that I have just mentioned.

Indeed, my remarks about consequence-regarding reasons, and about the normative conception of interpretation that introduces them, can happily serve to warn us against a type of theory that gives a *misplaced* emphasis to aesthetic absorption, and thus suggests that aesthetics can recognize no values save those that are inherent or intrinsic. It may be the case (or so I shall assume for purposes of argument) that an aesthetic enjoyment of poetry requires us to dwell with absorption on the immediacies of experience. But it is one thing to "dwell" in this manner and quite another thing to ask, for any given poem, *which* experiences we are to dwell upon. The latter cannot be separated from an interpretive question, which in turn cannot be separated from a question about what we *should bring to* the text that we are interpreting. The evaluations that attend our interpretations, then, need not resemble those intrinsic ones that attend (as so many have said) our immediate enjoyment of poetry. They involve inquiries that are usually *preparatory* to our poetic enjoyment; and any contention that they too must deal only with inherent or intrinsic values—that they too must "abstract from" all considerations of the consequences—could only spring from a confusion.

If my view seems in any way strange, then, that is presumably because interpretive criticism is usually conceived as a discipline that is narrower than I have suggested, and more self-contained. But my view is not, I think, strange even in that way. There can be no ground for repudiating narrower conceptions so long as they represent avowed efforts to select and emphasize, with a calculated risk, certain aspects of a total problem. Indeed, the need of such conceptions is beyond practical doubt. But there is also the need of keeping in mind the total problem; and there we must be careful not to exclude *any* of the considerations by which our interpretive judgments are influenced, whether actually or potentially. None of us, I suspect, is immune from the influence of just such broad considerations as I have been mentioning. If we ignore them we shall inevitably make tacit assumptions about them, and assumptions that, when tacitly changed, will leave us unable to understand why our present interpretations are not the same as our old ones.

VII

My consequence-regarding reasons are potentially open, of course, to the same inductive methods that bear on consequences quite generally, and they show the elaborate use that interpretive criticism could make of these methods. They may or may not, on the other hand, show that interpretive criticism falls *wholly* within an inductive pattern. For interpretive conclusions, as I am here viewing them, remain *normative;* and there are a number of theories—namely, those that oppose an unqualifiedly naturalistic theory of value—that point to a gap, as it were, between inductively supported reasons and any normative conclusion that the reasons, in their turn, are intended to support.

There will be no such gap, of course, if we add to the inductively supported reasons some supplementary normative principle, for the latter can be chosen, and sometimes plausibly chosen, in a way that makes the argument *de*ductive. But in cases where the supplementary normative principle is again controversial (as we have seen in Section V) we have a need of further reasons. Will this process have a termination, or will the further reasons, too, require a supplementary normative principle, the latter again requiring reasons . . . ? Some theorists (namely, the intuitionists) hope for a quite decisive termination—one in which the supplementary normative principles in question are "seen," a priori, to be acceptable. Other theorists (I among them) feel unable to guarantee a termination in this way, and hope for no more than a practical termination—one in which the supplementary normative principles, though they still *could* be questioned, will not in fact be questioned. In either case, it will be noted, the inductively established premises, though manifestly relevant to the argument, do not establish a normative conclusion in quite the way that they might establish a factual conclusion.

I have said nothing to imply, then, that interpretive criticism is a "science." I think that it differs from a science, and wish only to show that it need not, on that account, turn away from a *use* of science. A normative conception can speak of a "science of interpretation" only if it goes on to analyze normative judgments naturalistically—i.e., in a manner that reduces them to factual statements. And the latter view, though it still has respectable adherents, is one that I myself consider implausible.

But these are matters that I cannot (as I have previously suggested) undertake to develop within the scope of the present paper.[9] It will be sufficient to point out that almost all theorists, however much they may differ in other respects, acknowledge that we need to illuminate our evaluations by inquiries into the facts of the case. And the broader reasons that I have been mentioning have always an interest in *that* way—an interest that those holding divergent theories of value may nevertheless be expected to share.

Any such interest, however, is limited by some practical considerations, and I must not conclude my paper without mentioning them.

There can be no doubt that my broader reasons lead into regions that we can rarely explore. We cannot hope to know *all* the consequences of the habits of mind that we bring to poetry, and we shall be fortunate if we can become reasonably confident about certain aspects of some of them. So if practical reasons must be free from uncertainty, then those that I have mentioned are at best (here and now, at least) only half-practical.

But that is only to say, for our special case, what can be said of evaluative problems in general. When we vote in an election, for instance, there is an even greater discrepancy between what we know and what we need to know. And to know *that*, which is a kind of Socratic wisdom, has its own kind of practicality. It is not to be confused with a ground for discouragement. In common life we get along in spite of our imperfect knowledge; we trust our tentative evaluations for the time, but allow for our fallibility. And there is no reason to suppose that we cannot do the same thing in interpreting poetry.

In our approach to criticism, then, I am not suggesting that we make all the needed inquiries today, using them tomorrow to explain what poetry

[9] See footnote 6. Let me supplement the comment in that note by this further one: I take reasons for value-judgments to be reasons for favoring or disfavoring, and not just reasons for believing or disbelieving. When the reasons are purely factual (i.e., when they are themselves in no part evaluative) their relation to the value-judgments is one that I take to be only *psycho*logical; so although they can be judged as good or bad reasons, they cannot be shown so by the rules of logic alone.

really means. My moral, if I must have one, lies rather in the reminder that allegedly final interpretations are less final than they may seem. And I for one do not regret this. If final answers could readily be given, perhaps our reading of poetry would cease to be a living thing. Our successively altered answers are of interest long before they can make a pretense, even, of being "the" answer.

Bibliography

Stevenson has presented his views on the present topic in an earlier paper:
> "Interpretation and Evaluation in Aesthetics," in Max Black (ed.), *Philosophical Analysis* (Ithaca, 1950).

There is also an important clue to the bearing of his general theory of value upon his aesthetics in:
> *Ethics and Language* (New Haven, 1944), Chapter VII.

Other current discussions of interest include:
> Monroe C. Beardsley, *Aesthetics* (New York, 1958), Chapter X;
> Bernard C. Heyl, "Relativism Again," *Journal of Aesthetics and Art Criticism,* Volume V (1946), 54-61;
> Isabel C. Hungerland, *Poetic Discourse* (Berkeley, 1958), Chapter III;
> Margaret Macdonald, "Some Distinctive Features of Arguments Used in Criticism of the Arts," reprinted (revised) in William Elton (ed.), *Aesthetics and Language* (Oxford, 1954);
> Harold Osborne, *Aesthetics and Criticism* (London, 1955), Chapter I.

VIII

VALUE JUDGMENTS

VALUE judgments are ubiquitous in aesthetics. In a sense, one thinks of the analysis of these as the aesthetician's most distinctive concern. The discussions of recent years still show the marked influence of Immanuel Kant's neat division of moral and aesthetic judgments and of G. E. Moore's exposure of the so-called Naturalistic Fallacy. Nevertheless, to some extent, the Kantian emphasis loses some of its force as it becomes clear that moral judgments may well be appreciative and not, as such, concerned to direct anyone's conduct and that aesthetic judgments (as in the criticism of a work in progress) may well be intended to direct another's efforts and, in doing so, come to construe these efforts as the solving of a practical problem. Also, the force of Moore's criticism declines as philosophers attempt (as they do) to treat evaluation in terms of certain distinctive uses sentences are put to rather than in terms of the qualities that may be found in things.

Value-laden remarks range themselves in an extensive spectrum. There are comments that merely express our taste; there are comments that express our appreciation; there are comments that appraise and rank and grade works of art; there are commendations and recommendations that we make. We may expect, therefore, that there will be no simple comprehensive theory of evaluation that will hold for the variety of remarks we are to account for.

We may, perhaps, simplify certain of the principal distinctions required in the following way. Let us admit that, sometimes, remarks that assign some value to a work of art are merely expressions of one's own particular taste, that is, of one's own likes and dislikes. These are, surely, idiosyncratic, at best matters of fact, and call for no justification (though taste may itself be evaluated). Let us admit, further, that some remarks are appreciative, that is, assign some value to a work of art for relevant reasons. One's taste will not be mentioned here: the reasons one supplies to another will not include mention of one's own likes and dislikes (though these will be expected to be in accord with the remarks made). Another may confirm that the reasons given do mention features that can be noticed in the work and that reasons of the sort given are pertinent to appreciation. But since taste is involved, no one else is bound to appreciate the work for the same reasons and in the same way. Hence, one may be called on to defend or make plausible and clear his own appreciative attitude toward a given work, but he cannot be called on to show that his appreciation is true or correct; his appreciative remarks cannot be disputed, except in the uninteresting sense that he may have contradicted himself or made an error regarding some quality of the work in question. Finally, we may admit that works of art may be evaluated, that is, judged to have this or that sort of merit on grounds that do not concern one's own likes and dislikes (whatever they may be). And these judgments may be open to dispute.

One of the prime models suggested for value-judgments is that of reaching a verdict. The adequacy of such a model for aesthetic judgments is instructive to explore. Arnold Isenberg has attempted to apply it to the range of relevant sorts of judgment.

Critical Communication

ARNOLD ISENBERG[1]

T HAT questions about meaning are provisionally separable, even if finally inseparable, from questions about validity and truth, is shown by the fact that meanings can be exchanged without the corresponding cognitive decisions. What is imparted by one person to another in an act of communication is (typically) a certain idea, thought, content, meaning, or claim—not a belief, expectation, surmise, or doubt; for the last are dependent on factors, such as the checking process, which go beyond the mere understanding of the message conveyed. And there is a host of questions which have to do with this message: its simplicity or complexity, its clarity or obscurity, its tense, its mood, its modality, and so on. Now, the theory of art criticism has, I think, been seriously hampered by a kind of headlong assault on the question of validity. We have many doctrines about the objectivity of a critical judgment but few concerning its import, or claim to objectivity, though the settlement of the first of these questions probably depends on the clarification of the second. The following remarks are for the most part restricted to meeting such questions as: What is the content

From *The Philosophical Review*, Volume LVIII (July, 1949), 330-344. Reprinted with the permission of the author and *The Philosophical Review*.
[1] The author is indebted to Mr. Herbert Bohnert for assistance with this paper.

of the critic's argument? What claim does he transmit to us? How does he expect us to deal with this claim?

A good point to start from is a theory of criticism, widely held in spite of its deficiencies, which divides the critical process into three parts. There is the value judgment or *verdict* (V): "This picture or poem is good—." There is a particular statement or *reason* (R): "—because it has such-and-such a quality—." And there is a general statement or *norm* (N): "—and any work which has that quality is *pro tanto* good."[2]

V has been construed, and will be construed here, as an expression of feeling—an utterance manifesting praise or blame. But among utterances of that class it is distinguished by being in some sense conditional upon R. This is only another phrasing of the commonly noted peculiarity of aesthetic feeling: that it is "embodied" in or "attached" to an aesthetic content.

R is a statement describing the content of an art work; but not every such descriptive statement will be a case of R. The proposition, "There are just twelve flowers in that picture" (and with it nine out of ten descriptions in Crowe and Cavalcaselle), is without critical relevance; that is, without any bearing upon V. The description of a work of art is seldom attempted for its own sake. It is controlled by some purpose, some interest; and there are many interests by which it might be controlled other than that of reaching or defending a critical judgment. The qualities which are significant in relation to one purpose—dating, attribution, archaeological reconstruction, clinical diagnosis, proving or illustrating some thesis in sociology—might be quite immaterial in relation to another. At the same time, we cannot be sure that there is any *kind* of statement about art, serving no matter what main interest, which cannot also act as R; or, in other words, that there is any *kind* of knowledge about art which cannot influence aesthetic appreciation.

V and R, it should be said, are often combined in sentences which are at once normative and descriptive. If we have been told that the colors of a certain painting are garish, it would be astonishing to find that they were all very pale and unsaturated; and to this extent the critical comment conveys information. On the other hand, we might find the colors bright and intense, as expected, without being thereby forced to admit that they are garish; and this reveals the component of valuation (that is, distaste) in

---

[2] Cf., for instance, C. J. Ducasse, *Art, the Critics, and You* (p. 116): "The statement that a given work possesses a certain objective characteristic expresses at the same time a judgment of value if the characteristic is one that the judging person approves or, as the case may be, disapproves; and is thus one that he regards as conferring, respectively, positive or negative value on any object of the given kind that happens to possess it." See, further, pp. 117-20.

the critic's remark. This feature of critical usage has attracted much notice and some study; but we do not discuss it here at all. We shall be concerned solely with the descriptive function of R.

Now if we ask what makes a description critically useful and relevant, the first suggestion which occurs is that it is *supported by N*. N is based upon an inductive generalization which describes a relationship between some aesthetic quality and someone's or everyone's system of aesthetic response. Notice: I do not say that N *is* an inductive generalization; for in critical evaluation N is being used not to predict or to explain anybody's reaction to a work of art but to vindicate that reaction, perhaps to someone who does not yet share it; and in this capacity N is a precept, a rule, a *generalized value statement*. But the *choice* of one norm, rather than another, when that choice is challenged, will usually be given some sort of inductive justification. We return to this question in a moment. I think we shall find that a careful analysis of N is unnecessary, because there are considerations which permit us to dismiss it altogether.

At this point it is well to remind ourselves that there is a difference between *explaining* and *justifying* a critical response. A psychologist who should be asked "why X likes the object y" would take X's enjoyment as a datum, a fact to be explained. And if he offers as explanation the presence in y of the quality Q, there is, explicit or latent in this causal argument, an appeal to some generalization which he has reason to think is true, such as "X likes any work which has that quality." But when we ask X as a critic "why he likes the object y," we want him to give us some reason to like it too and are not concerned with the causes of what we may so far regard as his bad taste. This distinction between genetic and normative inquiry, though it is familiar to all and acceptable to most of us, is commonly ignored in the practice of aesthetic speculation; and the chief reason for this—other than the ambiguity of the question "Why do you like this work?"—is the fact that some statements about the object will necessarily figure both in the explanation and in the critical defence of any reaction to it. Thus, if I tried to explain my feeling for the line

> But musical as is Apollo's lute,

I should certainly mention "the pattern of *u*'s and *l*'s which reinforces the meaning with its own musical quality"; for this quality of my sensations is doubtless among the conditions of my feeling response. And the same point would be made in any effort to convince another person of the beauty of the line. The remark which gives a reason also, in this case, states a cause. But notice that, though as criticism this comment might be very effective, it is practically worthless as explanation; for we have no phonetic or psychological laws (nor any plausible "common-sense" generalizations) from which we might derive the prediction that such a pattern of u's and l's should be pleasing to me. In fact, the formulation ("pattern of u's and l's," etc.) is so vague that one could not tell just what general hypothesis it is that is being invoked or assumed; yet it is quite sharp enough for critical purposes. On the other hand, suppose that someone should fail to be "convinced" by my argument in favor of Milton's line. He might still readily admit that the quality of which I have spoken might have something to do with my pleasurable reaction, given my peculiar mentality. Thus the statement which is serving both to explain and to justify is not equally effective in the two capacities; and this brings out the difference between the two lines of argument. Coincident at the start, they diverge in the later stages. A $complete$ explanation of any of my responses would have to include certain propositions about my nervous system, which would be irrelevant in any critical argument. And a critically relevant observation about some configuration in the art object might be useless for explaining a given experience, if only because the experience did not yet contain that configuration.[3]

Now it would not be strange if, among the dangers of ambiguity to which the description of art, like the rest of human speech, is exposed, there should be some which derive from the double purpose—critical and psychological—to which such description is often being put. And this is, as we shall see, the case.

The necessity for sound inductive generalizations in any attempt at aesthetic explanation is granted. We may now consider, very briefly, the parallel role in normative criticism which has been assigned to N. Let us limit our attention to those metacritical theories which $deny$ a function in criticism to N. I divide these into two kinds, those which attack existing standards and those which attack the very notion of a critical standard.

(1) It is said that we know of no law which governs human tastes and preferences, no quality shared by any two works of art that makes those works attractive or repellent. The point might be debated; but it is more

[3] I should like to add that when we speak of "justifying" or "giving reasons" for our critical judgments, we refer to something which patently does go on in the world and which is patently different from the causal explanation of tastes and preferences. We are not begging any question as to whether the critical judgment can "really" be justified; that is, established on an objective basis. Even if there were no truth or falsity in criticism, there would still be agreement and disagreement; and there would be argument which arises out of disagreement and attempts to resolve it. Hence, at the least there exists the purely "phenomenological" task of elucidating the import and intention of words like 'insight,' 'acumen,' 'obtuseness,' 'bad taste,' all of which have a real currency in criticism.

important to notice what it assumes. It assumes that if N *were* based on a sound induction, it would be (together with R) a real ground for the acceptance of V. In other words, it would be reasonable to accept V on the strength of the quality Q if it could be shown that works which possess Q tend to be pleasing. It follows that criticism is being held back by the miserable state of aesthetic science. This raises an issue too large to be canvassed here. Most of us believe that the idea of progress applies to science, does not apply to art, applies, in some unusual and not very clear sense, to philosophy. What about criticism? Are there "discoveries" and "contributions" in this branch of thought? Is it reasonable to expect better evaluations of art after a thousand years of criticism than before? The question is not a simple one: it admits of different answers on different interpretations. But I do think that some critical judgments have been and are every day being "proved" as well as in the nature of the case they ever can be proved. I think we have already numerous passages which are not to be corrected or improved upon. And if this opinion is right, then it could not be the case that the validation of critical judgments waits upon the discovery of aesthetic laws. Let us suppose even that we had some law which stated that a certain color combination, a certain melodic sequence, a certain type of dramatic hero has everywhere and always a positive emotional effect. To the extent to which this law holds, there is of course that much less disagreement in criticism; but there is no better method for resolving disagreement. We are not more fully convinced in our own judgment because we know its explanation; and we cannot hope to convince an imaginary opponent by appeal to this explanation, which by hypothesis does not hold for him.

(2) The more radical arguments against critical standards are spread out in the pages of Croce, Dewey, Richards, Prall, and the great romantic critics before them. They need not be repeated here. In one way or another they all attempt to expose the absurdity of presuming to judge a work of art, the very excuse for whose existence lies in its *difference* from everything that has gone before, by its degree of *resemblance* to something that has gone before; and on close inspection they create at least a very strong doubt as to whether a standard of success or failure in art is either necessary or possible. But it seems to me that they fail to provide a positive interpretation of criticism. Consider the following remarks by William James on the criticism of Herbert Spencer: "In all his dealings with the art products of mankind he manifests the same curious dryness and mechanical literality of judgment. . . . Turner's painting he finds untrue in that the earth-region is habitually as bright in tone as the air-region. Moreover, Turner scatters

his detail too evenly. In Greek statues the hair is falsely treated. Renaissance painting is spoiled by unreal illumination. Venetian Gothic sins by meaningless ornamentation." And so on. We should most of us agree with James that this is bad criticism. But *all* criticism is similar to this in that it cites, as reasons for praising or condemning a work, one or more of its qualities. If Spencer's reasons are descriptively true, how can we frame our objection to them except in some such terms as that "unreal illumination does not make a picture bad"; that is, by attacking his standards? What constitutes the relevance of a reason but its correlation with a norm? It is astonishing to notice how many writers, formally committed to an opposition to legal procedure in criticism, *seem* to relapse into a reliance upon standards whenever they give reasons for their critical judgments. The appearance is inevitable; for as long as we have no alternative interpretation of the import and function of R, we must assume *either* that R is perfectly arbitrary *or* that it presupposes and depends on some general claim.

With these preliminaries, we can examine a passage of criticism. This is Ludwig Goldscheider on *The Burial of Count Orgaz:*

> Like the contour of a violently rising and falling wave is the outline of the four illuminated figures in the foreground: steeply upwards and downwards about the grey monk on the left, in mutually inclined curves about the yellow of the two saints, and again steeply upwards and downwards about . . . the priest on the right. The depth of the wave indicates the optical centre; the double curve of the saints' yellow garments is carried by the greyish white of the shroud down still farther; in this lowest depth rests the bluish-grey armor of the knight.

This passage—which, we may suppose, was written to justify a favorable judgment on the painting—conveys to us the idea of a certain quality which, if we believe the critic, we should expect to find in a certain painting by El Greco. And we do find it: we can verify its presence by perception. In other words, there is a quality in the picture which agrees with the quality which we "have in mind"—which we have been led to think of by the critic's language. But the same quality ("a steeply rising and falling curve," etc.) would be found in any of a hundred lines one could draw on the board in three minutes. It could not be the critic's purpose to inform us of the presence of a quality as obvious as this. It seems reasonable to suppose that the critic is thinking of another quality, no idea of which is transmitted to us by his language, which he *sees* and which by his use of language he *gets us to see*. This quality is, of course, a wavelike contour; but it is not the quality designated by the *expression* 'wavelike contour.' Any object which has this quality will have a wavelike contour; but it is not true that any object which has a wavelike contour will have this quality. At the same time, the expression 'wavelike contour' *excludes* a great many things: if anything is a wavelike contour, it is not a color, it is not a mass, it is not a straight line. Now the critic, besides imparting to us the idea of a wavelike contour, gives us directions for perceiving, and does this *by means* of the idea he imparts to us, which narrows down the field of possible visual orientations and guides us in the discrimination of details, the organization of parts, the grouping of discrete objects into patterns. It is as if we found both an oyster and a pearl when we had been looking for a seashell because we had been told it was valuable. It *is* valuable, but not because it is a seashell.

I may be stretching usage by the senses I am about to assign to certain words, but it seems that the critic's *meaning* is "filled in," "rounded out," or "completed" by the act of perception, which is performed not to judge the truth of his description but in a certain sense to *understand* it. And if *communication* is a process by which a mental content is transmitted by symbols from one person to another, then we can say that it is a function of criticism to bring about communication at the level of the senses; that is, to induce a sameness of vision, of experienced content. If this is accomplished, it may or may not be followed by agreement, or what is called "communion" —a community of feeling which expresses itself in identical value judgments.

There is a contrast, therefore, between critical communication and what I may call normal or ordinary communication. In ordinary communication, symbols tend to acquire a footing relatively independent of sense-perception. It is, of course, doubtful whether the interpretation of symbols is at any time completely unaffected by the environmental context. But there is a difference of degree between, say, an exchange of glances which, though it means "Shall we go home?" at one time and place, would mean something very different at another—between this and formal science, whose vocabulary and syntax have relatively fixed connotations. With a passage of scientific prose before us, we may be dependent on experience for the definition of certain simple terms, as also for the confirmation of assertions; but we are not dependent on experience for the interpretation of compound expressions. If we are, this exposes semantical defects in the passage—obscurity, vagueness, ambiguity, or incompleteness. (Thus: "Paranoia is marked by a profound egocentricity and deep-seated feelings of insecurity"—the kind of remark which makes every student think he has the disease—is suitable for easy comparison of notes among clinicians, who know how to recognize the difference between paranoia and other conditions; but it does not explicitly set forth the criteria which they employ.) Statements about immediate experience, made in ordinary communication, are no exception. If a theory requires that a certain flame should be blue, then we have to report whether it is or is not blue—regardless of shades or variations which may be of enormous importance aesthetically. We are bound to the letters of our words. Compare with this something like the following:

"The expression on her face was delightful."

"What was delightful about it?"

"Didn't you see that smile?"

The speaker does not mean that there is something delightful about smiles as such; but he cannot be accused of not stating his meaning clearly, because the clarity of his language must be judged in relation to his purpose, which in this case is the *evaluation* of the immediate experience; and for that purpose the reference to the smile will be sufficient if it gets people to feel that they are "talking about the same thing." There is understanding and misunderstanding at this level; there are marks by which the existence of one or the other can be known; and there are means by which misunderstanding can be eliminated. But these phenomena are not identical with those that take the same names in the study of ordinary communication.

Reading criticism, otherwise than in the presence, or with direct recollection, of the objects discussed is a blank and senseless employment—a fact which is concealed from us by the cooperation, in our reading, of many non-critical purposes for which the information offered by the critic is material and useful. There is not in all the world's criticism a single purely descriptive statement concerning which one is prepared to say beforehand, "If it is true, I shall like that work so much the better"—and *this* fact is concealed by the play of memory, which gives the critic's language a quite different, more specific, meaning than it has as ordinary communication. The point is not at all similar to that made by writers who maintain that value judgments have no objective basis because the reasons given to support them are not logically derivable from the value judgments themselves. I do not ask that R be related *logically* to V. In ethical argument you have someone say, "Yes, I would condemn that policy if it really did cause a wave of suicides, as you maintain." Suppose that the two clauses are here only psychologically related—still, this is what you never have in criticism. *The truth of R never adds the slightest weight to V,* because R does not designate any quality the perception of which might induce us to assent to V. But if it is not R, or what it designates that makes V acceptable, then R cannot possibly require the support of N. The critic is not committed to the general claim that the quality named Q is valuable because he never makes the particular claim that a work is good in virtue of the presence of Q.

But he, or his readers, can easily be misled into *thinking* that he has made such a claim. You have, perhaps, a conflict of opinion about the merits of a poem; and one writer defends his judgment by mentioning vowel sounds, metrical variations, consistent or inconsistent imagery. Another critic, taking this language at its face value in ordinary communication, points out that "by those standards" one would have to condemn famous passages in *Hamlet* or *Lear* and raise some admittedly bad poems to a high place. He may even attempt what he calls an "experiment" and, to show that his opponents' grounds are irrelevant, construct a travesty of the original poem in which its plot or its meter or its vowels and consonants, or whatever other qualities have been cited with approval, are held constant while the rest of the work is changed. This procedure, which takes up hundreds of the pages of our best modern critics, is a waste of time and space; for it is the critic abandoning his own function to pose as a scientist —to assume, in other words, that criticism explains experiences instead of clarifying and altering them. If he saw that the *meaning* of a word like 'assonance'—the quality which it leads our perception to discriminate in one poem or another—is in critical usage never twice the same, he would see no point in "testing" any generalization about the relationship between assonance and poetic value.

Some of the foregoing remarks will have reminded you of certain doctrines with which they were not intended to agree. The fact that criticism does not actually designate the qualities to which it somehow directs our attention has been a ground of complaint by some writers, who tell us that our present critical vocabulary is woefully inadequate.[4] This proposition clearly looks to an eventual improvement in the language of criticism. The same point, in a stronger form and with a different moral, is familiar to readers of Bergson and Croce, who say that it is impossible by means of concepts to "grasp the essence" of the artistic fact; and this position has seemed to many people to display the ultimate futility of critical analysis. I think that by returning to the passage I quoted from Goldscheider about the painting by El Greco we can differentiate the present point of view from both of these. Imagine, then, that the painting should be projected on to a graph with intersecting co-ordinates. It would then be possible to write complicated mathematical expressions which would enable another person who knew the system to construct for himself as close an approximation to the exact outlines of the El Greco as we might desire. Would this be an advance towards precision in criticism? Could we say that we had devised a more specific terminology for drawing and painting? I think not, for the most refined

[4] See D. W. Prall, *Aesthetic Analysis*, p. 201.

concept remains a concept; there is no vanishing point at which it becomes a percept. It is the idea *of* a quality, it is not the quality itself. To render a critical verdict we should still have to perceive the quality; but Goldscheider's passage already shows it to us as clearly as language can. The idea of a new and better means of communication presupposes the absence of the sensory contents we are talking about; but criticism always assumes the presence of these contents to both parties; and it is upon this assumption that the vagueness or precision of a critical statement must be judged. Any further illustration of this point will have to be rough and hasty. For the last twenty or thirty years the "correct" thing to say about the metaphysical poets has been this: They think with their senses and feel with their brains. One hardly knows how to verify such a dictum: as a psychological observation it is exceedingly obscure. But it does not follow that it is not acute criticism; for it increases our awareness of the difference between Tennyson and Donne. Many words—like 'subtlety,' 'variety,' 'complexity,' 'intensity'—which in ordinary communication are among the vaguest in the language have been used to convey sharp critical perceptions. And many expressions which have a clear independent meaning are vague and fuzzy when taken in relation to the content of a work of art. An examination of the ways in which the language of concepts mediates between perception and perception is clearly called for, though it is far too difficult to be attempted here.

We have also just seen reason to doubt that any aesthetic quality is ultimately ineffable. 'What can be said' and 'what cannot be said' are phrases which take their meaning from the purpose for which we are speaking. The aesthetics of obscurantism, in its insistence upon the incommunicability of the art object, has never made it clear what purpose or demand is to be served by communication. If we devised a system of concepts by which a work of art could be virtually reproduced at a distance by the use of language alone, what human intention would be furthered? We saw that *criticism* would not be improved: in the way in which criticism strives to "grasp" the work of art, we could grasp it no better then than now. The scientific *explanation* of aesthetic experiences would not be accomplished by a mere change of descriptive terminology. There remains only the *aesthetic* motive in talking about art. Now if we set it up as a condition of communicability that our language should *afford* the experience which it purports to describe, we shall of course reach the conclusion that art is incommunicable. But by that criterion all reality is unintelligible and ineffable, just as Bergson maintains. Such a demand upon thought and language is not only preposterous in that its fulfilment is logically impossible;

it is also baneful, because it obscures the actual and very large influence of concepts upon the process of perception (by which, I must repeat, I mean something more than the ordinary *reference* of language to qualities of experience). Every part of the psychology of perception and attention provides us with examples of how unverbalized apperceptive reactions are engrained in the content and structure of the perceptual field. We can also learn from psychology how perception is affected by verbal cues and instructions. What remains unstudied is the play of critical comment in society at large; but we have, each of us in his own experience, instances of differential emphasis and selective grouping which have been brought about through the concepts imparted to us by the writings of critics.

I have perhaps overstressed the role of the critic as teacher, i.e., as one who affords *new* perceptions and with them new values. There is such a thing as discovering a community of perception and feeling which already exists; and this can be a very pleasant experience. But it often happens that there are qualities in a work of art which are, so to speak, neither perceived nor ignored but felt or endured in a manner of which Leibniz has given the classic description. Suppose it is only a feeling of monotony, a slight oppressiveness, which comes to us from the style of some writer. A critic then refers to his "piled-up clauses, endless sentences, repetitious diction." This remark shifts the focus of our attention and brings certain qualities which had been blurred and marginal into distinct consciousness. When, with a sense of illumination, we say "Yes, that's it exactly," we are really giving expression to the *change* which has taken place in our aesthetic apprehension. The post-critical experience is the true commentary on the pre-critical one. The same thing happens when, after listening to Debussy, we study the chords that can be formed on the basis of the whole-tone scale and then return to Debussy. New feelings are given which bear some resemblance to the old. There is no objection in these cases to our saying that we have been made to "understand" why we liked (or disliked) the work. But such understanding, which is the legitimate fruit of criticism, is nothing but a second moment of aesthetic experience, a retrial of experienced values. It should not be confused with the psychological study which seeks to know the causes of our feelings.

Note

In this article I have tried only to mark out the direction in which, as I believe, the exact nature of criticism should be sought. The task has been largely negative: it is necessary to correct preconceptions, obliterate false trails. There remain questions of two main kinds. Just to establish the adequacy of my analysis, there would have to be a detailed examination of critical phenomena, which present in the gross a fearful complexity. For example, I have paid almost no attention to large-scale or summary judgments—evaluations of artists, schools, or periods. One could quote brief statements about Shakespeare's qualities as a poet or Wagner's as a composer which seem to be full of insight; yet it would be hard to explain what these statements do to our "perception"—if that word can be used as a synonym for our appreciation of an artist's work as a whole.

But if the analysis is so far correct, it raises a hundred new questions. Two of these—rather, two sides of one large question—are especially important. What is the semantical relationship between the language of criticism and the qualities of the critic's or the reader's experience? I have argued that this relationship is not designation (though I do not deny that there *is* a relationship of designation between the critic's language and *some* qualities of a work of art). But neither is it denotation: the critic does not *point* to the qualities he has in mind. The ostensive function of language will explain the exhibition of *parts* or *details* of an art object but not the exhibition of abstract *qualities;* and it is the latter which is predominant in criticism. The only positive suggestion made in this paper can be restated as follows. To say that the critic "picks out" a quality in the work of art is to say that if there did exist a designation for that quality, then the designation which the critic employs would be what Morris calls an analytic implicate of that designation. (Thus, 'blue' is an analytic implicate of an expression 'H3B5S2' which designates a certain point on the colour solid.) This definition is clearly not sufficient to characterize the critic's method; but, more, the antecedent of the *definiens* is doubtful in meaning. A study of terms like 'Rembrandt's chiaroscuro,' 'the blank verse of *The Tempest*,' etc., etc., would probably result in the introduction of an idea analogous to that of the proper name (or of Russell's "definite description") but with this difference, that the entity uniquely named or labelled by this type of expression is not an object but a quality.

If we put the question on the psychological plane, it reads as follows: How is it that (*a*) we can "know what we like" in a work of art without (*b*) knowing what "causes" our enjoyment? I presume that criticism enlightens us as to (*a*) and that (*b*) would be provided by a psychological explanation; also that (*a*) is often true when (*b*) is not.

Contrary to Ducasse[5] and some other writers I cannot see that the critic has any competence as a self-psychologist, a specialist in the explanation of his own responses. There is no other field in which we admit the existence of such scientific insight, unbridled by experimental controls and unsupported by valid general theory; and I do not think we can admit it here. (For that reason I held that critical insight, which does exist, cannot be identified with scientific understanding.) The truth is that, in the present stone age of aesthetic inquiry, we have

[5] *Op. cit.*, p. 117.

not even the vaguest idea of the form that a "law of art appreciation" would take.
Consider, "It is as a *colorist* that Titian excells"; interpret this as causal hypothesis—for example, "Titian colors give pleasure"; and overlook incidental
difficulties, such as whether 'color' means tone or the hue (as opposed to the
brightness and the saturation) of a tone. Superficially, this is similar to many low-
grade hypotheses in psychology: "We owe the *color* of the object to the retinal
rods and cones," "It is the *brightness* and not the color that infuriates a bull,"
"Highly *saturated* colors give pleasure to American schoolboys." But the difference is that we do not know what test conditions are marked out by our chosen
proposition. Would it be relevant, as a test of its truth, to display the colors of a
painting by Titian, in a series of small rectanguler areas, to a group of subjects in
the laboratory? I cannot believe this to be part of what is meant by a person who
affirms this hypothesis. He is committed to no such test.

Anyone with a smattering of Gestalt psychology now interposes that the colors
are, of course, pleasing *in* their context, not out of it. One has some trouble in
understanding how in that case one could know that it is the *colors* that are
pleasing. We may believe in studying the properties of wholes; but it is hard
to see what scientific formulation can be given to the idea that a quality should
have a certain function (that is, a causal relationship to the responses of an observer) in one and only one whole. Yet that appears to be the case with the color
scheme in any painting by Titian.

We can be relieved of these difficulties simply by admitting our ignorance and
confusion; but there is no such escape when we turn to criticism. For it *is* as a
colorist that Titian excels—this is a fairly unanimous value judgment, and we
should be able to analyze its meaning. (I should not, however, want the issue to
turn on this particular example. Simpler and clearer judgments could be cited.)
Now when our attention is called, by a critic, to a certain quality, we respond to
that quality *in its context*. The context is never specified, as it would have to be
in any scientific theory, but always assumed. Every descriptive statement affects
our perception of—and our feeling for—the work as a whole. One might say, then,
that we agree with the critic if and when he gets us to like the work about as
well or as badly as he does. But this is clearly not enough. For he exerts his influence always through a specific discrimination. Art criticism is analytic, dis-
criminating. It concerns itself less with over-all values than with merits and faults
in specified respects. It is the quality and not the work that is good or bad; or, if
you like, the work is good or bad "on account of its qualities." Thus, we may agree
with his judgment but reject the critic's grounds (I have shown that the "grounds,"
to which he is really appealing are not the same as those which he explicitly states
or designates); and when we do this, we are saying that the qualities which he
admires are not those which we admire. But then we must know what we
admire: we are somehow aware of the special attachment of our feelings to certain
abstract qualities rather than to others. Without this, we could never reject a
reason given for a value judgment with which we agree—we could never be dis-

satisfied with descriptive evaluation. There must therefore exist an analyzing, sifting, shredding process within perception which corresponds to the conceptual distinctness of our references to "strong form but weak color," "powerful images but slovenly meter," and so on.

This process is mysterious; but we can get useful hints from two quarters. Artists and art teachers are constantly "experimenting," in their own way. "Such a bright green at this point is jarring." "Shouldn't you add more detail to the large space on the right?" We can compare two wholes in a single respect and mark the difference in the registration upon our feelings. Implicit comparisons of this kind, with shifting tone of feeling, are what are involved in the isolation of qualities from the work, at least in *some* critical judgments. I am afraid that as psychology, as an attempt to discover the causes of our feelings, this is primitive procedure; but as a mere analysis of what is meant by the praise and blame accorded to special qualities, it is not without value.

If, in the second place, we could discover what we mean by the difference between the "object" and the "cause" of an emotion, *outside* the field of aesthetics; if we could see both the distinction and the connection between two such judgments as "I hate his cheek" and "It is his cheek that inspires hatred in me"; if we knew what happens when a man says, "Now I know why I have always disliked him—it is his pretence of humility," there would be a valuable application to the analysis of critical judgments.

Bibliography

Discussions of value judgments are rarely bound to aesthetic considerations alone. The following however are comparatively restricted to our domain:

Monroe C. Beardsley, *Aesthetics* (New York, 1958), Chapter XI;

Bernard Harrison, "Some Uses of 'Good' in Criticism," *Mind,* Volume LXIX (1960), 206-222;

Isabel C. Hungerland, *Poetic Discourse* (Berkeley, 1958), Chapter III;

William E. Kennick, "Does Traditional Aesthetics Rest on a Mistake?," *Mind* (1958), 317-334;

Helen Knight, "The Use of 'Good' in Aesthetic Judgments," reprinted in William Elton (ed.), *Aesthetics and Language* (Oxford, 1954);

Margaret Macdonald, "Some Distinctive Features of Arguments Used in Criticism of the Arts," reprinted (revised) in William Elton, *loc. cit.;*

J. A. Passmore, "The Dreariness of Aesthetics," reprinted in William Elton, *loc. cit.*

Another discussion of considerable relevance but bearing more indirectly on aesthetics is to be found in:

P. H. Nowell-Smith, *Ethics* (London, 1954), Chapter XII.

IX

APPRECIATION AND EVALUATION

IT IS an obvious truth that music is for listening and paintings for viewing. But if one reflects on it, consequences may be drawn for the theory
of criticism. Can we not also say that the point of criticism is to indicate
what to listen for and what to view? That is, perhaps criticism is primarily
designed (or ought to be) to indicate what we may appreciate in particular
works of art. We are led, then, to consider the variety of tasks critics of
fine art, both professional and amateur, may undertake and also the special
logical features of appreciative remarks. Inquiry here will take the form
of sorting out distinctions among the describing, interpreting, analyzing,
comparing, and classifying of works of art, among the activities associated
with the educative role of critics, as well as among the expressing of taste
and appreciation and the various ways of judging and evaluating works
of art.

The distinction of appreciative remarks, however, seems to lie in the fact
that one cannot properly be said to be mistaken in what one appreciates
(though he may be mistaken about the properties of what he is favorably
disposed to). Nevertheless, one may be called on to defend his appreciative
remark (for example, "That's a rather good painting"). And he will supply
reasons, in the sense of detailing features of the work that can be perceived
and that support his comment.

156

Questions may be raised about what is relevant to the support of such a comment. These are not easy to answer, because one cannot say that remarks of this or that sort will invariably be relevant or irrelevant. Sometimes, it seems, much the same comment may bear on identifying and classifying works of art as would bear on supporting an evaluative remark. Nevertheless, it will be important to form some sense of the characteristic ways in which we do defend appreciative and evaluative remarks.

The chief questions, then, are probably these. What sorts of reasons are generally relevant in asserting that a work of art is good or bad? And how closely related, logically, are appreciation and evaluation? And are there general principles available for judging such characteristic values as subtlety, delicacy, ingenuity, boldness, inventiveness, control, and the like? Or are we obliged to mention only particular reasons for particular works? And if there are only particular reasons for particular works, is it possible to dispute judgments rendered and what form will such disputes take?

Paul Ziff has dealt with this issue in a somewhat elliptical and allusive way. But since the relevant puzzles are admittedly involved ones, there may be a distinct advantage in his having provided numerous specimens, which will repay scrutiny, of the kind of talk we associate with criticism in the arts.

Reasons in Art Criticism

PAUL ZIFF

Hsieh ho said one of the principles of painting is that "through organization, place and position should be determined." Le Brun praised
Poussin's paintings to the French Academy, saying the figures were faithful
copies of Roman and Greek statues.

If someone now says "P.'s painting is a faithful copy of a Roman statue,"
he is not apt to be offering a reason why the work is either good or bad.
"The painting has a touch of blue," ". . . is a seascape," ". . . a picture of
peasants," ". . . conforms to the artist's intentions," ". . . will improve men's
morals": these too are not apt to be offered, and if offered cannot be accepted as reasons why the painting is good or bad.

But if someone says "P.'s painting is disorganized," he is apt to be offering a reason why the work is bad (he need not be; this might be part of an
answer to "Which one is P.'s?"). Even if it is right to say "P.'s painting is
disorganized," it may be wrong to conclude "P.'s painting is bad," or even
"P.'s painting is not good." Some good paintings are somewhat disorganized;
they are good in spite of the fact that they are somewhat disorganized. But

From *Philosophy and Education,* edited by I. Scheffler (Boston: Allyn and Bacon, 1958),
pp. 219-236. Reprinted with the permission of the author.

no painting is good because it is disorganized and many are bad primarily because they are disorganized.

To say "P.'s painting is disorganized" may be to offer a good reason why P.'s painting is bad. It is a consideration. It need not be conclusive. But it is a reason nonetheless. Much the same may be said of reference to the balance, composition, proportions, etc., of a painting; but much the same may not be said of certain references to the subject matter, of any reference to the size, shape, effect on morals, etc., of a painting. Why is this so? Is this so?

I

Someone might say this: "If a painting were disorganized and had no redeeming features, one would not call it 'a good painting.' To understand the relevant uses of the phrase 'a good painting' is to understand, among other things, that to say 'P.'s painting is disorganized' may be to offer a reason in support of an unfavorable opinion of P.'s painting."

This won't do at all even though it is plainly true that someone would not—I would not—call a painting "a good painting" if it were disorganized and had no redeeming features.

Maybe certain persons use the phrase "a good painting" in such a way that they would call a painting "a good painting" even if it were disorganized and had no redeeming features. Maybe some or even many or most in fact use the phrase "a good painting" in a way that no painting is good if it is not a seascape. Many people probably use the phrase "a good painting" in many different ways.

It is true that I and my friends would not call a painting "a good painting" if it were merely disorganized, unredeemed. That is no reason why anyone should accept the fact that a painting is disorganized as a reason in support of an unfavorable opinion of it. To say one would not call it "a good painting" if it were disorganized and had no redeeming features is primarily a way of indicating how strongly one is committed to the acceptance of such a fact as a reason, it is a way of making clear precisely what attitude one has here: it does not show the attitude is reasonable.

Why use the phrase in one way rather than another? Why bother with organization? Why not concentrate on seascapes? on pictures of peasants? Is it merely a linguistic accident that one is concerned with organization? This is not a matter of words. (And this is not to say that the words do not matter: "That is a good painting" can be queried with "According to what standards?"; "That is a magnificent painting" cannot be so queried

and neither can "That is an exquisite painting," ". . . a splendid painting," etc.)

Only some of the remarks sometimes made while discussing a work of
art are reasons in support of a critical evaluation of the work: to evaluate
a work one must understand it, appreciate it; much of what is said about a
work is directly relevant only to an appreciation of it.

Any fact is relevant to an appreciation of a work if a knowledge of it is
likely to facilitate, to enhance, the appreciation of the work. A critic may
direct attention to many different facts: the role of the supporting continuo is a central point in Tovey's discussion of Haydn's chamber music.
Tovey points out that the supporting continuo was used to fill a crucial gap
in the musical structure:

> The pioneers of instrumental music in the years 1600-20 showed an accurate
> instinct by promptly treating all groups of instruments as consisting of a
> firm bass and a florid treble, held together by an unobstrusive mass of
> harmony in the middle. Up to the death of Handel and beyond, through-
> out Haydn's boyhood, this harmonic welding was entrusted to the con-
> tinuo player, and nobody ever supposed that the polyphony of the "real"
> orchestral parts could, except accidentally or by way of relief, sound well
> without this supplement.[1]

When Tovey then says: in the later chamber music Haydn abandoned
the use of a supporting continuo, he is saying something of relevance to an
appreciation of any one of Haydn's chamber works: who can then listen
to an early Haydn quartet and not hear it in a new way? The supporting
continuo acquires a new prominence; for a time, an undue prominence in
the structure of the whole work. But the end product of this process of re-
examining the interrelations of the various parts, to which one has been
impelled by the critic's information, is a keener feeling for the texture of
the whole.

This is one instance of how historical information can be of value in
directing and enlightening the appreciation of a work; there are others:
the music of Bach has been compared with that of Schütz, Donne's poetry
with that of Cavalcanti, Matisse's work with Egyptian wall paintings. Comparative studies are useful; they provide fresh means of directing and
arousing interest in certain aspects of the works under consideration. When
a critic shows that work *A* is intimately related or similar in some important
respects to work *B*, this is of interest not only in that one is then aware of
this particular relation between *A* and *B*, but more significantly, one may

---

[1] *Essays and Lectures on Music,* pp. 3-4.

then see both *A* and *B* in a different way: *A* seen in the light of its relation to *B* can acquire a new lucidity.

Any fact may be relevant to an appreciation of a work, may thereby be indirectly relevant in evaluating it. Presumably every fact directly relevant in evaluating the work is also relevant to an appreciation of it. But the converse is not true, e.g., that the work was executed while the artist was in Rome may be relevant to an appreciation of it but is likely to be relevant in no other way to an evaluation of it. What further requirements must a fact relevant to an appreciation of a work satisfy if it is also to be relevant in evaluating the work?

To say a painting is a good painting is here simply to say it is worth contemplating. (Strictly speaking, this is false but for the time being I am not concerned to speak strictly, but only for the time being. See II below.) Nothing can be a reason why the painting is good unless it is a reason why the painting is worth contemplating. (One can add: for its own sake, but that is redundant.)

Suppose we are in a gallery with a friend looking at P.'s painting; he somewhat admires the work, is inclined to claim it is good; we wish to deny this, to claim it is a bad painting. We might attempt to support our counterclaim by saying "The painting is clearly disorganized," offering this as a reason in support of our opinion of the work.

Saying this to him would be a way of drawing his attention to the organization of the painting, to the lack of it, a way of pointing to this aspect of the painting, saying "Notice this, see the disorder," not merely this, of course, but at least this.

> (Here you see a single great curving diagonal holds together in its sweep nearly everything in the picture. And this diagonal is not built up by forms that are at the same distance from the eye. The forms are arranged so as to lead the eye gradually backwards until we pass out of the stable into the open air beyond. Here . . .[2]

said Roger Fry, discussing a painting by Rubens, focusing the listening eye on the single great curving diagonal, drawing it back and forth across the picture plane, levelling the attention, directing it freely throughout the painting.)

This pointing is a fundamental reason why "The painting is clearly disorganized" is a reason, and the fact that it is indicates why "The work was executed while the artist was in Rome," ". . . conforms to the artist's in-

[2] *French, Flemish and British Art*, p. 125.

tentions," ". . . is liked by Bernard," even though possibly relevant to an appreciation of the work, are not reasons why the painting is good or bad; for all this is not directly relevant. One cannot contemplate the fact that the work was done while the artist was in Rome in the painting; this is not an aspect of the painting, not a characteristic of it which one can either look at or look for. Suppose one were told: "Notice that the work was done while the artist was in Rome," one could only reply: "But what am I supposed to look at?"

Of course one could do this: I say to you "Think of Rome; then look for things in the picture that will fit in with what you've just been thinking"; you might find a great deal in some pictures, little in others. If I want you to make out a lion in the picture which you seem not to have seen I could say this: "Remember the work was done in Africa," "The artist was much interested in animals," etc. So it won't do, in one sense, to say that remarks like "Notice that the work was done while the artist was in Rome" are not reasons because they do not direct or guide one in the contemplation of the work. But in another sense it is obvious that such remarks do not guide or direct one in the contemplation of a work; to suppose that they do is to suppose certain familiar locutions to be signifying in somewhat extraordinary ways.

What is important here is this: one looks at paintings; nothing can be a reason why a painting is good or bad unless it is concerned with what can be looked at in the painting, unless it is concerned with what can, in some sense, be seen.

If it be asked: "Why insist on this? How does this show that 'The work was done while the artist was in Rome' is not a reason why the painting is good?," a sufficient answer is: only in this way can the reason direct or guide one in the contemplation of the work; a "reason" that failed to do this would not be worth asking for, not worth giving; there would be no reason to be concerned with such a "reason."

But this is not to say that "The work was done while the artist was in Rome," ". . . is liked by Bernard," etc., are necessarily, apart from questions of appreciation, altogether irrelevant; these matters may in many ways be indirectly relevant to an evaluation of a work.

That the work was done while the artist was in Rome, is liked by Bernard, was done in the artist's old age, is detested by people of reputed good taste . . . may be indications, signs, that it is a poor work; these may be very good and important reasons to suppose the work is defective. It is for such reasons as these that one decides not to see a certain exhibition, not to read a certain book, not to hear a certain concert. But such facts as these do not in themselves constitute reasons why the painting is a poor work: indications or signs are never reasons why the painting is good or bad, but at best only reasons to suppose it is good or bad. The fact that *C* cannot remember *D*'s name is often an indication or a sign of the fact that *C* dislikes *D*; it is a reason to suppose *C* dislikes *D*; in odd cases it may also be a reason why *C* dislikes *D* in that it is a contributing cause of the dislike: an indication or a sign is a reason why only when it is a cause. But one is not here concerned with causes: "What causes this to be a good painting?" has no literal meaning; "What makes this a good painting?" asks for a reason why it is a good painting, and this kind of question cannot be answered by citing indications or signs.

This pointing is not the only reason why certain facts are, and others are not, reasons why a painting is good or bad: "The painting is a seascape" points to a characteristic of the painting, directs one's attention to certain features of the work; for saying this to him could be a way of saying "Notice this, see that it is a seascape," yet this is not a reason why the painting is either good or bad.

To say to him "The painting is a seascape" could be a way of directing his attention to the subject matter of the painting, indicating that the painting was of a certain kind. While contemplating a painting one may consider what kind of work it is, who painted it, what kind of organization it has, what kind of subject matter (if any), what kind of pigmentation, etc. To learn that a painting is by a certain artist, has a certain kind of organization, subject matter, pigmentation, etc., may be relevant to an appreciation of the work; it may enable one to recognize, discern, make out, identify, label, name, classify things in the painting, aspects of the painting; such recognition, identification, classification, may be important in the appreciation of a painting; one who failed to recognize or discern or make out the man in Braque's *Man with a Guitar,* the printed letters in a cubist painting, a horse in *Guernica,* would be apt to misjudge the balance and organization of these works, would fail to appreciate or understand these works, would be in no position to evaluate them.

That a painting is of a certain kind may be an excellent reason to suppose it is good or bad. But is it ever a reason why the painting is good or bad? Is the fact that the painting is of a certain kind directly relevant to the contemplation of the painting? Does "The painting is a seascape" direct or guide one in the contemplation of the painting?

Being of a certain kind matters here primarily in connection with the recognition, identification, classification, etc., of various elements of the work.

Shall we then say: "Contemplating the subject matter of a painting (or its organization, or its pigmentation, etc.) is not merely a matter of recognizing, identifying, the subject matter, not merely a matter of labelling, naming, classifying"?

That is not enough: it is not that contemplating a painting is not merely a matter of this or that, it is not a matter of recognizing or identifying or classifying or labelling at all.

Contemplating a painting is something one does, something one may be engaged in; one can and does say things like "I am contemplating this painting," "I have been contemplating this painting for some time." But in this sense, recognizing is not something one does; even though it may be true that while contemplating a painting (which has subject matter) I may recognize, or fail to recognize, or simply not recognize, the subject matter of the painting, it is never true that I am recognizing the subject matter; and this is a way of saying one cannot say "I am recognizing the subject matter of this painting," or "I am recognizing this painting," or "I have been recognizing it for some time," etc.

Recognition is like an event, whereas contemplation is like an activity (much the same may be said of identification, classification, etc., in certain relevant senses, though not in all senses, of these terms); certain events may occur during the course of an activity, recognition may or may not take place during the course of contemplation. While contemplating Braque's *Man with a Guitar* one may suddenly (or slowly and at great length) recognize, discern, make out, a figure in the painting; analytical cubistic works often offer such difficulties. If on Monday one recognizes a figure in the Braque painting, on Tuesday there is ordinarily no question of recognition; it has occurred, is over and done with, for the time being; "I recognize it every time I see it" would be sensible if each time it appeared in a fresh disguise, if I suffered from recurrent amnesia, if it appeared darkly out of a haze. (In the sense in which one can speak of "recognizing" the subject matter of an abstract or semi-abstract work, one often cannot speak of "recognizing" the subject matter of a characteristic Chardin still-life: one can see, look at, study, examine the apple in the Chardin painting, but there is not likely to be any "recognition.")

This is not to deny that if a work has recognizable elements, recognition may occur during the course of contemplation, nor that if it does occur then the contemplation of the work is, for some people at least, likely to be somewhat enhanced. If recognition is ever a source of delight, that is certainly true; this, too, would be true: the second time one contemplates the work the contemplation of it may be less worthwhile. But whether this is true or not does not really matter here. It appears to be of interest owing only to an ambiguity of "contemplating."

"Contemplating" may be employed to refer simply to contemplating, or to someone's contemplation of a work at a certain time and place and under certain conditions. "In contemplating the work one attends to the organization" is about contemplating, about what one is doing in contemplating the work; to speak of "contemplating a work," or of "the contemplation of a work," is a way of referring only to certain aspects of one's contemplation of a work at a certain time and place and under certain conditions; it is a way of abstracting from considerations of person, place and time. "In contemplating the work one recognizes a figure in the foreground" is not about contemplating the work; it is not about what one is doing in contemplating the work; it is about something like an event that may occur while someone is contemplating the work for the first or second time under certain conditions. (Contrast "In walking one's leg muscles are continually being tensed and relaxed" with "In walking one finds an emerald.")

To say "Since the work has recognizable elements, recognition is likely to occur while contemplating the work and thus the contemplation of the work will be enhanced" would not be to refer to the contemplation of the work, it would not be to abstract from considerations of time; for it is not the contemplation of the work that would be enhanced, but only and merely the contemplation of the work on that particular occasion when recognition occurred. It is for this reason the fact that the work has recognizable elements—and thus admits of the possibility of recognition occurring during the course of contemplation, so enhancing the contemplation—is not a reason why the work is worth contemplating. To say "The work is worth contemplating," or "Contemplating the work is worthwhile," is here and ordinarily to speak of contemplating the work, it is here and ordinarily to abstract from considerations of person, place, and time.

Were *Guernica* hung in Hell, contemplating it would hardly be worthwhile, would there be altogether tedious; yet it is not the work that would be at fault, rather the contemplation of the work in the galleries of Hell. But whether this would be the case has no bearing on whether *Guernica* is worth contemplating. It would ordinarily be at best foolish to reply to "*Guernica* is well worth contemplating" by asking "When?" or "Where?" or even "For whom?" That a certain person, at a certain time and place, finds *Guernica* not worth contemplating may be a slight reason to suppose *Guernica* is not worth contemplating; but it is not a reason why the work is not worth contemplating. If one knows that no one ever has found, or ever will find, *Guernica* worth contemplating, one has excellent reason to suppose *Guernica* is not worth contemplating; one can be absolutely sure it is not worth contemplating; yet this is not even the most trifling reason why *Guernica* is not worth contemplating. This does not ever entitle anyone to say "I know *Guernica* is not worth contemplating." All this is but an elaborate way of saying that in saying "The work is worth contemplating" one is abstracting from considerations of person, place, and time.

What has been said of "recognition" could be said, in one way or another, of "identification," "classification," "labelling," "naming," etc.; thus identification, as well as recognition, may occur during the course of contemplation, may enhance the contemplation, is over and done with after a time. But this is never a reason why the painting is good or bad. If recognition, identification, classification, etc., all fail, as they do in fact all fail, to be such a reason, and if nothing can be such a reason unless it is a fact about the work that directs or guides one in the contemplation of the work—thus comparisons, associations, etc., are out of order—it follows that the fact that a work is of a certain kind is also incapable of being a reason why the work is worth contemplating. "There can be no objective rule of taste by which what is beautiful may be defined by means of concepts" said Kant,[3] and he was right (but for the wrong reasons).

Let it be clear that nothing has been said to deny that one can be concerned only with recognition, or identification, or classification, or comparisons, etc., when contemplating paintings; one can treat a painting in the way an entomologist treats a specimen spider, or be concerned only with puzzle pictures, with conundrums. Nor has it been maintained that to say "The work is worth contemplating" is necessarily to abstract from considerations of person, place, and time; that this is what is here and ordinarily intended in speaking of "contemplating a painting" is primarily (though not exclusively) a verbal point and does not signify. There are other ways of speaking: a person may choose to say "The work is worth contemplating" and abstract only from considerations of person, or of place, or of time, or not at all. But if so, he cannot then say what one now wants to say and does say about paintings; for if a person fails or refuses to abstract from such considerations at all, it will be impossible either to agree or disagree with him about the worth of paintings; refusing to abstract from considerations of person, place, and time is tantamount to refusing ever to say, as one now says, "The work is worth contemplating," but insisting always on saying things like "The work is worth contemplating for me, here and now," or ". . . for him, yesterday, at two o'clock," etc. One can speak in this way if one

[3] *Critique of Aesthetic Judgement*, Bk. I, sec. 17.

chooses; one can do what one wills with paintings. But none of this has anything to do with art.

To state that a painting is a seascape, if it is simply to state that the work is of a certain kind, is not to state a reason why it is good or bad; for that the painting is of a certain kind cannot be such a reason. What can?

Contrast "The painting is a seascape" with "The painting is disorganized." To say the former to someone could be a way of directing his attention to the subject matter of the painting, indicating that it had a certain kind of subject matter; to say the latter not only could but would be a way of directing his attention to the organization of the painting, but it would not be indicating that it had a certain kind of organization.

The sense of "organization" with which one is here primarily concerned is that in which one can say of any painting "Notice the organization" without thereby being committed to the view that the painting is in fact organized; one can and does say things like "The main fault to be found with Pollock's paintings is in the organization: his work is completely disorganized." (Just so one can on occasion say "Notice the balance" of a certain painting, and yet not be committed to saying the painting is balanced.) Every work has an organization in the sense that no matter what arrangement there may be of shapes, shades, etc., there is necessarily a particular configuration to be found in the painting. In this sense, the organization is an aspect, a feature, of every painting; something that may be contemplated, studied, and observed, in every painting.

There are various kinds of organization, for the organization of a work is something which may be described, classified, analyzed:

> The chief difference between the classical design of Raphael and the Baroque lay in the fact that whilst the artists of the high Renaissance accepted the picture plane and tended to dispose their figures in planes parallel to that—Raphael's cartoons, for instance, almost invariably show this method—the Baroque designers disposed their figures along lines receding from the eye into the depths of the picture space.[4]

"Horizontally, crossing the picture plane," or "Primarily rectangular," or "Along a single curving diagonal," could be answers to the question "What kind of organization does it have?" in a way that "Organized" or "Disorganized" could not. "Organized" and "Disorganized" are more like states than like kinds of organization ("organized" is more like "happy" than like "healthy," and more like "healthy" than like "human").

Yet this is not to deny what cannot be denied, that a sensible answer to

[4] R. Fry, *op. cit.*, p. 22.

"What kind of painting is it?" might be "A fairly well organized seascape, somewhat reminiscent of the Maine coast." "What kind of painting is it?" is often a request not only to describe the painting, to identify it, name it, classify it, point out its similarities and dissimilarities to other paintings, but also to evaluate the painting, to say whether it is worth bothering with, etc.

But seascapes are a kind of painting in a way disorganized or organized paintings are not; crocodiles are a kind of animal in a way healthy animals are not: unlike "seascape" and "crocodile," "organized" and "healthy" admit of questions of degree; one can say "He is quite healthy," "It is somewhat disorganized," "It would be less well organized if that were done," etc.; there are and can be no corresponding locutions employing the terms "seascape" and "crocodile." (One could introduce the terms "seascapish" and "crocodilish," but this is to say: one could invent a use for them.) One cannot discriminate between seascapes on the basis of their being seascapes, whereas one can and does discriminate between disorganized paintings on the basis of their being disorganized, for some are more and some are less.

That "organized," and "disorganized," unlike "seascape," admit of questions of degree is important (thus Tolstoi, who knew what art was, and knowing crucified it, spoke of ". . . those infinitely minute degrees of which a work of art consists"[5]); here it indicates that determining whether a painting is disorganized, unlike determining whether it is a seascape, is not a matter of recognition or identification, though it may, on occasion, presuppose such recognition or identification. In order to determine whether a painting is disorganized, it is necessary to contemplate the organization of the painting. To determine whether a painting is a seascape, it is sufficient to recognize or identify the subject matter of the work; it is not necessary to contemplate the subject matter. To say to someone "The painting is a seascape" could be a way of drawing his attention to the subject matter of the painting, but it would be a way of inviting recognition or identification of certain things in the painting, not a way of inviting contemplation of an aspect of the painting.

"Disorganized," unlike "seascape," reports on an aspect of the painting; one might also say: it refers to a point in a dimension, the particular dimension being that of organization; another point in this dimension is referred to by "clearly organized," another by "an incoherent organization," etc.; to say "The organization of the painting is defective," or "The painting has a defective organization," or "The painting is defectively organized," are ways—different ways—of attributing approximately the same location to

[5] *What is Art?*, Oxford University Press, p. 201.

the painting in the dimension of organization. To say "The painting is a sea-scape" is not to direct attention to a certain dimension, that of subject matter; it may direct attention to the subject matter, but not to the dimension of subject matter: such a dimension is found when one considers not the kind but the treatment or handling of subject matter (contrast "The painting is a seascape" with "The figures are too stiff, too impassive"); for it does not refer to a point in that dimension; it does not locate the painting in that dimension. (Just so to say "The painting has a diagonal organization" is not to direct attention to a certain dimension.)

But not any report on any aspect of the painting can be a reason why the painting is good or bad; "The painting is quite green, predominantly green" reports on an aspect of the painting, yet it is not a reason why the work is good or bad.

To say "The painting is quite green" could be somewhat like saying "Notice the organization of the painting" for it could serve to direct attention to an aspect of the painting; but it is not apt to be the relevant kind of report on this aspect. It is not such a report if it does not lead one either to or away from the work: if it were a reason, would it be a reason why the painting is a good painting or a reason why the painting is a bad painting?

But it would not be correct to say it is never a report, in a relevant sense; it is not apt to be, but it might; if someone were to claim that a painting were good and if, when asked why, replied "Notice the organization!" it could be clear he was claiming that the painting was organized, perhaps superbly organized, that the organization of the work was delightful, etc.; just so if he were to claim "The painting is quite green, predominantly green," it could be quite clear he was claiming that the greenness of the painting was delightful, that the work was "sufficiently green," etc.: "The painting is quite green" would here be a report on an aspect of the painting, a report leading in one direction. Even so, it is not a reason why the painting is good or bad.

This is not to deny that someone might offer such a statement as the statement of a reason why the painting is good. Nor is it to deny that "The painting is quite green" has all the marks of such a reason: it points to the painting; it directs one's attention to an aspect of the painting, an aspect that can be contemplated; it reports on this aspect of the painting and thus directs one to the contemplation of the painting. It could be a reason why the painting is good. But it is not. Is it because one simply does not care whether the painting is quite green? because it makes no difference?

One would not ordinarily say to someone "The painting is clearly disorganized" unless one supposed he had somehow not sufficiently attended to the organization of the work. But more than this: ordinarily one would not attempt to draw his attention to the organization of the painting, to the lack of it, unless one took for granted that if he did sufficiently attend to the organization and did in fact find the work to be disorganized, he would then realize that the painting was indeed defective.

One sometimes takes for granted that the absence of organization in a painting, once it is attended to, will in fact make much difference to a person; that he will be less inclined and perhaps even cease to find the work worth contemplating. And this is in fact sometimes the case; what one sometimes takes for granted is sometimes so.

This is one reason that a reference to the organization of the work may be a reason, and why a reference to the greenness of the painting is not; one ordinarily neither finds nor takes for granted one will find the fact that the painting is or is not quite green will make any such difference.

Being green or not green is not likely to make any difference to anyone in his contemplation of the painting; but the same is not true of being huge, or of having a sordid subject. Suppose a work were three miles high, two miles long: one simply could not contemplate it; suppose the subject matter of a work were revolting: certainly many could not contemplate it; or again, what if one knew that contemplating a work would have an insidious and evil influence: could one, nonetheless, contemplate it calmly?

There are many factors that may prevent and hinder one from contemplating a work; there are also certain factors that may facilitate the contemplation of a work, e.g., figure paintings, the Italian treatment of the figure, Raphael's, Signorelli's, Piero's handling, smoothes the path of contemplation.

> Therefore, the nude, and best of all the nude erect and frontal, has through all the ages in our world—the world descended from Egypt and Hellas—been the chief concern of the art of visual representation.[6]

One is inclined to contemplate the nude (though not the naked—there is a difference).

That a painting has revolting subject matter, may seduce the beholder, is too large, too small, etc., does make much difference, but a difference of a different kind. That a painting is too large is in fact a reason why the painting is not good; yet it is a reason of a different kind, for it is also a reason why the painting is not bad: that the painting is too large is not a reason

[6] B. Berenson, *Aesthetics and History*, pp. 81-82.

why the contemplation of the work is not worthwhile; rather it is a reason why one cannot contemplate the painting, a reason why one simply cannot evaluate the work.

That a painting is not too large, not too small, is not apt to seduce and is even apt to improve one, has splendid subject matter, etc., are not, in themselves, or in isolation, reasons why a work is a good work, why the work is worth contemplating. Yet such factors as these, by rendering the work accessible to contemplation, can tend to enhance its value. (Memling's *Lady with a Pink* would be less lovely were it larger; *Guernica* would be less majestic were it smaller.) Such factors as these cannot stand alone; alone they are not reasons why the painting is a good painting. That the neighboring woods are nearby does not prove them lovely, but if lovely, then by being nearby they are that much lovelier, and if ugly, that much uglier.

It is here, perhaps, that the locus of greatness, of sublimity, is to be found in art; a painting with a trivial subject, a shoe, a cabbage, may be a superb work, but its range is limited: even if it succeeds, it is not great, not sublime; and if it fails, its failure is of no consequence; it may be trivial, it may be delightful—nothing more. But a figure painting, Signorelli's *Pan,* was a great, a sublime painting; had it failed, its failure would have been more tragic than trivial.

Such factors as these often do make a difference, but unlike the fact that the work is well or poorly organized, they do not indicate that the work is or is not worth contemplating: they indicate only that if the work is worth contemplating, it will be well worth contemplating; and if it is not worth contemplating, then possibly it will be not merely not worth contemplating, but distressing.

One sometimes takes for granted that the presence or absence of organization will make a difference to the person. But what if it does not?

It is quite possible that it will not. It is possible that to some people it makes no difference at all whether a painting is disorganized. It may even be that some people prefer what are in fact disorganized paintings (though they might not call them "disorganized"). Perhaps some people greatly admire quite green paintings; the fact that a painting is or is not quite green will make much difference to them.

Someone might now want to say this: "Even though you may happen to like a disorganized painting at a time, you won't like it after a time; disorganized paintings do not wear well." Or this: "Even though you may happen to like a disorganized painting, your liking of it will interfere with and narrow the range of your appreciation of many other paintings." Or even this: ". . . your liking of it is unlike that of someone who likes an organized painting; for such a person will not only like it longer, but will like it in a different and better way: 'not merely a difference in quantity, but a difference in quality.' Thus the satisfaction, the value, he finds in contemplating an organized painting is unlike and better than that you find in contemplating a disorganized painting."

It is sometimes true that disorganized paintings do not wear well, but it sometimes is not true; some people persist in liking unlikable paintings. Will perseverance do to transmute vice to virtue? It is sometimes true that a taste for disorganized paintings is apt to interfere with and narrow the range of one's appreciation of other paintings; but is it not likely that one who likes both organized and disorganized paintings will have the more catholic taste? Is it wise to be a connoisseur of wine and cut one's self off from the pleasures of the poor? There is a sense in which it is certainly true that the satisfaction one finds in contemplating an organized painting is unlike and superior to that one finds in contemplating a disorganized painting, but in the sense in which it is, it is here irrelevant: for of course it is certainly true that the satisfaction and value found in connection with a good painting is superior to that found in connection with a bad painting—this of course being a necessary statement. But apart from the fact that the satisfaction found in connection with a good painting is of course superior to that found in connection with a bad painting, what reason is there to suppose in fact—and not merely of course—this is the case? I find no satisfaction in connection with a bad painting, so how shall I compare to see which is superior?

One sometimes says: "Last year I found satisfaction in connection with what I now see to be a bad painting. Now I can see that my satisfaction then was inferior to my satisfaction now found in connection with a good painting." So you might predict to someone: "Just wait! Cultivate your taste and you will see that the satisfaction found in connection with good-*A* will be superior to the satisfaction, value, you now find in connection with bad-*B*."

And what if he does not? (Is it not clear that here aesthetics has nothing to do with consequences?) A man might say: "I find the very same kind of satisfaction in this 'disorganized' painting that you find in that 'organized' one: I too am greatly moved, greatly stirred. You may say of course your satisfaction, the value you find, is superior to mine; in fact it is not." He might be lying, but could he be mistaken?

There is then an inclination to say this: "If being organized or being disorganized does make much difference to a person then for him it is a reason, whereas if it does not make any such difference, it is not." This would be to say that instead of speaking of "the reasons why the painting is good," one would have to speak of "his reasons why" and "my reasons why" and "your reasons why" if one wished to speak precisely. This will not do at all.

I or you or he can have a reason to suppose (think, believe, etc.) the work is worth contemplating; but neither I nor you nor he can have a reason why the work is worth contemplating; anyone may know such a reason, discover, search for, find, wonder about such a reason, but no one can ever have such a reason; even when one has found such a reason, one can only point to it, present it, never appropriate it for one's own; "What are your reasons?" makes sense in reply to "I believe it is worth contemplating," but it has no literal sense if asked of "I know it is worth contemplating." "My reasons why the work is worth contemplating . . . ," "The reason for me the work is worth contemplating . . . ," are also here without relevant literal meaning.

(It would be absurd to describe this fact by saying that what is a reason for me must be a reason for everyone else—as though what no one ever could own must therefore be owned by all alike. What one could say here is that a reason must be as abstract as the judgment it supports.)

If being organized or being disorganized does make much difference to a person then, not "for him" nor "in that case," nor "then and there," it is apt to be a reason; for in that case, then and there, one can forget about him then and there; whereas if it does not make any such difference then, for him, in that case, then and there, it is not apt to be a reason, for in that case, then and there, one cannot forget about him then and there.

To say "The work is worth contemplating" is here and ordinarily to abstract from considerations of person; but such abstraction is, as it were, a minor achievement, an accomplishment possible only when there either is or can be a community of interest. I can ignore the ground I walk on so long as it does not quake. This fact cannot be ignored: contemplating a painting is something that people do, different people.

Paradise gardens are not ever simply a place (one could not be there not knowing it, and it is in part because I know I am not there that I am not there); not being simply a place, paradise gardens are proportioned to everyman's need, even though these requirements may at times be incompatible. But these lesser perfections that paintings are are less adaptable, answer only to some men's need.

Reasoning about works of art is primarily a social affair, an attempt to build and map our common Eden; it can be carried on fruitfully only so long as there is either a common care or the possibility of one. But Kant was wrong in saying aesthetic judgments presuppose a common sense: one cannot sensibly presuppose what is often not the case. A community of interest and taste is not something given, but something that can be striven for.

II

And now I can be more precise, and that is to say, more general, for we speak of "good poems," "good quartets," "good operas," etc., as well as "good painting." But the problem is always the same. A good any-thing is something that answers to interests associated with it. In art, this is always a matter of performing certain actions, looking, listening, read-ing, etc., in connection with certain spatio-temporal or temporal entities, with paintings, poems, musical compositions, etc.

Formulaically, there is only this: a person p_i, performs an action, a_i, in connection with an entity, e_i, under conditions, c_i; e.g. George contem-plates Fouquet's *Madonna* in the gallery at Antwerp. e_i is good if and only if the performance of the relevant a_i by p_i under c_i is worthwhile for its own sake. To state a reason why e_i is good is simply to state a fact about e_i in virtue of which the performance of the relevant a_i by p_i under c_i is worthwhile for its own sake.

Someone says, pointing to a painting, "That is a good painting." There is (at least) a triple abstraction here, for neither the relevant persons, nor actions, nor conditions, have been specified. Is it any wonder we so often disagree about what is or is not a good painting?

Persons: George and Josef disagree about a Breughel. Say Josef is color-blind. Then here I discount Josef's opinion: I am not color-blind. But if they were concerned with a Chinese ink drawing, color-blindness would be irrelevant. George is not a peasant, neither does he look kindly on peas-ants, not even a Breughel painting of peasants. Well, neither do I, so I would not, for that reason, discount his opinion. Josef is a prude, that is, a moralist, and he looks uncomfortably at the belly of a Titian nude. I would discount his opinion, for I am not. (This is why it is horrible nonsense to talk about "a competent observer" in matters of art appreciation: no one is competent or not competent to look at the belly of a Titian nude.) But George has no stomach for George Grosz's pictures of butchers chopping up pigs, and neither do I, so I would not discount his opinion there. George has a horror of churches: his opinion of stained glass may be worthless. Not having an Oedipus complex, George's attitude towards *Whistler's Mother* is also eccentric. And so on.

If e_i is good then the performance of a_i by p_i under c_i is worthwhile for its own sake. But this obviously depends on the physical, psychological, and intellectual characteristics of p_i. If p_i and p_j are considering a certain work then the relevant characteristics of p_i depend on the particular p_j, e_i, a_i, and c_i involved. It is worse than useless to stipulate that p_i be "normal": what is that to me if I am not normal? and who is? To be normal is not necessary in connection with some limited works, and it is not enough to read *Finnegan's Wake*. Different works make different demands on the person. The popularity of "popular art" is simply due to the fact that it demands virtually nothing: one can be as ignorant and brutish as a savage and still deal with it.

But there is no point in worrying about persons for practically nothing can be done about them. Actions are what matter. Art education is a matter of altering the person's actions, and so, conceivably, the person.

Actions: here we have a want of words. Aestheticians are fond of "contemplate," but one cannot contemplate an opera, a ballet, a cinema, a poem. Neither is it sensible to contemplate just any painting, for not every painting lends itself to contemplation. There is only one significant problem in aesthetics, and it is not one that an aesthetician can answer: given a work e_i under conditions c_i, what are the relevant a_i? An aesthetician cannot answer the question because it depends on the particular e_i and c_i: no general answer exists.

Roughly speaking, I survey a Tintoretto, while I scan an H. Bosch. Thus I step back to look at the Tintoretto, up to look at the Bosch. Different actions are involved. Do you drink brandy in the way you drink beer? Do you drive a Jaguar XKSS in the way you drive a hearse?

A generic term will be useful here: "aspection," to aspect a painting is to look at it in some way. Thus to contemplate a painting is to perform one act of aspection; to scan it is to perform another; to study, observe, survey, inspect, examine, scrutinize, etc., are still other acts of aspection. There are about three hundred words available here in English, but that is not enough.

Generally speaking, a different act of aspection is performed in connection with works belonging to different schools of art, which is why the classification of style is of the essence. Venetian paintings lend themselves to an act of aspection involving attention to balanced masses; contours are of no importance, for they are scarcely to be found. The Florentine school demands attention to contours, the linear style predominates. Look for light in a Claude, for color in a Bonnard, for contoured volumes in a Signorelli.

George and Josef are looking at Van der Weyden's *Descent from the Cross*. Josef complains "The figures seem stiff, the Christ unnatural." George replies "Perhaps. But notice the volumes of the heads, the articulation of the planes, the profound movement of the contours." They are not looking at the painting in the same way, they are performing different acts of aspection.

They are looking at the *Unicorn Tapestry*. Josef complains "But the organization is so loose!" So Spenser's great *Faerie Queene* is ignored because fools try to read it as though it were a sonnet of Donne, for the *Queene* is a medieval tapestry, and one wanders about in it. An epic is not an epigram.

George says "A good apple is sour" and Josef says "A good apple is sweet," but George means a cooking apple, Josef means a dessert apple. So one might speak of "a scanning-painting," "a surveying-painting," etc., and just so one speaks of "a Venetian painting," "a sonata," "a lyric poem," "an improvisation," etc.

If e_i is good then the performance of a_i by p_i under c_i is worthwhile for its own sake. If p_i performs a_i under c_i in connection with e_i, whereas p_j performs a_j under c_i in connection with e_i, p_i and p_j might just as well be looking at two different paintings (or poems, etc.) It is possible that the performance of a_i under c_i in connection with e_i is worthwhile for its own sake, while the performance of a_j under c_i in connection with e_i is not worthwhile for its own sake.

There is no easy formula for the relevant actions. Many are possible: only some will prove worthwhile. We find them by trial and error. The relevant actions are those that prove worthwhile in connection with the particular work, but we must discover what these are.

Imagine that *Guernica* had been painted in the time of Poussin. Or a Mondrian. What could the people of the time have done with these works? The question the public is never tired of asking is: "What am I to look at? look for?" and that is to say: what act of aspection is to be performed in connection with e_i?

Before 1900, El Greco was accredited a second-rate hack whose paintings were distorted because he was blind in one eye. Who bothered with Catalonian frescoes? The Pompeian murals were buried.

Modern art recreates the art of the past, for it teaches the critics (who have the ear of museum and gallery directors who pick the paintings the public consents to see) what to look for and at in modern works. Having been taught to look at things in a new way, when they look to the past, they usually find much worth looking at, in this new way, that had been ignored. So one could almost say that Lehmbruck did the portal of Chartres, Daumier gave birth to Hogarth, and someone (unfortunately) did Raphael in.

Artists teach us to look at the world in new ways. Look at a Mondrian, then look at the world as though it were a Mondrian and you will see what I mean. To do this, you must know how to look at a Mondrian.

And now I can explain why a reason why a work is good or bad is worth listening to. One reason why a (good) Mondrian is good is that it is completely flat. If that sounds queer to you, it is because you do not know how to look at a Mondrian. And that is why the reason is worth considering.

A reason why e_i is good is a fact about e_i in virtue of which the performance of a_i by p_i under c_i is worthwhile for its own sake. So I am saying that the fact that the Mondrian is completely flat indicates that the performance of a_i by p_i under c_i is worthwhile in connection with the Mondrian painting. In telling you this, I am telling you something about the act of aspection to be performed in connection with the work, for now you know at least this: you are to look at the work spatially, three-dimensionally. (Without the painting to point to, I can only give hints: look at it upside down! Right side up, each backward movement into space is counterbalanced by an advancing movement. The result is a tense, dynamic, and dramatic picture plane held intact by the interplay of forces. Turn the painting upside down and the spatial balance is destroyed: the thing is hideous.)

Reasons in criticism are worthwhile because they tell us what to do with the work, and that is worth knowing. Yao Tsui said:

> It may seem easy for a man to follow the footsteps of his predecessors, but he does not know how difficult it is to follow the movements of curved lines. Although one may chance to measure the speed of the wind which blows through the Hsiang valley, he may have difficulty in fathoming the water-courses of the Lü-liang mountain. Although one may make a good beginning by the skilful use of instruments, yet the ultimate meaning of an object may remain obscure to him until the end. Without knowing the song completely, it is useless to crave for the response of the falling dust.

Bibliography

Discussions of appreciation range typically from such topics as the educative function of the critic to the involvement and excitement of the audience. The following items are therefore somewhat assorted:

Stuart Hampshire, "Logic and Appreciation," reprinted in William Elton, *Aesthetics and Language* (Oxford, 1954);

Bernard C. Heyl, "Relativism Again," *Journal of Aesthetics and Art Criticism,* Volume V (1946), 54-61;

Arnold Isenberg, "Perception, Meaning, and the Subject-Matter of Art," *Journal of Philosophy,* Volume XLI (1944), 561-575;

Margaret Macdonald, "Some Distinctive Features of Arguments Used in Criticism of the Arts," reprinted (revised) in William Elton, *loc. cit.*

Possibly (and paradoxically) the most effective discussion of questions of appreciation in a large sense appears in:

John Wisdom, "Gods," reprinted in his *Philosophy and Psycho-analysis* (Oxford, 1953).

Other discussions of considerable interest include:

George Boas, *Wingless Pegasus* (Baltimore, 1950);

Ralph Church, *An Essay on Critical Appreciation* (Ithaca, 1938);

John Dewey, *Art as Experience* (New York, 1934), Chapter XIII;

Curt J. Ducasse, *The Philosophy of Art* (New York, 1929), Chapter XI;

Stephen C. Pepper, *The Work of Art* (Bloomington, 1955), Chapters II, V.

X

FICTION

Philosophically considered, fiction interests us chiefly in the respects in which the sentences of a story may or may not function as do statements of fact. This is not to restrict the sort of sentences that appear in a story but rather to draw attention to the logical peculiarities involved in conceding that what is being told is a story. On the face of it, then, stories are not lies or false statements. The question is, what are the properties of sentences that enter into a story, in so far merely as fiction is concerned?

Whatever the account put forward, complications of at least two distinct sorts will have to be examined. One concerns the fact that stories are based on an experience of the world, sometimes even cast as historical or biographical novels. So one sometimes declares a story to be "true" or "true to life" or some such thing and even considers that the story may refer to the things of the world. The master question here is verisimilitude; and the philosophical puzzle, in a nutshell, is to reconcile the facts about these sorts of stories with the apparently fundamental thesis that fiction, as fiction, cannot be true or false.

A second set of questions arises from the fact that, sometimes, statements of fact or moral maxims and the like may be told in story form, statements and maxims that are, on independent grounds, true or false, accurate or inaccurate, defensible or indefensible. And these questions call for a distinction between the special logical features of sentences in so far as they are used to tell a story and the features of a fictional style of speaking that is bound to some ulterior use of language—a distinction, say, between *Alice in Wonderland* and Aesop's *Fables*. One comes then to consider the differences between a fictional use of sentences and a fictional style that may relate to any use of sentences, such as stating a fact or prescribing a moral rule.

And once a contrast of this sort is admitted, the study of fiction suggests interesting comparisons. What, for instance, are the differences between telling a story and speaking jokingly or ironically? For all of these clearly concern ways of waiving or reversing considerations of truth and falsity and the like. And what, furthermore, may one say about poetry and drama? Do these concern uses of language like the fictional use of language or are they rather styles of language that may be fitted to any otherwise legitimate use of language, like making statements or judgments or recommendations?

The late Margaret Macdonald provides, in her contribution to the Aristotelian Society's symposium on fiction, a challengingly clear analysis of the distinction of fictional language. The point at stake is the reducibility of fictional language to other well-known uses of language and the propriety of viewing all admissible specimens of fiction as exhibiting whatever essential distinction is claimed for fiction as such.

The Language of Fiction

MARGARET MACDONALD

I

Emma Woodhouse, handsome, clever and rich, with a comfortable house and happy disposition seemed to unite some of the best blessings of existence and had lived nearly twenty-one years in the world with very little to distress or vex her.

THE OPENING sentence of Jane Austen's novel *Emma* is a sentence from fiction. *Emma* is a work in which the author tells a story of characters, places and incidents almost all of which she has invented. I shall mean by "fiction" any similar work. For unless a work is largely, if not wholly, composed of what is invented, it will not correctly be called "fiction." One which contains nothing imaginary may be history, science, detection, biography, but not fiction. I want to ask some questions about how an author uses words and sentences in fiction. But my interest is logical, not literary. I shall not

From *Proceedings of the Aristotelian Society*, Supplementary Volume XXVII (1954), 165-184. Reprinted with the permission of the Aristotelian Society and Bedford College, University of London.

discuss the style or artistic skill of any storyteller. Mine is the duller task of trying to understand some of the logic of fictional language; to determine the logical character of its expressions. How do they resemble and differ from those in other contexts? What are they understood to convey? Are they, e.g., true or false statements? If so, of or about what are they true or false? If not, what other function do they perform? How are they connected? These are the questions I shall chiefly discuss.

First of all, "fiction" is often used ambiguously both for what is fictitious and for that by which the fictitious is expressed. Thus "fiction" is opposed to "fact" as what is imaginary to what is real. But one must emphasize that a work of fiction itself is not imaginary, fictitious or unreal. What is fictitious does not exist. There are no dragons in the zoo. But the novels of Jane Austen do exist. The world, fortunately, contains them just as it contained Jane Austen. They occupy many bookshelves. Works of fiction, stories, novels are additions to the universe. Any unreality attaches only to their subject matter.[1]

Secondly, everyone understands the expressions of fiction. Or, if they do not, the reason is technical, not logical. One may find it hard to understand some of the expressions of Gertrude Stein or *Finnegan's Wake* but this is due to the peculiar obscurity of their style and not to the fact they occur in works of fiction. No one who knows English could fail to understand the sentence quoted from *Emma*. That Emma Woodhouse was handsome, clever, and rich is understood just as easily as that Charlotte Brontë was plain, sickly and poor. Both are indicative sentences which appear to inform about their subjects. But while the sentence containing "Charlotte Brontë" expresses a true statement of which Charlotte Brontë is the subject, that containing "Emma Woodhouse," cannot work similarly, since Jane Austen's Emma did not exist and so cannot be the logical subject of any statement. "Emma Woodhouse" does not and cannot designate a girl of that name of whom Jane Austen wrote. This has puzzled philosophers.[2] If apparent statements about Emma Woodhouse are about no one, of what is Jane Austen writing and how is she to be understood? Perhaps a subsistent wraith in a logical limbo is her subject? This will not do; or, at least not in this form. Jane Austen is certainly "pretending" that there was a girl called Emma Woodhouse who had certain qualities and adventures. According to one view she is understood because we understand from non-fictional contexts the use of proper names and the general terms in which she describes Emma

---

[1] Cf. also "Art and Imagination," *Proc. Aris. Soc.*, 1952-53, p. 219.
[2] See earlier Symposium on "Imaginary Objects," *Proc. Aris. Soc.*, Supp. Vol. 12, 1933, by G. Ryle, R. B. Braithwaite and G. E. Moore.

Woodhouse and her adventure. There is no Emma Woodhouse, so Jane Austen is not writing about her; rather is she writing about a number of properties, signified by the general terms she uses, and asserting that they belonged to someone. Since they did not, "Emma Woodhouse" is a pseudo-designation and the propositions are false, though significant. Readers of *Emma* need not, and usually do not, believe falsely that its propositions are true. A work of fiction is, or is about, "one big composite predicate" and is so understood by readers who need neither know nor believe that any subject was characterized by it. If, however, there had been, by chance, and unknown to Jane Austen, a girl called Emma Woodhouse who conformed faithfully to all the descriptions of the novel, its propositions would have been about and true of her and Jane Austen would have "accidentally" written biography and not fiction.[3]

This seems a somewhat strained account of a story. As Moore says,[4] it does seem false to deny that Jane Austen wrote about Emma Woodhouse, Harriet Smith, Miss Bates, Mr. George Knightley and the rest, but is, instead, about such a peculiar object as a "composite predicate." He would, surely, find this quite unintelligible. It is also false to say that a work of fiction may be "accidentally" history or biography. For if there were ten girls called "Emma Woodhouse" of whom all that Jane Austen wrote were true, they are not the subject of *Emma*, for Jane Austen is not telling a story of any of them, but of a subject of her own invention. Moreover, it would not only be necessary that Emma Woodhouse should have a real counterpart but that such counterparts should exist for every other element of the novel. You cannot separate Emma from Highbury, her companions and the ball at the Crown. They all belong to the story. Such a coincidence would be almost miraculous. So Moore seems to be right when he says:[5]

> I think that what he (Dickens) meant by "Mr. Pickwick" and what we all understand is: "There was only one man of whom it is true both that *I am going to tell you about him* and that he was called 'Pickwick' *and that, etc.*" In other words, he is saying from the beginning, that he has one and only one man in his mind's eye, about whom he is going to tell you a story. That he has is, of course, false; it is part of the fiction. It is this which gives unique reference to all subsequent uses of "Mr. Pickwick." And it is for this reason that Mr. Ryle's view that if, by coincidence, there happened to be a real man of whom everything related of Mr. Pickwick in the novel were true then "we could say that Dickens' propositions were true of

---

[3] *Loc. cit.*, G. Ryle, pp. 18-43.
[4] *Ibid.*, p. 59.
[5] *Loc. cit.*, p. 68.

somebody" is to be rejected . . . . . . *since Dickens was not telling us of him:* and that this is what is meant by saying that it is only "by coincidence" that there happened to be such a man.

I think this can be seen to be true even in circumstances which might appear to support Ryle's view. *Jane Eyre* and *Villette* are known to contain much autobiographical material. Charlotte Brontë knew her original as Dickens did not know of a "coincidental" Mr. Pickwick. Yet *Jane Eyre* and *Villette* are still works of fiction, not biography. They are no substitute for Mrs. Gaskell's *Life of Charlotte Brontë*. For although she may be *using* the facts of her own life, Charlotte Brontë is not writing "about" herself, but "about" Jane Eyre, Helen Burns, Mr. Rochester, Lucy Snowe, Paul Emmanuel and the rest. Or, she is writing about herself in a very different sense from that in which she is writing about the subject matter of her novels.

Ryle and Moore agree, with many others, that the sentences of fiction express false statements and Moore adds, I think rightly, that, so far, at least, as these are fictional, they could not be true. But there is a more radical view for which there is also some excuse. If a storyteller tells what he knows to be false, is he not a deceiver and his works a "tissue of lies?" That storytelling is akin to, if not a form of, lying is a very common view. "To make up a tale," "to tell a yarn" are common euphemisms for "to tell a lie." A liar knows what is true, but deliberately says what is false. What else does the storyteller who pretends that there was a girl called "Emma Woodhouse," etc., when she knows this is false? A liar intends to, and does, deceive a hearer. Does not a storyteller do likewise? "Poets themselves," says Hume, "though liars by profession, always endeavor to give an air of truth to their fictions."[6] Hume is contrasting all other expressions as indifferently lies or fiction, with those which are true of matters of fact. Hume is quite wrong to classify all poetry with fiction, though some stories may be told in verse. But no one could correctly call, e.g., Shakespeare's Sonnets, Keats' Odes or Eliot's Four Quartets, works of fiction. Nor are they statements of fact, but their analysis is not my task here. I wish only to protest against a common tendency to consign to one dustbin all expressions which do not conform to the type of statement found in factual studies. Even though they are not factual statements, expressions in literature may be of many different logical types. It is clear, however, that for Hume storytelling is a form of lying. And, indeed, a storyteller not only says what he knows to be false but uses every device of art to induce his audience

[6] *Treatise of Human Nature,* Bk. I, Pt. 3, Sec. 10.

to accept his fancies. For what else are the ancient incantatory openings, "Once upon a time . . . ," "Not yesterday, not yesterday, but long ago . . . ," and their modern equivalents, but to put a spell upon an audience so that the critical faculties of its members are numbed and they willingly suspend disbelief to enter the state which Coleridge called "illusion" and likened to dreaming?[7] All this is true. Everyone must sometimes be informed, instructed, exhorted by others. There are facts to learn and attitudes to adopt. However dull, these processes must be endured. But no one is obliged to attend to another's fancies. Unless, therefore, a storyteller can convince, he will not hold an audience. So, among other devices, he "endeavors to give an air of truth to his fictions." It does not follow that what he says *is* true, nor that he is a deceiver. One must distinguish "trying to convince" from "seeking to mislead." To convince is a merit in a work of fiction. To induce someone to accept a fiction, however, is not necessarily to seduce him into a belief that it is real. It is true that some people may be deceived by fiction. They fail to distinguish conviction from deception. Such are those who write to the B.B.C. about Mrs. Dale and the Archers as if they believe themselves to be hearing the life histories of real families in these programs. But this does not show that the B.B.C. has deliberately beguiled these innocents. Finally, a liar may be "found out" in his lie. He is then discredited and his lie is useless. Nor is he easily believed again. But it would be absurd for someone to complain that since *Emma* was fiction he had "found out" Jane Austen and could never trust her again. The conviction induced by a story is the result of a mutual conspiracy, freely entered into, between author and audience. A storyteller does not lie, nor is a normal auditor deceived. Yet there are affinities between fiction and lying which excuse the comparison. Conviction, without belief or disbelief, as in art, is like, but also very different from, unwitting deception. And a liar, too, pretends but not all pretending is lying.

A fictional sentence does not, then, express a lying statement. Does it express a false statement which is not a lie? False statements are normally asserted from total or partial ignorance of the facts. Those who assert them mistakenly believe they are true. This is not true of the storyteller. Neither he nor his auditor normally believes that his statements are true. It is false that Jane Austen wrote *Pickwick Papers* but it is not nonsense to suggest that it might have been true. As already seen, however, no factual discovery can verify a fictional statement. It can then never be true. So it would seem to be necessarily false or logically impossible. But the expressions of fiction

[7] Cf. Notes on *The Tempest* from *Lectures on Shakespeare.*

are neither self-contradictory nor nonsensical. Most of them are perfectly intelligible. Those which are not are so for reasons quite unconnected with truth and falsity. It is not because James Joyce's statements are false that they are unintelligible. For those of Jane Austen and Dickens are equally false, but not obscure.

Alternatively, it might be said that the propositions of fiction are false, but neither believed nor asserted. Their fictional character consists in the fact that they are merely proposed for consideration, like hypotheses. "Let us suppose there was a girl called Emma Woodhouse, who . . . etc." For a proposition may be entertained, but yet be false. So an author puts forward and his audience considers, but neither affirm, the false propositions of fiction.[8] Now, a storyteller does invite his audience to "Imagine that . . . ," "Pretend that . . ." and even "Suppose that . . ." or "Let it be granted that . . ." He does not often preface his story with just these remarks, but he issues a general invitation to exercise imagination. So far one may liken his attitude to that of some one proposing an hypothesis in other fields. An hypothesis, like a lie or a story, requires some invention; it is not a report of observed fact. But these suggested fictional hypotheses are also very different from all others. Non-fictional hypotheses are proposed to explain some fact or set of facts. "If the picture is by Van Dyck, then . . ."; "Suppose that malaria is transmitted by mosquitoes, then . . ." They suggest, e.g., the origin of a painting or the cause of a disease. But a story is not told to solve any such problem. Moreover, a non-fictional hypothesis must be testable or be mere speculation without explanatory value. But, obviously, nothing can count as evidence in favor of a fictional story. And what no fact can confirm none can disconfirm either. So, if a story consists of propositions entertained for consideration, the purpose of such entertainment must be for ever frustrated since they can never be asserted as true, false, probable or improbable. I conclude, therefore, that the expressions of fiction do not function either as propositions or hypotheses.

Nevertheless, as I have said, one can easily understand why people are tempted to identify fictional expressions with lies, falsehoods, unverifiable hypotheses. For what it is worth, the English dictionary appears to support this view. "Fiction," it says, "the act of feigning, inventing or imagining: that which is feigned, i.e., a fictitious story, fable, fabrication, falsehood." If the last four terms are intended as synonyms, this certainly suggests that all fiction is falsehood. Both rationalist and religious parents have forbidden children to read fairy stories and novels lest they be led astray into false

---

[8] I understood Professor Moore to hold such a view in a discussion in 1952. I do not, however, claim his authority for this version. Nor do I know if he is still of the same opinion.

and immoral beliefs. Yet its logical difference from these seems to show that fiction is not false, lying or hypothetical statement. It is clear that "S pretends that p" cannot entail p. This is, again, the point of saying that the truth of p must be "coincidental." When discovered, no future S (or storyteller) could pretend that p, for one cannot pretend that a proposition is true when it is, and is known to be, true. But neither, in fiction, can "S pretends that p" entail "not-p," or even "Perhaps-p." So, fictional expressions must be of a different type from statements.

An alternative is the familiar emotive answer. This is associated chiefly with the name of I. A. Richards. I can mention it only briefly. According to it, sentences in fiction, as in all non-informative contexts, express an emotional state of their author and seek to induce a similar state in his audience. A work is judged better or worse according to the amount of harmonious mental adjustment by which it was caused and which it effects. This view is difficult to estimate because of its vague use of the word "express." It tends to suggest that the expressions of fiction are disguised exclamations such as "Hurrah!" or "Alas!" Or that these could be substituted for them. This, of course, is impossible. No one could tell the story of *Emma* in a series of smiles, sighs, tears, shouts or the limited vocabulary which represents such emotive expressions. Most stories, one must reiterate, are told in normal English sentences which are common to fact and fiction and appropriately understood. This is, indeed, just the problem. If the expressions of Jane Austen were as easily distinguishable from factual statement as exclamation from articulate utterance no one would be puzzled. "Emotive expression" must, therefore, be compatible with understood sense.[9] It is true that emotional relationships play a large part in most fiction, but so does much else. Nor need these subjects coincide with the experience of either author or audience. No story, even though told in the first person, can be completely autobiographical without ceasing to be fiction. And whether or not a work of fiction uses autobiographical material, the actual, or suspected, direct intrusion of personal feeling by the author is liable to be fatal to the work.

> I opened it at chapter twelve and my eye was caught by the phrase "Anybody may blame me who likes." What were they blaming Charlotte Brontë for, I wondered? And I read how Jane Eyre used to go up on the roof when Mrs. Fairfax was making jellies and look over the fields at the distant view. And then she longed—and it was for this that they blamed her—that "then I longed for a power of vision which might overpass that limit . . . I desired more of practical experience . . . more of intercourse with my kind . . . I believed in the existence of other and more vivid

[9] Cf. also Empson, *The Structure of Complex Words*, London, 1951, ch. 1.

kinds of goodness and what I believed in I wished to behold . . . Who
blames me? Many no doubt and I shall be called discontented . . . When
thus alone I not infrequently heard Grace Poole's laugh."

That is an awkward break, I thought. It is upsetting to come upon
Grace Poole all of a sudden. The continuity is disturbed. One might say,
I continued . . . That the woman who wrote these pages had genius . . .
but if one reads them over and marks that jerk in them, that indignation,
one sees . . . that her books will be deformed and twisted. (Virginia
Woolf; *A Room of One's Own*, p. 104.)

In short, Charlotte Brontë will, or will appear to, express her own feelings
too nakedly through her heroine, in order to induce a sympathetic emotional
response in her readers, instead of telling her story. Someone may protest
that this amounts to *describing*, not expressing, her emotions. But this is not
ostensibly so. The passage is still a soliloquy by Jane Eyre, not an introspective report by Charlotte Brontë. Virginia Woolf is giving an interpretation
of the passage, but this would not be necessary if it were a simple description of Charlotte Brontë's feelings. If her critic is right and if, nevertheless,
the passage is not what is meant by an expression of the author's emotion
by fiction, this cannot be because it is a straightforward description of fact.
Another objection might be that this is a crude example of expression and
does not prove that the task of fiction is not to express emotion. Skilful
expression is impersonal, almost anonymous. One cannot tell from their
works what Shakespeare or Jane Austen felt. Hence the floods of speculation
by critics. One knows only too well from her novels what Charlotte Brontë
felt, so she is not truly expressing, but merely venting, her emotions. But
then, if one so often cannot tell whose, or even what, emotion is being
expressed, what is the point of saying that all fictional expressions are emotive? Should the criterion be solely the effect on their audience? Certainly, a
tale may amuse, sadden, anger, or otherwise move a hearer. But is the fact
that *Emma* may cause one to laugh or sigh what distinguishes it as a work
of fiction from a statement of fact? This must be false for much that is
not fiction has the same effect. The answer to the theory is that a work of
fiction, like any work of literary art, causes a very special emotional effect,
an harmonious adjustment of impulses, a personal attitude, not otherwise
obtainable. But no independent evidence of any such pervasive effect is
offered, nor can I, for one, provide it from experience of reading fiction. So,
if one cannot distinguish fiction from fact by the normal emotional effects
which fiction sometimes causes, nor by the pervasive changes it is alleged
to cause, the theory only reformulates and does not explain this distinction.

But the theory does emphasize that language has less pedestrian uses than those of the laboratory, record office, police court and daily discourse. Also, that to create and appreciate fiction requires more than intellectual qualities. Most fiction would be incomprehensible to a being without emotions. One must be able to enter imaginatively into its emotional situations though its emotions need not be felt. One need not feel jealousy either to construct or understand Mr. Knightley's censorious attitude to Frank Churchill, but someone who had never felt this might find an account of it unconvincing. Authors differ, too, in what may vaguely be called "climate" or "atmosphere," which is emotional and moral as well as intellectual. The "worlds" of Jane Austen and Henry James, e.g., differ considerably from those of Emily Brontë and D. H. Lawrence. Also, much of the language of fiction is emotionally charged. For it depicts emotional situations which are part of its story. But none of these facts is positively illuminated by a theory which limits the language of fiction to the expression of an emotion transferred from author to auditor even if such a transaction were fully understood. It does not seem to be the feeling which generates them nor that which they cause which wholly differentiates the ironies of Gibbon from those of I. Compton Burnett. Nor is it either Tolstoy or ourselves in whom we are primarily interested when reading *War and Peace*. Rather is it the presentation of characters, actions and situations. The vast panorama of the novel shrinks into triviality as the instrument of the emotional adjustments of Tolstoy and his readers. I conclude, therefore, that the characteristic which differentiates fictional sentences from those which state facts is not that the former exclusively express anybody's emotions, though many of them have a very vital connection with emotion.

II

When someone reports a fact he may choose the language or symbolism of his report. He may choose to use this carefully or carelessly. But there is a sense in which he cannot choose what he will say. No one could report truly that Charlotte Brontë died in 1890; that she wrote *Villette* before *Jane Eyre;* that she was tall, handsome and a celebrated London hostess. No biography of Charlotte Brontë could contain such statements and remain a biography. For what is truly said of Charlotte Brontë must be controlled by what she was and what happened to her. But Jane Austen was under no such restraints with Emma Woodhouse. For Emma Woodhouse was her own invention. So she may have any qualities and undergo any adventures her author pleases. It is not even certain that these must be logically possible, i.e., not self-contradictory. For some stories, and not the worst, are extremely wild. There is *Finnegan's Wake* as well as *Emma*. A storyteller chooses not only the words and style but also, and I suggest with them, provides the material of a fictional story. I want to stress this fact that in fiction language is used to *create*. For it is this which chiefly differentiates it from factual statement. A storyteller performs; he does not—or not primarily—inform or misinform. To tell a story is to originate, not to report. Like the contents of dreams, the objects of fiction may pre-suppose, but do not compete with, those of ordinary life. Unlike those of dreams, however, they are deliberately contrived. Hence, they differ too from lunatic frenzies. A lunatic unintentionally offends against fact and logic. He intends to respect them. He thinks he is right, however wild his fancies, when he is always wrong. But a storyteller, though equally wild, is never deluded. He invents by choice, not accident.

As I have already said, most of a storyteller's words and sentences are understood to have the same meanings as the same words and grammatical forms in non-fictional contexts. For all who communicate use the same language, composed mainly of general terms. But language may be used differently to obtain different results. When a storyteller "pretends" he simulates factual description. He puts on an innocent air of informing. This is part of the pretence. But when he pretends, e.g., that there was a Becky Sharp, an adventuress, who finally came to grief, he does not inform or misinform about a real person called "Becky Sharp" or anyone else: he is creating Becky Sharp. And this is what a normal audience understands him to be doing. Of course, he does not thereby add to the population of the world. Becky Sharp is not registered at Somerset House. But this, too, is shown by language. A storyteller, like a dramatist, is not said to create persons, human beings, but *characters*. Characters, together with their settings and situations, are parts of a story. According to Ryle, although "it is correct to say that Charles Dickens created a story, it is wholly erroneous to speak as if Dickens created Mr. Pickwick."[10] But Dickens *did* create Mr. Pickwick and this is not equivalent to saying, as Ryle does, that what Dickens created was a "complex predicate." No one would ever say this. But it is perfectly ordinary and proper to say that an author has created certain characters and all that is required for them to function. "In Caliban," said Dryden, "Shakespeare seems to have *created* a being which was not in nature."[11] He was not in nature because he was part of *The Tempest*. To create a story is to use language to create the contents of that story.

[10] *Loc. cit.*, p. 32.
[11] Quoted by Logan Pearsall Smith. S.P.E. Tract XVII, 1924.

To write "about" Emma Woodhouse, Becky Sharp, Mr. Pickwick, Caliban, and the rest is to "bring about" these characters and their worlds. Human beings are not normally called "characters." If they are, it is by analogy with art. One might say, "I met a queer character the other day; he might have been created by Dickens." This does not show that Dickens wrote or tried to write about such a person, but that his readers now view their fellows through Dickens' works. So may one now see Constable and Cézanne pictures in natural landscapes, which would not have been seen without these artists. Characters play a rôle; human beings live a life. A character, like all else in pure fiction, is confined to its rôle in a story. Not even the longest biography exhausts what could be told of any human person, but what Jane Austen tells of Emma Woodhouse exhausts Emma Woodhouse. A character may be completely understood, but the simplest human being, if any human being is simple, is somewhere opaque to others. A character has no secrets but what are contained within five acts or between the covers of a book or the interval from supper to bedtime.[12] A story may, indeed, have a sequel, but this is a new invention, not a report of what was omitted from the original.

This may be challenged. Surely, it will be said, many characters in fiction are as complex as human beings? Do not critics still dispute about the motives of Iago and the sex of Albertine? But to say that a character is limited to what is related of it in a story does not imply that this must always be indisputably obvious. All it implies is that the only way to find out about a character is to consult the author's text. This contains all there is to discover. No one can find independent evidence which the author has missed. Not even Dr. Ernest Jones for the alleged "complexes" of Hamlet. Assuming that the text is complete and authentic, there may be different interpretations of it and thus of a character but no new evidence such as may render out of date a biography. No one will find a diary or a cache of letters from Hamlet to his mother which will throw light upon his mental state. Nor must this be forever secret in the absence of such evidence. For Hamlet is what Shakespeare tells and what we understand from the text, and nothing more.

What is true of characters is true also of other fictional elements of a story. "Barchester" does not name a geographical place. It is the setting or scene of a number of Trollope's characters. So is his magic island for Prospero and his companions. The words used to "set the scene" of a story paint as it were the backcloth to its incidents. "Scene" is a term of art, a

---

[12] See also E. M. Forster, *Aspects of the Novel*, Chs. 3 and 4.

word from the language of the theatre. One would naturally say "The scene of Archdeacon Grantley's activities is laid in Barchester," but not, unless affecting histrionics, "The scene of this Conference is laid in Oxford." It would be more normal to say "This Conference is being held in Oxford." "Scene" is used of natural situations only when they are being treated artificially. Finally, the situations and incidents of a story form its plot. They conform to a contrived sequence of beginning, middle and end —or have some modern variety of this shape. But human life and natural events do not have, or conform to, a plot. They have no contrived shape.

It is thus, then, that we talk of works of fiction and their fictional contents. They are contrivances, artefacts. A story is more like a picture or a symphony than a theory or report. Characters, e.g., might for a change, be compared with musical "themes" rather than with human flesh and blood. A composer creates a symphony, but he also creates all its several parts. So does a storyteller, but his parts are the characters, settings and incidents which constitute his story. The similarity is obscure just because the storyteller does, and must, use common speech with its general terms, so that he appears to assert propositions about an independent reality in a manner similar to that of one who does or fails to report what is true. So, philosophers conclude, since pure fiction cannot be about physical objects, it must be about wraith-like simulacra of real objects or equally attentuated "predicates." I do not, however, want to claim a special mode of existence for fictional objects as the contents of fiction. And though it is obvious that fiction writers use our common tongue I do not think that what they do is illuminated by saying that they write about predicates or properties. It is agreed that a storyteller both creates a story, a verbal construction, and the contents of that story. I want to say that these activities are inseparable. Certainly, no one could create pure fiction without also creating the contents which are its parts. One cannot separate Emma Woodhouse from *Emma* as one can separate Napoleon from his biography. I do not say that Emma is simply identical with the words by which she is created. Emma is a "character." As such she can, in appropriate senses, be called charming, generous, foolish, and even "lifelike." No one could sensibly use these epithets of words. Nevertheless, a character is that of which it makes no sense to talk except in terms of the story in which he or she is a character. Just as, I think, it would make no sense to say that a flock of birds was carolling "by chance" the first movement of a symphony. For birds do not observe musical conventions. What is true of characters applies to the settings and incidents of pure fiction. To the questions "Where will they be found?"; "Where do they exist?," the answer is "In such and such a story," and that is all. For they are the elements or parts of stories and this is shown by our language about them.

But the content of very little fiction is wholly fictitious. London also forms part of the setting of *Emma* as it does of many of Dickens' novels; Russia of *War and Peace* and India of *A Passage to India*. Historical persons and events also seem to invade fiction. They are indeed the very stuff of "historical" novels. Do not the sentences in which the designations or descriptions of such places, persons and incidents occur express true or false statements? It is true that these real objects and events are mentioned in such fictional expressions. Nevertheless, they certainly do not function wholly as in a typographical or historical record. They are still part of a story. A storyteller is not discredited as a reporter by rearranging London's squares or adding an unknown street to serve his purpose. Nor by crediting an historical personage with speeches and adventures unknown to historians. An historical novel is not judged by the same standards as a history book. Inaccuracies are condemned, if they are, not because they are bad history or geography, but because they are bad art. A story which introduces Napoleon or Cromwell but which departs wildly from historical accuracy will not have the verisimilitude which appears to be its object and will be unplausible and tedious. Or if, nevertheless, interesting will provoke the question, "But why call this character Oliver Cromwell, Lord Protector of England?" Similarly, for places. If somewhere called "London" is quite unrecognizable, its name will have no point.

So I am inclined to say that a storyteller is not making informative assertions about real persons, places and incidents even when these are mentioned in fictional sentences. But rather that these also function like purely fictional elements, with which they are always mingled in a story. Russia as the setting for the Rostovs differs from the Russia which Napoleon invaded which did not contain the Rostovs. There was a battle of Waterloo, but George Osborne was not one of its casualties, except in Thackeray's novel. Tolstoy did not create Russia, nor Thackeray the battle of Waterloo. Yet one might say that Tolstoy did create Russia-as-the-background-of-the-Rostovs and that Thackeray created Waterloo-as-the-scene-of-George-Osborne's-death. One might say that the mention of realities plays a dual rôle in fiction; to refer to a real object and to contribute to the development of a story. But I cannot pursue this, except to say that this situation differs from that in which, e.g., Charlotte Brontë uses the real events of her life in *Jane Eyre*. For she does not *mention* herself nor the real places and incidents upon which her story is modelled.

I have tried to say how the expressions of fiction operate and to show that they differ both from statements and emotive expressions. I also began by asking how they are connected. It is clear that their order need not be dictated by that of any matter of fact. Nor are they always even bound by the principles of logic. Do their connections, then, follow any rule or procedure? Is there a conception by which their transitions may be described? Since a work of fiction is a creative performance, however, it may be thought senseless to ask for such rules or such a conception. Is not the creation of that which is new and original, independent of logic and existence, just that to which no rules are appropriate and no conception adequate? But the creation of a work of fiction, however remarkable, is not a miracle. Nor is its author's use of language entirely lawless and vagabond but is directed by some purpose. Certainly, no set of rules will enable anyone to write a good novel or produce a good scientific hypothesis. But a scientist employs his ingenuity to invent a hypothesis to connect certain facts and predict others. He provides an organizing concept related to the facts to be organized and governed by the probability that it provides the correct explanation. As already emphasized, the situation of the storyteller is different.

In his Preface to *The Portrait of a Lady,* Henry James recalls that in organizing his "ado" about Isabel Archer, having conceived the character, he asked, "And now what will she *do?*" and the reply came immediately, "Why, the first thing she will do will be to come to Europe." He did not have to infer, guess, or wait upon observation and evidence; he *knew*. He knew because he had thus decided. He so decided, no doubt, for a variety of artistic reasons; to develop his conception of a certain character in relation to others, against a particular background, in accordance with his plot. His aim was to produce a particular, perhaps a unique, story; a self-contained system having its own internal coherence. There is certainly a sense in which every work of fiction is a law unto itself. Nevertheless, I think there is a general notion which governs these constructions though its application may give very different results. This is the Aristotelian notion which is usually translated "probability" but which I prefer to call "artistic plausibility." This is not an ideal phrase but it is preferable to "probability" which suggests an evidential relation between premises and conclusion and "possibility" which suggests a restriction to logical conceivability which might exclude some rare, strange and fantastic works. It is, moreover, a notion which applies only to what is verbal. Though some comparable notion may apply to them, one does not normally talk of "plausible" pictures, statues and symphonies, but does talk of "plausible stories." A plausible story is one which convinces; which induces acceptance. But since the plausibility is artistic plausibility, the conviction induced will not be the belief appropriate to factual statement. Nevertheless, one drawback to the notion is that it may suggest that all fiction is, or should be, realistic or naturalistic. It is true that although fiction does not consist of statements about life and natural events, yet much fiction does take lived experience as a model for its own connections. Sometimes, as with Charlotte Brontë's novels, using autobiographical material. Such stories convince by being "lifelike." But by no means all fiction is thus naturalistic. Nor is a story allegedly founded on fact necessarily fictionally convincing. To repeat the Aristotelian tag, "a convincing impossibility is better than an unconvincing possibility." There is, in fact, a range of plausible connections in fiction, varying from the purest naturalism to the wildest fantasy. If any convinces then it is justified. Much should obviously be said about who is convinced and whether he is a reliable judge, but I can do little more here than indicate the type of connection which differentiates works of fiction from descriptions of fact. It is the task of the literary critic to analyze the different types of plausibility, exemplified by, e.g., *Emma, War and Peace, The Portrait of a Lady, Wuthering Heights, Moby Dick, Alice in Wonderland* and *Grimm's Fairy Stories*. And though, perhaps, no rules can be given for attaining any particular type of plausibility, yet it is sometimes possible to say what does or would make a work unplausible. A mixture of elements from different plausible systems would, e.g., have this result. It is quite plausible that Alice should change her size by drinking from magic bottles, but it would be absurd that Emma Woodhouse or Fanny Price should do so. Or, to make such an incident plausible, Jane Austen's novels would need to be very different. For it would have needed explanation in quite different terms from the conventions she uses. This also applies to more important plausibilities. Emma Woodhouse could not suddenly murder Miss Bates after the ball, or develop a Russian sense of sin, without either destroying the plausibility of the novel or bringing about a complete revolution in its shape, though these incidents are in themselves more likely than that which befell Alice. But such examples raise questions about fiction and fact; art and life which I cannot now discuss.

Bibliography

Two quite interesting symposia on fiction have appeared in the *Proceedings of the Aristotelian Society:*

"Imaginary Objects," Supplementary Volume XII (1933), including contributions by R. B. Braithewaite, Gilbert Ryle, and G. E. Moore;

"The Language of Fiction," Supplementary Volume XXVII (1954), including the paper by Margaret Macdonald printed here and a contribution by Michael Scriven.

The first of these symposia contains what are very nearly the only contributions of Moore and Ryle to aesthetics. A convenient resumé of the principal issues may be found in:

Monroe Beardsley, *Aesthetics* (New York, 1958), Chapter III.

Also of interest are:

John Hospers, "Literature and Human Nature," *Journal of Aesthetics and Art Criticism,* Volume XVII (1958), 45-57;

Arnold Isenberg, "The Esthetic Function of Language," *Journal of Philosophy,* Volume XLVI (1949), 5-20;

Morris Weitz, *Philosophy of the Arts* (Cambridge, 1950), Chapter 8.

XI

TRUTH IN LITERATURE

IT IS a persistent view that holds poetry and drama and stories to preserve, in some way or other, significant truths about the world. The thesis has been generalized for all the arts (including architecture) and has even been held in a form in which works of art are taken, in effect, to be translatable into discursive statements. But these extreme views seem hardly tenable or promising. Also, those who wish to maintain that literature contains truths about the world do not particularly wish to trade on the obvious fact that statements may be put poetically. They are thinking rather of more difficult, but also more interesting, cases in which, somehow, though these literary works may not themselves directly state this or that to be true of the world, it would nevertheless be appropriate to say that they were true or false, or provided for true or false statements about the world. And the question is, what is the fair sense in which we are entitled to infer these statements from the literary works themselves?

It will not do to say the relationship is merely one of association or suggestion, for this would trivialize the question, at least in a philosophical sense. And it will not do to say that literary works are true to life or some such thing, because this would amount to a concession that 'true' is not

197

being used in a sense appropriate to the logical properties of statements. There may very well be an important (even a philosophically important) use for such locutions, but they will not provide for the hardest challenge, namely, that there is a sense in which literary works may be true or may *imply* true statements and that this sense, at one and the same time, preserves the distinctive nature of the literary piece (for instance, that it is a piece of fiction or dramatic fiction) and accords with the sense of 'true' appropriate to the logic of statements. This at least is the challenge, which would seem, on the face of it, to accommodate well-known ways of speaking about literary works.

The problem has consequences that go beyond the scope of literature, because it is generally conceded that there is a great variety of relationships that one might reasonably call implication. And, corresponding to this variety, there must be a variety of types of argument that will not readily reduce to the sorts of argument already codified in classical logical theory. In effect, to investigate the question raised is to turn to particular aspects of the logic of ordinary language. The general label suggested for the informal sorts of implication, of which the present instance is perhaps merely one specimen, is contextual implication; and one of the first clues about its properties, in comparatively recent literature, was undoubtedly provided by some remarks by G. E. Moore: that, for example, if I say I did something during a certain day, I imply that I believe I did. The likelihood is that a philosophical description of the sort of implication involved in saying that a literary piece contains truths about the world will have to be compared with other kinds of cases in order to sort out the general properties of what has come to be called contextual implication.

John Hospers' account of the issue in literature seeks to preserve the thesis in that most difficult and interesting form, already noted, in which it may be put. It is also developed with an awareness of the cognate forms in which the question of implication has been raised elsewhere.

Implied Truths in Literature

JOHN HOSPERS

M ANY THINGS have been identified as "the function of art": to express emotions, to edify or ennoble mankind, to promote communism, to bring about a moral society. But among the functions it has often been supposed to have is to give us *truth*. This claim for art was made by Aristotle when he said that art (poetry) gives us universal truth; and a long line of critics and philosophers since Aristotle has defended this view.

When one examines this claim, however, it seems highly peculiar. One would have thought that the task of the natural sciences was to give us truth in the form of general laws and theories about the physical universe; of history, to give us truth about what has happened in the past; and of philosophy, to give us truth about—well, opinions differ on this point. Perhaps even aesthetics gives us truth about the arts; but what is it that the arts give us truth about?

I

One of the arts at any rate, literature, uses words as its medium, and thus it can make statements; therefore, it would seem, it is in an excellent posi-

From *The Journal of Aesthetics and Art Criticism,* Volume XIX (Fall, 1960), 37-46. Reprinted with the permission of the author and the editor of *The Journal of Aesthetics and Art Criticism.*

tion to make true statements, that is, to state truths. Whether true or false, statements do indeed occur in literature,

> Life is real! Life is earnest!
> And the grave is not its goal.
> "Dust thou art, to dust returneth"
> Was not spoken of the soul.

If a poem is defined as whatever doesn't extend all the way across the page, the above passage may be called poetry. But whether or not one decides to call it poetry, one could not ask for a more outright statement anywhere. Many statements occurring in poetry are undoubtedly true; so it can hardly be denied that poetry gives us truth in this sense.

Of course, it is not always clear what the sentences in poems mean:

> Life, like a dome of many-colored glass,
> Stains the white radiance of eternity.

True or false? We must first know what is being stated. Some would say that nobody can tell for sure what is being stated; others would say that this is not a statement at all, that we are merely being regaled with exotic images. No doubt this sometimes occurs; whether the above couplet is a case of it is for critics to determine. When it does occur, no question of truth, of course, arises. Nor does it arise in the case of sentences which contain only exclamations, suggestions, commands, or questions.

Such sentences, however, constitute only a small minority of the sentences in literature, as in daily discourse. For the vast remainder, questions of truth do arise. Some of these questions, as we shall see, are extremely puzzling. But it is important at the outset that we should not dismiss literature as "non-cognitive." (1) First, we cannot easily relegate poetry to the category of "emotive language."

> Stars, I have seen them fall.
> And when they drop and die,
> No star is lost at all
> From all the star-sown sky.
> The tears of all that be
> Help not the primal fault.
> It rains into the sea,
> And still the sea is salt.

These lines of Housman are, to be sure, deeply moving. But to understand their meaning we do not suddenly have to "shift gears" from ordinary discourse into an entirely different domain (or "function") of language. We understand what these sentences mean as we understand any other sentences in the language. They have meaning—or, if one wants the usual qualifying adjective, "descriptive meaning"—just as non-poetic sentences do. Perhaps the author of them is expressing a feeling, but this does not prevent him from making statements which he believes to be true. In daily life also we often express feelings by making true-or-false statements: "I wish the war would end," "She's changed so much in the last few years," and so on. Whether the author uses the sentences to express a feeling (or to arouse feeling in others) is something we would have to ask the author to discover. Whether the sentence contains a true or false statement, however, is something for which we examine not the author but the sentence itself. The words, especially in the combinations and juxtapositions we find them in the poem, may, then, move us emotionally, as do many expressions of deep feeling, but this does not prevent them from being true or false. (2) Nor do they fall into the category that has sometimes been called "pictorial meaning." It is true that a poem may present us with an interesting array of mental pictures, but this is something that may or may not occur, depending on the pictorial capacities of the reader; and many readers who have no mental pictures at all while reading poems still claim that they get the full impact of the poems. Even the use of metaphor, which is so important in poetry that poetry has often been defined in terms of it, does not imply that language is being used pictorially. Some metaphors evoke no pictures whatever, and even if one claims that they should, the fact is that metaphor is not to be defined in terms of mental pictures but in terms of linguistic devices. The whole attempt to relegate poetry to the realms of "emotive meaning" or "pictorial meaning" is, I believe, a mistake.

To be sure, the sentences in poetry are richer in suggestion than most of the sentences we utter, but this does not make them "mean" in a different way; it only shows that we respond to them somewhat differently. We are moved, but not (usually) to action. When we read that "Poor Tom's a-cold," we do not go out to fetch a blanket, nor do we gather flowers to put on Cordelia's casket. But the problem of how we do or should *respond* to various linguistic utterances (to religious language, to political speeches, to statements in textbooks, etc.)—and our responses are varied indeed—is not to be confused with understanding the *meaning* of these utterances. The meaning of a sentence does not vary with the use to which it happens to be put on a particular occasion. In particular, the meaning does not vary with either (a) the feelings of the speaker, which it may express, or (b) the response which it evokes in the listener. If two readers respond differently to the same sentence, this does not show that the sentence has two different meanings. Talk about "emotive meaning" would be far less misleading if the term "meaning" were scrapped in favor of the term "effects." A sentence in a poem may powerfully affect the emotions, but it does not follow that its *meaning* is "emotive." (The term "emotive" is misleading even in describing the effects. As the term "emotive" is ordinarily used, at any rate, I would suggest that the language of poetry is considerably more emotive in its effects than the telephone directory, somewhat more emotive than scientific treatises, not quite as emotive as day-to-day conversations—consisting as they usually do of an inelegant mixture of assertion, persuasion, suggestion, and loaded language—and not nearly as emotive as propaganda or the language of political and moral persuasion.)

Let us say no more about the explicit statements that occur in literature. Some of them may well be true, and may thus give us knowledge we did not previously possess, whether or not the imparting of such knowledge was the intent of the author when he wrote.[1] The main problem that confronts us now has to do not with explicit statements, but with statements which the author nowhere makes.

We are probably convinced that the novels of Balzac give us a reasonably accurate picture of certain aspects of life in Paris in the early nineteenth century, that in fact they were intended to do this; but whether or not they were so intended, they do. Yet we do not encounter, on reading any of these novels, any sentence such as "This is a true picture of life in Paris in my time; I do hereby assert it." Nor do the novels of Thomas Hardy contain sentences telling us what Hardy's view of life and human destiny was; yet, from the way the novels are plotted, and the chance character of the events upon which the major developments turn, even the least perceptive reader, before he finishes even one of the novels, has a pretty good idea of what that view was. Psychological novels customarily contain many remarks describing the psychological traits of the characters; these are stated, but what seems actually to be the concern of such novels is not singular propositions about the characters but general, even universal, propositions about human nature; yet none of these general propositions is stated out-

---

[1] The language of fiction seems to raise special problems: Is it true that Hamlet was the prince of Denmark? Of course; just read the play. But how can it be true, since there never was a Hamlet at all? But then it's false. Still, Shakespeare's Hamlet *was* prince of Denmark, wasn't he? These have been dealt with abundantly in the recent literature. (See Monroe C. Beardsley, *Aesthetics,* pp. 411-414, and the numerous references on the topic listed on pp. 441-443, 446-447.) Once the peculiar logic of fictional sentences has been cleared up, no *special* problem of truth, I think, arises.

right.[2] These statements often seem to contain the most important things in the novel, and are often the novel's chief excuse for existing; yet they seem to operate entirely behind the scenes. The most important statements, views, theories in a work of literature are seldom stated in so many words. What is more natural, then, than to say that they are *implied*?

We can say it, and doubtless it is true. The difficulty, however, is to track down the relevant meaning of the term "imply." The logic-book senses of implication will not suffice here. There are, of course, statements in works of literature which imply other statements, just as they do anywhere else. If the sentence "Jones is a father" occurred in a novel, it would surely imply "Jones is a male." And if we read "If Smith was surprised, he gave no sign of it" and were later told that Smith was surprised (on this same occasion) but gave no sign of it, we could accuse the author of inconsistency in his narrative. But this is hardly the kind of case we are interested in here. What those who talk about implied truths in literature are referring to is seldom individual propositions at all; they talk about large segments of a work of literature, sometimes an entire novel or drama, as all together implying certain propositions. But what is the meaning of such a claim? What sense of "imply" is being used?

II

Let us try a few obvious candidates. Perhaps what you imply is what you *meant* to say, or intended to say, even though you did not actually say it. If someone says to a student in a somewhat sarcastic tone of voice after an examination, "Some people don't do their own work," the student may retort, "Are you implying that I cheat?" The proposition "You cheat" is the one he *meant* to convey to the student, though without having said it. Similarly, when I say during a miserable rain, "Lovely weather, isn't it?" I may be said to imply (intend) the opposite of what I said—what I meant to communicate to my hearer is that the weather is foul. So, it may be said, it can be the same in a work of literature. When we say that the author implied this proposition even though he did not state it, perhaps we mean simply that this is the proposition he wanted or intended to get across to his hearers through his work.

Why should people say one thing and mean (intend) another, either in daily conversation or in works of literature? Why should the proposition

---

[2] For example, the psychological observations of Marcel Proust are excellently described by Morris Weitz in his paper "Truth in Literature," *Revue Internationale de Philosophie*, IX (1955), 116-129.

they most want to impress upon their hearers or readers be never stated? Because, surely, they can often impress it on their readers with greater force and effectiveness by this means. When Jonathan Swift wrote *A Modest Proposal,* his words would not have been so devastatingly effective had he said outright what he meant; he said, with multiplied examples, just the opposite. Sometimes, indeed, when an author has meant to communicate something throughout an entire work, and then goes on to say it explicitly, we are pained and disappointed. "The President of the Immortals had had his sport with Tess," wrote Thomas Hardy, thus spoiling at the end (as Collingwood quite rightly, I think, points out in a different connection) the effect of what was otherwise a fine novel. The reader who has not surmised for himself by page 300 that this is what Hardy wants to communicate to us, hardly deserves to be told it at the end.

But this sense of "imply" is subject to an interesting objection. The test of whether a given proposition is implied in a work of art, as thus far explained, is simply whether the artist meant to communicate it to his audience by means of the work. If p is the proposition he meant to convey, then p is the proposition implied in the work. But can't the artist be wrong? Suppose he meant to convey one proposition, p, but didn't succeed, or succeeded in conveying to his readers another one, q, which he never intended or even thought of. And if all readers agree that q is the proposition implied, are we still to say that it is p that is implied because the author said so?

The main trouble here is that what is implied (in this sense) seems to require no connection with the words and sentences that are actually to be found in the work of literature. If Hardy (in a document just discovered) were to tell us that what he meant to convey in his novels is that humanity is nearing perfection, then this is implied in the novels, even though the novels seem to contradict such an assertion utterly at every point. If the poet says sincerely that what he meant to say in the poem is that reality is circular (and artists have said stranger things than this about their work), then this proposition is what is implied in the poem; and if the poet changes his mind and says that what he meant to convey is that blue is seven, then this (if it can be called a proposition at all) is implied. He said that he meant p or q; but does it follow that p or q is implied? Is he the final test? We might read the poem till doomsday without any such notion entering our heads as that reality is circular; but, one might say, this only shows that the poet did not *succeed* in communicating this proposition to us, not that he did not mean to communicate it; and thus far what he meant to communicate has been the test of what proposition or propositions are implied.

III

Let us, then, try to find a criterion of implication other than what the artist meant or wanted to convey; following the hint just given, why not say that the criterion is what proposition he *succeeded in conveying*? What he meant to convey and what he did actually convey to his readers may, after all, be two very different things.

But now another objection occurs at once: here the criterion of what is implied does not depend on the author, but it does depend on his readers. If the poem does not succeed in communicating to the readers proposition *p,* then the poem does not imply *p.* Moreover, it would follow that the poem may imply one proposition to one reader and a very different one (or none at all) to another reader, or even to the same reader at a different time. If the audience is dull, stupid, or sleepy, no proposition is implied no matter how much the poet meant to convey one and how much care he took to convey it, while if the audience is sensitive, alert, and imaginative, that same poem may imply a whole host of propositions, including many that never occurred to the poet at all or to any reader but one. This is, to say the least, an extremely relativistic kind of implying. Surely, one is tempted to say, a proposition is implied or it is not, and whether it is or is not doesn't vary with the intelligence or imaginative capacity of the audience or whether they have just been fed tranquillizing pills and taken the road to Miltown. I do not deny that we *can,* if we please, use the word "imply" in this sense, but I doubt very much whether it is a sense which anyone ever gives the word in practice, and it is certainly not a sense which (once we realize what it involves) would be at all acceptable to those who speak of propositions as being implied in works of literature.

IV

The trouble with the attempts at pinpointing the notion of implication we have considered thus far is that whether or not something is implied is determined by the artist's intention or by the audience's response, but not by the work of art itself. We want to be able to say that something is implied even though the author may not intend it and be quite unaware of it, and even though the audience may be so unperceptive as not to grasp it. In that way we shall at least be released from having to know the author's intentions to know what is implied.

Let us begin again with our previous example. "Some people don't do their own work," the person says to the student in an accusing tone of voice. Doubtless he intended to accuse him of cheating. But one might well allege that quite apart from this, he implied it: by what he said, by his tone of voice, by the whole context of the utterance (in connection with having finished an examination, and so on). A speaker uttering these words in this tone and in this context *does,* we would say, imply this, and if he later says that he didn't imply it because he didn't intend to, this does not exonerate him from the charge of implying it just the same.

It is surely this sense that G. E. Moore had in mind when he gave his classic example of implication: when I say that I went to the pictures last Tuesday, I thereby imply that I believe I went. Of course I did not *say* that I believed it; this is no part of the statement I made, and one cannot formally deduce the proposition that I believed I went (q) from the proposition that I went (p). It is not the proposition *per se* that implies this, but my *utterance* of the proposition, in a normal tone of voice, without evidence of joking or playing tricks on my listener. I do imply q when I utter p in this way, in that anyone who knows the language and can interpret facial expression and manner is *entitled,* by virtue of all these, to infer q. If I later disavow this and claim that I was only exercising my vocal cords, I would not be excused (say, in a court of law) from having implied q in my utterance. "But you implied that you believed it by what you said and the way you said it. So you did imply it, whether you intended to or not."

Can we apply this kind of implication to works of literature? There is one difficulty at the outset: there is an enormous difference between literature and the examples we have just considered from everyday conversation, in that when Jones speaks to us, we have not only his spoken utterance to go by but all the other cues such as his facial expression and gestures and tone of voice and the environmental circumstances accompanying the utterance. When Jones writes us a letter, however, we have only his written word as a guide. There are many inferences we might make if we *saw* him speaking that we are unable to make when we have before us only the sentences he has recorded. There are not as many clues in the written word alone. This makes things more difficult; but still, it is not as if there were *no* clues. What a person writes *may* give us good evidence of what he thinks or believes, even though he nowhere tells us that he thinks or believes these things.

Works of literature, of course, are a special case of the written word, and we can sometimes make inferences from them. We can infer many things about Theodore Dreiser's beliefs, without knowing anything about him as a man, by reading his novels: that his view of life was (roughly) materialistic; that he saw man as a pawn of destiny, caught in a tangled web of circumstances not of his own making which nevertheless lead him to his doom;

that he was a champion of the underdog and the downtrodden, a humanitarian, even a sentimentalist. How can we infer these things? By observing carefully which passages contain the greatest passion and intensity, which themes are most often reiterated, how the plot is made to evolve, which characters are treated with the greatest sympathy, and so on. There are countless clues in the novels themselves that we could cite as evidence for the author's beliefs. (Not for the truth of the beliefs, but for the truth of the proposition that the author entertained them.) And there are no contrary clues. From observing all this, we can say with considerable confidence that the work implies that the author had these beliefs. We are entitled to make this inference, even if by some chance it should turn out that he actually did not have these beliefs. The belief-clues are still there, even if (though this would be surprising, for normally they would not get there if he had not purposely put them there) the beliefs in this case did not exist. (A somewhat analogous kind of case is well-known in discussions of scientific method: our judgment that the next raven will be black is one we are entitled to make on the basis of the thousands of ravens already observed to be black and the absence of any contrary cases; and we are justified in making this inference, even if the next raven should turn out to be an albino.)

"Perhaps, however," an objector may say, "the point is not so much that the author believed this as that he wants *us* to believe it. As long as he can make us believe it, his own beliefs are irrelevant." This introduces the topic of the aesthetic relevance of belief, which is not my subject now. But I would venture this suggestion: Perhaps it doesn't matter whether the author believed *p*. But neither is it necessary, for understanding a work of literature, that *we* believe what the author may have wanted us to believe. Some would say that if we are in a state of belief or conviction, we are already far removed from a state of aesthetic receptivity. Do we know what beliefs Shakespeare had, or what beliefs (if any) he was trying to instill in us? And as far as the appreciation of his plays is concerned, who cares? There are many beliefs stated by the *characters* in Shakespeare's plays; but these cannot all be Shakespeare's beliefs, unless Shakespeare was pathologically addicted to changing his mind, for they constantly conflict with one another; nor can they all be our beliefs, unless we are so irrational as to believe whatever we hear regardless of whether it contradicts what we heard just before. Rather, it is necessary that we *understand* the beliefs to which the characters give voice, that we appreciate why they believe it, and what difference it makes to their motivation and behavior in the drama.

Whatever we may conclude, then, about the relevance of the author's beliefs, we can sometimes make highly probable inferences as to what they were; and when we do so, we can correctly say that the author was, in his written work, implying that he had these beliefs. But if we can infer what his beliefs were, why not his feelings, his attitudes, his intentions? Such inferences again are vulnerable, but they can often be made—perhaps not with Shakespeare, but with Dreiser. The written word often contains intent-clues as well as belief-clues.

Much of the writing of literary critics is given over to discovering, from these clues, what the author's intentions were (sometimes exclusively from these, and not from independent sources outside the work). The critic becomes a kind of sleuth, and from a careful reading of the work he tells us what the author probably felt or intended. Is this going back to intentions again? Not in the same way as before. Here we are not concerned with what he intended—i.e., in his intentions apart from the work—but with what he implied *in* the work *about* his intentions. (Not that there is anything sinful about discovering his intentions through outside sources, such as his autobiography. If we want to know what his intentions were, the work itself may offer no clues to this, and we have to discover it in other ways. There is no "fallacy" involved in this. We are in no position to cut ourselves off *a priori* from sources of information which may turn out to be useful, and if the author—outside his work—can enlighten us, we are cheating only ourselves if we refuse to accept this source of enlightenment. And if one objects, "But if you have to go outside the work to the artist to find such clues, the work is not self-sufficient, autonomous, etc., for the intentions should be embodied in the work and be wholly inferrable from it," we can reply that this is a counsel of perfection. Works of art may not be entirely self-sufficient—whatever exactly that is—and moreover there appears to be no compelling reason why they should be. Can we deny that some works, at any rate, mean more to us than they would if we had no such outside knowledge?)

A work of literature may also provide clues about the author's *unconscious* intentions, and a critic well-versed in psychiatry may discover them. Just as we say in daily life that a man does not intend, consciously, to be unpleasantly aggressive, he nevertheless has many such unconscious intentions (he says things in a hostile manner without meaning to, and unconsciously chooses situations for saying them that would strike any observer as calculated to arouse resentment), so we may make similar discoveries from the written word, though it takes someone who is both a sensitive critic and an astute psychiatrist to do this. (When Ernest Jones attempts it with *Hamlet*, I find his conclusions convincing, but when Ella Freeman-Sharpe attempts it with *King Lear,* I do not.) When this is well done, we have not merely a series of inferences about the author's personality—which would be of interest principally to clinicians—but clues to the interpretation of a work, or at least *an* interpretation of a work, which might otherwise have puzzled us forever.

One final point: although we sometimes draw inferences from works of literature to their authors, it may happen that we *think* we are doing this when we are actually doing something else.[3] Suppose that on walking through an empty building I see written on the blackboard a great many incendiary remarks and obscene epithets. I do not know who the author is, and presumably the words were not intended specifically for me. I may suspect that the author had vitriolic feelings when he wrote it, but this is not the inference that I normally make. He may have written it as a joke, or at random as a kind of verbal doodling, or seriously for someone's attention; I do not know. Accordingly I do not infer anything at all about the author. I conclude only that inflammatory language is being used— no matter by whom or for what purpose. Nor do I *infer* this; this language *is* inflammatory, and I do not so much infer this as *recognize* it as such; I make no inferences from it whatever.

We are sometimes in this situation with regard to works of literature. When we see the line "I fall upon the thorns of life! I bleed!" whether or not we know that Shelley wrote it, we can say that the lines are despairing in character. This is what they are, and they remain so even if neither Shelley nor the reader was despairing. We simply recognize them as lines of a certain character; the word "despairing" refers to a property of the poem, not of its author. Often what may first pass as inductive inference to propositions about the author is not only not inductive but is not inference at all.

V

But let us have an end of intentions. We have considered how an author's work, or parts thereof, can be said to imply that the author had certain beliefs, attitudes, or intentions. But this is not the end of the matter. Does not a work of literature often imply propositions, not about its author, but about the world, about human life, human traits, the human situation, the cosmos? Through reading the work we somehow arrive at these propositions—*not* the rather incidental proposition that the author believed them,

---

[3] This point was suggested to me by Professor Isabel Hungerland.

although we may infer this also. (We might say in such cases, not that the *author* implied this or that in his work, but that *the very words* imply it. But this distinction is not a sharp one, and I am not sure how far we would have to stretch our ordinary use of such expressions in order to make such a distinction sharp.)[4]

Before trying to be more precise about this, I shall give a few examples of sentences implying propositions which are never stated and which have nothing to do with the speaker's beliefs. A reporter asks an anthropologist, "Would you say that the Bongoese are a clean people?" and the anthropologist replies, "I would not say that the Bongoese are clean." Note that he did not say that they were *not* clean; he said only what he would *not* say—he would not say that they were clean, but he would not say that they were not clean either; perhaps he knew nothing one way or the other about the Bongoese. But though he did not say they were not clean, it does seem plausible to hold that the sentence *implies* this to anyone who is at all aware of the English idiom (whether or not the speaker intended any such thing). Or, the physician says, "Yes, of course the patient died. I wasn't his physician." He does not *say* that the patient would have lived if he had been the patient's physician, but this certainly seems to be what is implied. (Note that what the sentence implies is that the patient died because this man was not his physician, *not* that the physician *believed* that the patient died because he was not the physician.)

There is surely a relation here which in daily life we do not hesitate to call implication. Nor is it bizarre or mysterious; it is a garden variety sort of thing which we constantly recognize. What exactly does it consist in? There does not seem to be any term (other than "implication" itself) that describes it precisely; it seems to be closest to what, in one sense, we call *suggestion*.[5] Statements often suggest other statements, which need not at all be about the person who utters them. "They had children and got married" suggests that they had illegitimate children, even though the utterance was a slip of the tongue and the order of the two clauses should have been reversed. "He saw the dragon and fell down dead" suggests, though it does not state, that he fell down dead because he saw the dragon. What is actually *said* is usually very limited, and when pressure is applied it tends to narrow still further: "Did he actually *say* he was going to kill you? True, he said he was going to make mincemeat out of you, but . . ."

---

[4] See Max Black, "Presupposition and Implication," in S. Uyeda (ed.), *A Way to the Philosophy of Science* (Tokyo, 1958), pp. 443-448.
[5] See Monroe C. Beardsley, *Aesthetics*, p. 123.

And as our conception of what was actually said narrows, our conception of what was implied (suggested) tends to expand.

Why not conclude, then, that literature implies many propositions in the sense of suggesting them? The word "suggest," however, as it is presently employed, is not quite tailor-made for this job:

(1) The word "suggest" ordinarily has a far wider range than that of "imply" as we are now considering it. "To me this poem suggests the sounding surf, tropical islands, wine-red sunsets . . ." This is a perfectly legitimate sense of "suggest," one in which what is suggested is not a proposition at all, and it is not at all synonymous with "imply." Is this because what the poem suggests here is not a proposition? No, for most of the cases in which what is suggested *is* a proposition will not do either: "To me this play suggests that the hero was struggling, afraid to face the truth about himself, trying to repress it without knowing it himself . . ." This may indeed be what the play suggests to a particular reader, and it may do so even if the reader is just "imagining things" and there is not the slightest textual basis for such a claim. What a line suggests to you, it may not suggest to me; in our ordinary use of "suggest" there is virtually unlimited subjectivity, whether what is suggested is or is not a proposition. But this is not true of the cases we are now concerned with. I want to say that a line suggests this or that, not to you or to me, but suggests, period; or at least that it suggests it to anyone who understands the words and is acquainted with the idiom of the language. "They had children and got married," though it does not *say* that they had illegitimate children, *does* suggest this, and if a person does not catch the suggestion (whether it is an intentional one on the part of the speaker or not), he is stupid or blind to any subtlety of linguistic expression. If we continue to use "suggest," then, we shall have to limit its application rather arbitrarily to these "objective" cases, excluding the to-you-but-not-to-me cases. And in view of our common use of this term, it is difficult to make this stricture stick.

(2) Even when the stricture is accepted, the term "suggest" seems unsatisfactory for another reason: it is far too pallid, too vanilla-flavored. The term "suggestion" suggests (!) something not quite there, lurking in the background, or visible through the trees if one squints. But works of literature, as well as sentences in daily discourse, may suggest in a far stronger way than this. The implied proposition, or thesis, or moral, of the work (when there is one), far from being "suggested" in this way, may be the most prominent thing in it; it may leap out at you, scream at you, bowl you over. Shall we say that Ibsen's *A Doll's House* only *suggests* that a woman should develop her personality and have a life of her own as much as her

husband, or that Swift's *A Modest Proposal* only *suggests* that perhaps England was not treating Ireland in a humane manner? Perhaps we should say, not that these propositions are suggested by the work, but that they are *intimated* by it.[6] Or perhaps simply, "He said it all right, but not in so many words!"

Still, subject to these severe limitations, and because "imply" seems to have no ready synonym for this context, let us proceed with "suggest." Swift's *A Modest Proposal* is an instance of irony. Must irony be defined intentionalistically, as saying the opposite of what one intends? The disadvantage of this is, of course, that to know whether a given work was ironical, one would have to know whether it was so intended. It seems preferable to define "irony" as implying (suggesting) the opposite of what one says. One can even apply this to parody, which is often used as an incontrovertible example of a genre in which reference to the author's intention is indispensable. "To know that something is a parody, you have to know whether the author *meant* to parody this or that. If he didn't, you can hardly criticize him for failing to do something he didn't intend to do." In the intentionalistic sense, this is true; but we *can* criticize the work for not suggesting an interpretation other than the one it bears on its face. A good parody always contains countless such marks, whether or not the author so intended.

A frustrating and at the same time fascinating aspect of complex works of literature is their resistance to a single interpretation, in that many propositions seem to be implied, some of them contradicting others. The work would be far less rich in texture without this feature. Nor need any of the conflicting interpretations be wrong; both of two contradictory propositions may really be suggested by a work of literature, and though of course they cannot both be true, they may both really be implied, and both may live in aesthetic harmony in the same work, giving it a kind of piquancy by the very tension which is thus set up. How is *Paradise Lost* to be interpreted? There is some evidence in the text that man's fall is a dire catastrophe, a work of Satan in defiance of God; there is other evidence that the entire series of events was foreordained by omnipotence, and thus, in view of divine benevolence, not a catastrophe at all; and there is some evidence that man's state after the Fall is much better, in that he has free-will in a sense which he lacked before ("a paradise within thee, happier farr"). It is, I think, only of marginal interest to ask, What did Milton believe? or what did Milton intend? The question is: Regardless of what he believed

---

[6] This term was suggested to me by Professor Max Black.

or intended, what beliefs got embodied in the poem? Which propositions are stated, and what further ones are implied?

One fruitful field of suggested propositions is the following: Works of literature are able, through the delineation of character and the setting forth of situations which are followed through in the details of the plot, to suggest *hypotheses* about human behavior, human motivation, human actions, and sometimes about the social structure. In doing so it doubtless enters upon the domain of the social sciences; but in the present undeveloped state of these sciences, I do not think that a bit of supplementation from the literary artists (who are, at the least, excellent observers of the human scene) will be thought to crowd the scientists unduly. In any event, many writers have believed themselves, and with good reason, to be commentators on and interpreters of human behavior and the social situation in their time. Zola certainly considered himself to be one, and John Dos Passos another. Works of literature may suggest hypotheses of various kinds. Some are empirical in character—for example, Tolstoy's *War and Peace,* even apart from the explicitly stated philosophy of history at the end, suggests a hypothesis about the genesis of great events in history in relation to their leaders; and Dreiser's novels suggest semi-empirical and semi-metaphysical hypotheses about the helplessness of human beings caught in a web of circumstances beyond their control and carried on willy-nilly to their destruction. Many works of literature suggest what one might call *moral* hypotheses— Dostoyevsky, George Eliot, Victor Hugo. Works of literature do not, of course, *verify* these hypotheses; that is the task of the empirical sciences. But they can suggest hypotheses which may be empirically fruitful; and this is, of course, a far more difficult task than verification.

Now, what has all this to do with the topic of truth in literature, with which we began? Simply this: we were looking for propositions, and especially true propositions, in works of literature, other than explicitly stated ones. And we have found, first, that works of literature may provide us with evidence for propositions about the author's beliefs, attitudes, and intentions, thus entitling us to infer these propositions; and, second, that quite apart from any reference to their authors, these works may suggest or intimate (say without saying) numerous propositions which are not about the author but about the world, about the subject-matter of the work itself. And since some of these suggested propositions are doubtless true, we have here, surely, an important sense of truth in literature, and one which it seems to me that many critics who have made claims for truth in literature have had in mind without being fully aware of it.

Two final precautions: (1) I am not saying that truth in literature is an important feature of these works *aesthetically*. On this point, as far as the present paper is concerned, I am quite content to agree with Professor Arnold Isenberg when he says, "What is so glorious about truth? Why should a quality which all except the demented commonly attain in the greater number of their ideas be considered so precious as to increase the stature of a Milton or a Beethoven if it can be ascribed to him?"[7] Though in fact I would not go so far as this, the matter would have to be separately argued. (Roughly, I would hold that the thesis implied in a work of literature may be the most important single feature of that work, and that it may be an important thesis, never before thought of by anyone; but not that we must accept the thesis as *true*.) (2) Nor am I saying that the author of the work of literature means to *assert* the propositions he implies. He may, and in most cases he certainly does, wish to assert them, or he would not have taken such pains to suggest them; but this has to be discovered by checking the relevant data (including the work itself) that will enlighten us about the author's beliefs. I am saying only that a work of literature may imply certain propositions and that these implied propositions may be true; it is not even necessary that the author mean to *assert* that they are true. This too is a separate consideration.

[7] *JAAC*, XIII (March 1955), 3, 400.

Bibliography

The principal theoretical adjustments include prescribing different senses of 'true' for factual statements and literature, chiefly poetry (or even, sometimes, for the other arts):

John Hospers, *Meaning and Truth in the Arts* (Chapel Hill, 1946), Chapters 5-8;

I. A. Richards, *Science and Poetry* (London, revised 1935);

or attempting to treat works of art, chiefly fiction, as statements:

Monroe Beardsley, *Aesthetics* (New York, 1958), Chapters VIII-IX;

T. M. Greene, *The Arts and the Art of Criticism* (Princeton, 1940), Chapter XXIII;

Gilbert Ryle, "Imaginary Objects," *Proceedings of the Aristotelian Society*, Supplementary Volume XII (1933).

The most recent tendency is to preserve a sense of 'true' proper to statements and to provide for truth in literature by way of what has come to be called contextual implication:

Isabel Hungerland, "Contextual Implication," *Inquiry*, Volume IV (1960), 211-258;

A convenient and exploratory summary of the issue in a context wider than that of aesthetics.

Morris Weitz, *Philosophy of the Arts* (Cambridge, 1950), Chapter 8.

XII

METAPHOR

THE STUDY of metaphor inevitably invites comment on the general nature of figurative language. It turns out, however, that figures of speech are often merely ornamental, in the sense that their analysis reveals no distinctive logical features that a comprehensive philosophical account of language would wish to accommodate. Metaphor does not seem to be ornamental in this sense. It undoubtedly has important implications for a theory of meaning.

It may be easily supposed that, since one speaks of metaphor as of a particular sort of figure, that all metaphors behave in the same way essentially. This may be disputed at once in at least one important respect. It is a matter of debate whether all metaphors may be paraphrased or not. To hold that metaphors can be correctly and more or less accurately paraphrased is, in effect, to hold that figurative language reduces to literal language, that the metaphoric remainder is merely an ornament, in a philosophically uninteresting sense. On the other hand, to hold that metaphors (at least certain sorts of metaphor) cannot be paraphrased is to suggest that a special account must be given of figurative sense, that metaphor is itself philosophically interesting and would provide specimen expressions whose

216

meaning cannot be determined in those ways appropriate to literal sense. The evidence seems to be that, particularly in poetry, non-paraphrasable metaphors abound. The question is, what is the meaning of such expressions which, if taken literally, may even appear as nonsense and how do we decide their meaning?

The most important clue lies in the parasitic nature of metaphor. Quite obviously, it trades on the literal meanings of the words it joins together in unexpected ways. We may also notice, incidentally, that the "literal sense" on which it trades has an enormous spread—from standard dictionary meanings to looser suggestions, associations, even private asides. The question is, how does metaphor trade on literal sense? To put the matter this way is to see at once the inadequacy (though not the irrelevance) of any talk of resemblance and similarity. Resemblance is the favorite theme among theories of metaphor, but by itself it fails to touch on the *use* of resemblance and similarity (possibly also the use of lack of resemblance) that distinguishes metaphor proper from literal comparison, analogy, catachresis, simile, possibly even synecdoche and metonymy.

One also notices, thinking along these lines, that the principal tropes—irony, synecdoche, metonymy, and metaphor—undoubtedly will not lend themselves to a single comprehensive analysis. One has only to see that irony directly affects the primary uses of language, such as making a statement or asking a question, that it need not otherwise involve any departure from the literal sense of the words it employs; but that, on the other hand, metaphor is not at all directly linked to such primary uses of language, that it is more a semantic than a syntactical matter. In this sense, it is more closely related to codes and slang (though it cannot be identified with these) than it is to telling a story, speaking jokingly or ironically, or stating a fact. Also, it may be noted, an inevitable quibble dogs all candidate theories. The distinctions between metaphor, synecdoche, and metonymy are construed in stricter and looser ways by the different theorists; in fact, some examples taken to be absolutely telling against a particular account may be found rejected as ineligible by the partisans of another theory. And this calls for caution in gauging the force of all arguments pro and con.

Max Black's discussion of metaphor is generally conceded to be one of the indispensable papers on the subject.

Metaphor

MAX BLACK

Metaphors are no arguments, my pretty maiden.

The Fortunes of Nigel, Book 2, Chapter 2.

To DRAW attention to a philosopher's metaphors is to belittle him—like
praising a logician for his beautiful handwriting. Addiction to metaphor is held to be illicit, on the principle that whereof one can speak only
metaphorically, thereof one ought not to speak at all. Yet the nature of the
offence is unclear. I should like to do something to dispel the mystery that
invests the topic; but since philosophers (for all their notorious interest in
language) have so neglected the subject, I must get what help I can from
the literary critics. They, at least, do not accept the commandment, "Thou
shalt not commit metaphor," or assume that metaphor is incompatible with
serious thought.

I

The questions I should like to see answered concern the "logical grammar"
of "metaphor" and words having related meanings. It would be satisfactory

From *Proceedings of the Aristotelian Society,* Volume LV (1954-1955), 273-294 (now,
with a minor correction). Reprinted with the permission of the author and the
Aristotelian Society.

to have convincing answers to the questions: "How do we recognize a case of metaphor?," "Are there any criteria for the detection of metaphors?," "Can metaphors be translated into literal expressions?," "Is metaphor properly regarded as a decoration upon 'plain sense'?," "What are the relations between metaphor and simile?," "In what sense, if any, is a metaphor 'creative'?," "What is the point of using a metaphor?" (Or, more briefly, "What do we *mean* by 'metaphor'?" The questions express attempts to become clearer about some uses of the word "metaphor"—or, if one prefers the material mode, to analyze the notion of metaphor.)

The list is not a tidy one, and several of the questions overlap in fairly obvious ways. But I hope they will sufficiently illustrate the type of inquiry that is intended.

It would be helpful to be able to start from some agreed list of "clear cases" of metaphor. Since the word "metaphor" has some intelligible uses, however vague or vacillating, it must be possible to construct such a list. Presumably, it should be easier to agree whether any given item should be included than to agree about any proposed analysis of the notion of metaphor.

Perhaps the following list of examples, chosen not altogether at random, might serve:

1. "The chairman ploughed through the discussion."
2. "A smokescreen of witnesses."
3. "An argumentative melody."
4. "Blotting-paper voices" (Henry James).
5. "The poor are the Negroes of Europe" (Chamfort).
6. "Light is but the shadow of God" (Sir Thomas Browne).
7. "Oh dear white children, casual as birds. Playing amid the ruined languages" (Auden).

I hope all these will be accepted as unmistakable *instances* of metaphor, whatever judgments may ultimately be made about the meaning of "metaphor." The examples are offered as clear cases of metaphor, but, with the possible exception of the first, they would be unsuitable as "paradigms." If we wanted to teach the meaning of "metaphor" to a child, we should need simpler examples like "The clouds are crying" or "The branches are fighting with one another." (Is it significant that one hits upon examples of personification?) But I have tried to include some reminders of the possible complexities that even relatively straightforward metaphors may generate.

Consider the first example—"The chairman ploughed through the discussion." An obvious point to begin with is the contrast between the word "ploughed" and the remaining words by which it is accompanied. This would be commonly expressed by saying that "ploughed" has here a metaphorical sense, while the other words have literal senses. Though we point to the whole sentence as an instance (a "clear case") of metaphor, our attention quickly narrows to a single word, whose presence is the proximate reason for the attribution. And similar remarks can be made about the next four examples in the list, the crucial words being, respectively, "smoke-screen," "argumentative," "blotting-paper," and "Negroes."

(But the situation is more complicated in the last two examples of the list. In the quotation from Sir Thomas Browne, "Light" must be supposed to have a symbolic sense, and certainly to mean far more than it would in the context of a text-book on optics. Here, the metaphorical sense of the expression, "the shadow of God" imposes a meaning richer than usual upon the subject of the sentence. Similar effects can be noticed in the passage from Auden [consider for instance the meaning of "white" in the first line]. I shall have to neglect such complexities in this paper.)

In general, when we speak of a relatively simple metaphor, we are referring to a sentence or another expression, in which *some* words are used metaphorically, while the remainder are used non-metaphorically. An attempt to construct an entire sentence of words that are used metaphorically results in a proverb, an allegory, or a riddle. No preliminary analysis of metaphor will satisfactorily cover even such trite examples as "In the night all cows are black." And cases of symbolism (in the sense in which Kafka's castle is a "symbol") also need separate treatment.

II

"The chairman ploughed through the discussion." In calling this sentence a case of metaphor, we are implying that at least one word (here, the word "ploughed") is being used metaphorically in the sentence, and that at least one of the remaining words is being used literally. Let us call the word "ploughed" the *focus* of the metaphor, and the remainder of the sentence in which that word occurs the *frame*. (Are *we* now using metaphors—and mixed ones at that? Does it matter?) One notion that needs to be clarified is that of the "metaphorical use" of the focus of a metaphor. Among other things, it would be good to understand how the presence of one frame can result in metaphorical use of the complementary word, while the presence of a different frame for the same word fails to result in metaphor.

If the sentence about the chairman's behavior is translated word for word into any foreign language for which this is possible, we shall of course want to say that the translated sentence is a case of the *very same* metaphor.

So, to call a sentence an instance of metaphor is to say something about its *meaning,* not about its orthography, its phonetic pattern, or its grammatical form.[1] (To use a well-known distinction, "metaphor" must be classified as a term belonging to "semantics" and not to "syntax"—or to any *physical* inquiry about language.)

Suppose somebody says, "I like to plough my memories regularly." Shall we say he is using the same metaphor as in the case already discussed, or not? Our answer will depend upon the degree of similarity we are prepared to affirm on comparing the two "frames" (for we have the same "focus" each time). Differences in the two frames will produce *some* differences in the interplay[2] between focus and frame in the two cases. Whether we regard the differences as sufficiently striking to warrant calling the sentences *two* metaphors is a matter for arbitrary decision. "Metaphor" is a loose word, at best, and we must beware of attributing to it stricter rules of usage than are actually found in practice.

So far, I have been treating "metaphor" as a predicate properly applicable to certain expressions, without attention to any occasions on which the expressions are used, or to the thoughts, acts, feelings, and intentions of speakers upon such occasions. And this is surely correct for *some* expressions. We recognize that to call a man a "cesspool" is to use a metaphor, without needing to know who uses the expression, or on what occasions, or with what intention. The rules of our language determine that some expressions must count as metaphors; and a speaker can no more change this than he can legislate that "cow" shall mean the same as "sheep." But we must also recognize that the established rules of language leave wide latitude for individual variation, initiative, and creation. There are indefinitely many contexts (including nearly all the interesting ones) where the meaning of a metaphorical expression has to be reconstructed from the speaker's intentions (and other clues) because the broad rules of standard usage are too general to supply the information needed. When Churchill, in a famous phrase, called Mussolini "that *utensil,*" the tone of voice, the verbal setting, the historical background, helped to make clear *what* metaphor was being used. (Yet, even here, it is hard to see how the phrase "that utensil" could ever be applied to a man except as an insult. Here, as elsewhere, the general rules of usage function as limitations upon the

---

[1] *Any* part of speech can be used metaphorically (though the results are meagre and uninteresting in the case of conjunctions); any form of verbal expression may contain a metaphorical focus.

[2] Here I am using language appropriate to the "interaction view" of metaphor that is discussed later in this paper.

speaker's freedom to mean whatever he pleases.) This is an example, though still a simple one, of how recognition and interpretation of a metaphor may require attention to the *particular circumstances* of its utterance.

It is especially noteworthy that there are, in general, no standard rules for the degree of *weight* or *emphasis* to be attached to a particular use of an expression. To know what the user of a metaphor means, we need to know how "seriously" he treats the metaphorical focus. (Would he be just as content to have some rough synonym, or would only *that* word serve? Are we to take the word lightly, attending only to its most obvious implications—or should we dwell upon its less immediate associations?) In speech we can use emphasis and phrasing as clues. But in written or printed discourse, even these rudimentary aids are absent. Yet this somewhat elusive "weight" of a (suspected or detected[3]) metaphor is of great practical importance in exegesis.

To take a philosophical example. Whether the expression "logical form" should be treated in a particular frame as having a metaphorical sense will depend upon the extent to which its user is taken to be conscious of some supposed analogy between arguments and other things (vases, clouds, battles, jokes) that are also said to have "form." Still more will it depend upon whether the writer wishes the analogy to be active in the minds of his readers; and how much his own thought depends upon and is nourished by the supposed analogy. We must not expect the "rules of language" to be of much help in such inquiries. (There is accordingly a sense of "metaphor" that belongs to "pragmatics," rather than to "semantics"—and this sense may be the one most deserving of attention.)

III

Let us try the simplest possible account that can be given of the meaning of "The chairman ploughed through the discussion," to see how far it will take us. A plausible commentary (for those presumably too literal-minded to understand the original) might run somewhat as follows:

"A speaker who uses the sentence in question is taken to want to say *something* about a chairman and his behavior in some meeting. Instead of saying, plainly or *directly,* that the chairman dealt summarily with objections, or ruthlessly suppressed irrelevance, or something of the sort, the speaker chose to use a word ('ploughed') which, strictly speaking, means

---

[3] Here, I wish these words to be read with as little "weight" as possible!

something else. But an intelligent hearer can easily guess what the speaker had in mind."[4]

This account treats the metaphorical expression (let us call it "*M*") as a substitute for some other literal expression ("*L*," say) which would have expressed the same meaning, had it been used instead. On this view, the meaning of *M*, in its metaphorical occurrence, is just the *literal* meaning of *L*. The metaphorical use of an expression consists, on this view, of the use of that expression in other than its proper or normal sense, in some context that allows the improper or abnormal sense to be detected and appropriately transformed. (The reasons adduced for so remarkable a performance will be discussed later.)

Any view which holds that a metaphorical expression is used in place of some equivalent *literal* expression, I shall call a *substitution view of metaphor*. (I should like this label to cover also any analysis which views the entire sentence that is the locus of the metaphor as replacing some set of literal sentences.) Until recently, one or another form of a substitution view has been accepted by most writers (usually literary critics or writers of books on rhetoric) who have had anything to say about metaphor.

To take a few examples. Whately defines a metaphor as "a word substituted for another on account of the Resemblance or Analogy between their significations."[5] Nor is the entry in the Oxford Dictionary (to jump to modern times) much different from this: "Metaphor: The figure of speech in which a name or descriptive term is transferred to some object different from, but analogous to, that to which it is properly applicable; an instance of this, a metaphorical expression."[6] So strongly entrenched is the view expressed by these definitions that a recent writer who is explicitly arguing for a different and more sophisticated view of metaphor, nevertheless

---

[4] Notice how this type of paraphrase naturally conveys some implication of *fault* on the part of the metaphor's author. There is a strong suggestion that he ought to have made up his mind as to what he really wanted to say—the metaphor is depicted as a way of glossing over unclarity and vagueness.

[5] Richard Whately, *Elements of Rhetoric* (7th revised ed., London, 1846), p. 280.

[6] Under "Figure" we find: "Any of the various 'forms' of expression, deviating from the normal arrangement or use of words, which are adopted in order to give beauty, variety, or force to a composition; *e.g.,* Aposiopesis, Hyperbole, Metaphor, etc." If we took this strictly we might be led to say that a transfer of a word not adopted for the sake of introducing "beauty, variety, or force" must necessarily fail to be a case of metaphor. Or will "variety" automatically cover *every* transfer? It will be noticed that the O.E.D.'s definition is no improvement upon Whately's. Where he speaks of a "word" being substituted, the O.E.D. prefers "name or descriptive term." If this is meant to restrict metaphors to nouns (and adjectives?) it is demonstrably mistaken. But, if not, what *is* "descriptive term" supposed to mean? And why has Whately's reference to "Resemblance or Analogy" been trimmed into a reference to analogy alone?

slips into the old fashion by defining metaphor as "saying one thing and meaning another."[7]

According to a substitution view, the focus of a metaphor, the word or expression having a distinctively metaphorical use within a literal frame, is used to communicate a meaning that might have been expressed literally. The author substitutes M for L; it is the reader's task to invert the substitution, by using the literal meaning of M as a clue to the intended literal meaning of L. Understanding a metaphor is like deciphering a code or unravelling a riddle.

If we now ask why, on this view, the writer should set his reader the task of solving a puzzle, we shall be offered two types of answer. The first is that there may, in fact, be no literal equivalent, L, available in the language in question. Mathematicians spoke of the "leg" of an angle because there was no brief literal expression for a bounding line; we say "cherry lips," because there is no form of words half as convenient for saying quickly what the lips are like. Metaphor plugs the gaps in the literal vocabulary (or, at least, supplies the want of convenient abbreviations). So viewed, metaphor is a species of *catachresis,* which I shall define as the use of a word in some new sense in order to remedy a gap in the vocabulary. Catachresis is the putting of new senses into old words.[8] But if a catachresis serves a genuine need, the new sense introduced will quickly become part of the *literal* sense. "Orange" may originally have been applied to the color by catachresis; but the word is now applied to the color just as "properly" (and unmetaphorically) as to the fruit. "Osculating" curves don't kiss for long, and quickly revert to a more prosaic mathematical contact. And similarly for other cases. It is the fate of catachresis to disappear when it is successful.

There are, however, many metaphors where the virtues ascribed to catachresis cannot apply, because there is, or there is supposed to be, some readily available and equally compendious literal equivalent. Thus in the somewhat unfortunate example,[9] "Richard is a lion," which modern writers have discussed with boring insistence, the literal meaning is taken to be the

---

[7] Owen Barfield, "Poetic Diction and Legal Fiction," in *Essays Presented to Charles Williams* (Oxford, 1947), pp. 106-127. The definition of metaphor occurs on p. 111, where metaphor is treated as a special case of what Barfield calls "turning." The whole essay deserves to be read.

[8] The O.E.D. defines catachresis as: "Improper use of words; application of a term to a thing which it does not properly denote; abuse or perversion of a trope or metaphor." I wish to exclude the pejorative suggestions. There is nothing perverse or abusive in stretching old words to fit new situations. Catachresis is surely a striking case of the transformation of meaning that is constantly occurring in any living language.

[9] Can we imagine anybody saying this nowadays and seriously meaning anything? I find it hard to do so. But in default of an authentic context of use, any analysis is liable to be thin, obvious and unprofitable.

same as that of the sentence, "Richard is brave."[10] Here, the metaphor is not supposed to enrich the vocabulary.

When catachresis cannot be invoked, the reasons for substituting an indirect, metaphorical, expression are taken to be stylistic. We are told that the metaphorical expression may (in its literal use) refer to a more concrete object than would its literal equivalent; and this is supposed to give pleasure to the reader (the pleasure of having one's thoughts diverted from Richard to the irrelevant lion). Again, the reader is taken to enjoy problem-solving—or to delight in the author's skill at half-concealing, half-revealing his meaning. Or metaphors provide a shock of "agreeable surprise"—and so on. The principle behind these "explanations" seem to be: When in doubt about some peculiarity of language, attribute its existence to the pleasure it gives a reader. A principle that has the merit of working well in default of any evidence.[11]

Whatever the merits of such speculations about the reader's response, they agree in making metaphor a *decoration*. Except in cases where a metaphor is a catachresis that remedies some temporary imperfection of literal language, the purpose of metaphor is to entertain and divert. Its use, on this view, always constitutes a deviation from the "plain and strictly appropriate style" (Whately).[12] So, if philosophers have something more important to do than give pleasure to their readers, metaphor can have no serious place in philosophical discussion.

IV

The view that a metaphorical expression has a meaning that is some transform of its normal literal meaning is a special case of a more general view about "figurative" language. This holds that any figure of speech involving semantic change (and not merely syntactic change, like inversion

[10] A full discussion of this example, complete with diagrams, will be found in Gustaf Stern's *Meaning and Change of Meaning* (Göteborgs Högskolas Årsskrift, vol. 38, 1932, part 1), pp. 300 ff. Stern's account tries to show how the reader is led by the context to *select* from the connotation of "lion" the attribute (bravery) that will fit Richard the man. I take him to be defending a form of the substitution view.

[11] Aristotle ascribes the use of metaphor to delight in learning; Cicero traces delight in metaphor to the enjoyment of the author's ingenuity in overpassing the immediate, or in the vivid presentation of the principal subject. For references to these and other traditional views, see E. M. Cope, *An Introduction to Aristotle's Rhetoric* (London, 1867), "Appendix B to Book III, Ch. II: On Metaphor."

[12] Thus Stern (*op. cit.*) says of all figures of speech that "they are intended to serve the expressive and purposive functions of speech better than the 'plain statement'" (p. 296). A metaphor produces an "enhancement" (*Steigerung*) of the subject, but the factors leading to its use "involve the expressive and effective (purposive) functions of speech, not the symbolic and communicative functions" (p. 290). That is to say, metaphors may evince feelings or predispose others to act and feel in various ways—but they don't typically say anything.

of normal word order) consists in some transformation of a *literal* meaning. The author provides, not his intended meaning, *m,* but some function thereof, *f(m)*; the reader's task is to apply the inverse function, f^{-1}, and so to obtain $f^{-1}(f(m))$, i.e., *m,* the original meaning. When different functions are used, different tropes result. Thus, in irony, the author says the *opposite* of what he means; in hyperbole, he *exaggerates* his meaning; and so on.

What, then, is the characteristic transforming function involved in metaphor? To this the answer has been made: either *analogy* or *similarity. M* is either similar or analogous in meaning to its literal equivalent *L.* Once the reader has detected the ground of the intended analogy or simile (with the help of the frame, or clues drawn from the wider context) he can retrace the author's path and so reach the original meaning (the meaning of *L*).

If a writer holds that a metaphor consists in the *presentation* of the underlying analogy or similarity, he will be taking what I shall call a *comparison view* of metaphor. When Schopenhauer called a geometrical proof a mousetrap, he was, according to such a view, *saying* (though not explicitly): "A geometrical proof is *like* a mousetrap, since both offer a delusive reward, entice their victims by degrees, lead to disagreeable surprise, etc." This is a view of metaphor as a condensed or elliptical *simile.* It will be noticed that a "comparison view" is a special case of a "substitution view." For it holds that the metaphorical statement might be replaced by an equivalent literal *comparison.*

Whately says: "The Simile or Comparison may be considered as differing in form only from a Metaphor; the resemblance being in that case *stated,* which in the Metaphor is implied."[13] Bain says that "The metaphor is a comparison implied in the mere use of a term" and adds, "It is in the circumstance of being confined to a word, or at most to a phrase, that we are to look for the peculiarities of the metaphor—in advantages on the one hand, and its dangers and abuses on the other."[14] This view of the metaphor, as condensed simile or comparison, has been very popular.

The chief difference between a substitution view (of the sort previously considered) and the special form of it that I have called a comparison view

---

[13] Whately, *loc. cit.* He proceeds to draw a distinction between "Resemblance, strictly so called, i.e. *direct* resemblance between the objects themselves in question, (as when we speak of '*table*-land,' or compare great waves to *mountains*)" and "Analogy, which is the resemblance of ratios—a similarity of the relations they bear to certain other objects; as when we speak of the '*light* of reason,' or of 'revelation'; or compare a wounded and captive warrior to a stranded ship."

[14] Alexander Bain, *English Composition and Rhetoric* (Enlarged edition, London, 1887), p. 159.

may be illustrated by the stock example of "Richard is a lion." On the first view, the sentence means approximately the same as "Richard is brave"; on the second, approximately the same as "Richard is *like* a lion (in being brave)," the added words in brackets being understood but not explicitly stated. In the second translation, as in the first, the metaphorical statement is taken to be standing in place of some *literal* equivalent. But the comparison view provides a more elaborate paraphrase, inasmuch as the original statement is interpreted as being about lions as well as about Richard.[15]

The main objection against a comparison view is that it suffers from a vagueness that borders upon vacuity. We are supposed to be puzzled as to how some expression (M), used metaphorically, can function in place of some literal expression (L) that is held to be an approximate synonym; and the answer offered is that what M stands for (in its literal use) is *similar* to what L stands for. But how informative is this? There is some temptation to think of similarities as "objectively given," so that a question of the form, "Is A like B in respect of P?" has a definite and predetermined answer. If this were so, similes might be governed by rules as strict as those controlling the statements of physics. But likeness always admits of degrees, so that a truly "objective" question would need to take some such form as "Is A more like B than like C in respect of P?"—or, perhaps, "Is A closer to B than to C on such and such a scale of degrees of P?" Yet, in proportion as we approach such forms, metaphorical statements lose their effectiveness and their point. We need the metaphors in just the cases when there can be no question as yet of the precision of scientific statement. Metaphorical statement is not a substitute for a formal comparison or any other kind of literal statement, but has its own *distinctive* capacities and achievements. Often we say, "X is M," evoking some imputed connection between M and an imputed L (or, rather, to an indefinite system, $L_1, L_2, L_3 \ldots$) in cases where, prior to the construction of the metaphor, we would have been hard put to it to find any *literal* resemblance between M and L. It would be more illuminating in some of these cases to say that the metaphor *creates* the similarity than to say that formulates some similarity antecedently existing.[16]

[15] Comparison views probably derive from Aristotle's brief statement in the *Poetics*: "Metaphor consists in giving a thing a name that belongs to something else; the transference being either from genus to species, or from species to genus, or from species to species, or on grounds of analogy" ($1457b$). I have no space to give Aristotle's discussion the detailed examination it deserves. An able defence of a view based on Aristotle will be found in S. J. Brown's *The World of Imagery* (London, 1927, especially pp. 67 ff).

[16] Much more would need to be said in a thorough examination of the comparison view. It would be revealing, for instance, to consider the contrasting types of case in which a formal comparison is preferred to a metaphor. A comparison is often a prelude to an explicit state-

V

I turn now to consider a type of analysis which I shall call an *interaction view* of metaphor. This seems to me to be free from the main defects of substitution and comparison views and to offer some important insight into the uses and limitations of metaphor.[17]

Let us begin with the following statement: "In the simplest formulation, when we use a metaphor we have two thoughts of different things active together and supported by a single word, or phrase, whose meaning is a resultant of their interaction."[18]

We may discover what is here intended by applying Richards' remark to our earlier example, "The poor are the Negroes of Europe." The substitution view, at its crudest, tells us that something is being *indirectly* said about the poor of Europe. (But what? That they are an oppressed class, a standing reproach to the community's official ideals, that poverty is inherited and indelible?) The comparison view claims that the epigram *presents* some comparison between the poor and the Negroes. In opposition to both, Richards says that our "thoughts" about European poor and (American) Negroes are "active together" and "interact" to produce a meaning that is a resultant of that interaction.

I think this must mean that in the given context the focal word "Negroes" obtains a *new* meaning, which is *not* quite its meaning in literal uses, nor quite the meaning which any literal substitute would have. The new context (the "frame" of the metaphor, in my terminology) imposes *extension* of meaning upon the focal word. And I take Richards to be saying that for the metaphor to work the reader must remain aware of

ment of the grounds of resemblance; whereas we do not expect a metaphor to explain itself. (Cf. the difference between *comparing* a man's face with a wolf mask, by looking for points of resemblance—and seeing the human face *as* vulpine.) But no doubt the line between *some* metaphors and *some* similes is not a sharp one.

[17] The best sources are the writings of I. A. Richards, especially Chapter 5 ("Metaphor") and Chapter 6 ("Command of Metaphor") of his *The Philosophy of Rhetoric* (Oxford, 1936). Chapters 7 and 8 of his *Interpretation in Teaching* (London, 1938) cover much the same ground. W. Bedell Stanford's *Greek Metaphor* (Oxford, 1936) defends what he calls an "integration theory" (see especially pp. 101 ff) with much learning and skill. Unfortunately, both writers have great trouble in making clear the nature of the positions they are defending. Chapter 18 of W. Empson's *The Structure of Complex Words* (London, 1951) is a useful discussion of Richards' views on metaphor.

[18] *The Philosophy of Rhetoric*, p. 93. Richards also says that metaphor is "fundamentally a borrowing between and intercourse of *thoughts,* a transaction between contexts" (p. 94). Metaphor, he says, requires two ideas "which co-operate in an inclusive meaning" (p. 119).

the extension of meaning—must attend to both the old and the new meanings together.[19]

But how is this extension or change of meaning brought about? At one point, Richards speaks of the "common characteristics" of the two terms (the poor and Negroes) as "the ground of the metaphor" (*op cit.*, p. 117), so that in its metaphorical use a word or expression must connote only a *selection* from the characteristics connoted in its literal uses. This, however, seems a rare lapse into the older and less sophisticated analyses he is trying to supersede.[20] He is on firmer ground when he says that the reader is forced to "connect" the two ideas (p. 125). In this "connection" resides the secret and the mystery of metaphor. To speak of the "interaction" of two thoughts "active together" (or, again, of their "interillumination" or "co-operation") is to *use* a metaphor emphasizing the dynamic aspects of a good reader's response to a non-trivial metaphor. I have no quarrel with the use of metaphors (if they are good ones) in talking about metaphor. But it may be as well to use several, lest we are misled by the adventitious charms of our favorites.

Let us try, for instance, to think of a metaphor as a *filter.* Consider the statement, "Man is a wolf." Here, we may say, are *two* subjects—the *principal subject,* Man (or: men) and the *subsidiary subject,* Wolf (or: wolves). Now the metaphorical sentence in question will not convey its intended meaning to a reader sufficiently ignorant about wolves. What is needed is not so much that the reader shall know the standard dictionary meaning of "wolf"—or be able to use that word in literal senses—as that he shall know what I will call the *system of associated commonplaces.* Imagine some layman required to say, without taking special thought, those things he held to be true about wolves; the set of statements resulting would approximate to what I am here calling the system of commonplaces associated with the word "wolf." I am assuming that in any given culture the responses made by different persons to the test suggested would agree rather closely, and that even the occasional expert, who might have unusual knowledge of the subject, would still know "what the man in the street thinks about the matter." From the expert's standpoint, the system of commonplaces may include half-truths or downright mistakes (as when a whale is classified as a fish); but the important thing for the metaphor's effectiveness is not that the commonplaces shall be true, but that they should be

---

[19] It is this, perhaps, that leads Richards to say that "talk about the identification or fusion that a metaphor effects is nearly always misleading and pernicious" (*op. cit.,* p. 127).

[20] Usually, Richards tries to show that similarity between the two terms is at best *part* of the basis for the interaction of meanings in a metaphor.

readily and freely evoked. (Because this is so, a metaphor that works in one society may seem preposterous in another. Men who take wolves to be reincarnations of dead humans will give the statement "Man is a wolf" an interpretation different from the one I have been assuming.)

To put the matter in another way: Literal uses of the word "wolf" are governed by syntactical and semantical rules, violation of which produces nonsense or self-contradiction. In addition, I am suggesting, literal uses of the word normally commit the speaker to acceptance of a set of standard beliefs about wolves (current platitudes) that are the common possession of the members of some speech community. To deny any such piece of accepted commonplace (e.g., by saying that wolves are vegetarians—or easily domesticated) is to produce an effect of paradox and provoke a demand for justification. A speaker who says "wolf" is normally taken to be implying in some sense of that word that he is referring to something fierce, carnivorous, treacherous, and so on. The idea of a wolf is part of a system of ideas, not sharply delineated, and yet sufficiently definite to admit of detailed enumeration.

The effect, then, of (metaphorically) calling a man a "wolf" is to evoke the wolf-system of related commonplaces. If the man is a wolf, he preys upon other animals, is fierce, hungry, engaged in constant struggle, a scavenger, and so on. Each of these implied assertions has now to be made to fit the principal subject (the man) either in normal or in abnormal senses. If the metaphor is at all appropriate, this can be done—up to a point at least. A suitable hearer will be led by the wolf-system of implications to construct a corresponding system of implications about the principal subject. But these implications will *not* be those comprised in the commonplaces *normally* implied by literal uses of "man." The new implications must be determined by the patterns of implications associated with literal uses of the word "wolf." Any human traits that can without undue strain be talked about in "wolf-language" will be rendered prominent, and any that cannot will be pushed into the background. The wolf-metaphor suppresses some details, emphasizes others—in short, *organizes* our view of man.

Suppose I look at the night sky through a piece of heavily smoked glass on which certain lines have been left clear. Then I shall see only the stars that can be made to lie on the lines previously prepared upon the screen, and the stars I do see will be seen as organized by the screen's structure. We can think of a metaphor as such a screen, and the system of "associated commonplaces" of the focal word as the network of lines upon the screen. We can say that the principal subject is "seen through" the metaphorical expression—or, if we prefer, that the principal subject is "projected upon" the field of the subsidiary subject. (In the latter analogy, the implication-system of the focal expression must be taken to determine the "law of projection.")

Or take another example. Suppose I am set the task of describing a battle in words drawn as largely as possible from the vocabulary of chess. These latter terms determine a system of implications which will proceed to control my description of the battle. The enforced choice of the chess vocabulary will lead some aspects of the battle to be emphasized, others to be neglected, and all to be organized in a way that would cause much more strain in other modes of description. The chess vocabulary filters and trans-forms: it not only selects, it brings forward aspects of the battle that might not be seen at all through another medium. (Stars that cannot be seen at all, except through telescopes.)

Nor must we neglect the shifts in attitude that regularly result from the use of metaphorical language. A wolf is (conventionally) a hateful and alarming object; so, to call a man a wolf is to imply that he too is hateful and alarming (and thus to support and reinforce dislogistic attitudes). Again, the vocabulary of chess has its primary uses in a highly artificial setting, where all expression of feeling is formally excluded: to describe a battle as if it were a game of chess is accordingly to exclude, by the choice of language, all the more emotionally disturbing aspects of warfare. (Similar by-products are not rare in philosophical uses of metaphor.)

A fairly obvious objection to the foregoing sketch of the "interaction view" is that it has to hold that some of the "associated commonplaces" themselves suffer metaphorical change of meaning in the process of transfer from the subsidiary to the principal subject. And *these* changes, if they occur, can hardly be explained by the account given. The primary metaphor, it might be said, has been analyzed into a set of subordinate metaphors, so the account given is either circular or leads to an infinite regress.

This might be met by denying that *all* changes of meaning in the "asso-ciated commonplaces" must be counted as metaphorical shifts. Many of them are best described as *extensions* of meaning, because they do not involve apprehended connections between two systems of concepts. I have not undertaken to explain how such extensions or shifts occur in general, and I do not think any simple account will fit all cases. (It is easy enough to mutter "analogy," but closer examination soon shows all kinds of "grounds" for shifts of meaning with context—and even no ground at all, sometimes.)

Secondly, I would not deny that a metaphor may involve a number of subordinate metaphors among its implications. But these subordinate meta-phors are, I think, usually intended to be taken less "emphatically," i.e., with less stress upon *their* implications. (The implications of a metaphor are like the overtones of a musical chord; to attach too much "weight" to them is like trying to make the overtones sound as loud as the main notes—and just as pointless.) In any case, primary and subordinate metaphors will normally belong to the same field of discourse, so that they mutually reinforce one and the same system of implications. Conversely, where substantially new metaphors appear as the primary metaphor is unravelled, there is serious risk of confusion of thought (cf. the customary prohibition against "mixed metaphors").

But the preceeding account of metaphor needs correction, if it is to be reasonably adequate. Reference to "associated commonplaces" will fit the commonest cases where the author simply plays upon the stock of common knowledge (and common misinformation) presumably shared by the reader and himself. But in a poem, or a piece of sustained prose, the writer can establish a novel pattern of implications for the literal uses of the key expressions, prior to using them as vehicles for his metaphors. (An author can do much to suppress unwanted implications of the word "contract," by explicit discussion of its intended meaning, before he proceeds to develop a contract theory of sovereignty. Or a naturalist who really knows wolves may tell us so much about them that *his* description of man as a wolf diverges quite markedly from the stock uses of that figure.) Metaphors can be supported by specially constructed systems of implications, as well as by accepted commonplaces; they can be made to measure and need not be reach-me-downs.

It was a simplification, again, to speak as if the implication-system of the metaphorical expression remains unaltered by the metaphorical statement. The nature of the intended application helps to determine the character of the system to be applied (as though the stars could partly determine the character of the observation-screen by which we looked at them). If to call a man a wolf is to put him in a special light, we must not forget that the metaphor makes the wolf seem more human than he otherwise would.

I hope such complications as these can be accommodated within the outline of an "interaction view" that I have tried to present.

VI

Since I have been making so much use of example and illustration, it may be as well to state explicitly (and by way of summary) some of the chief respects in which the "interaction" view recommended differs from a "substitution" or a "comparison" view.

In the form in which I have been expounding it, the "interaction view" is committed to the following seven claims:—

(1) A metaphorical statement has *two* distinct subjects—a "principal" subject and a "subsidiary" one.[21]

(2) These subjects are often best regarded as *"systems* of things," rather than "things."

(3) The metaphor works by applying to the principal subject a system of "associated implications" characteristic of the subsidiary subject.

(4) These implications usually consist of "commonplaces" about the subsidiary subject, but may, in suitable cases, consist of deviant implications established *ad hoc* by the writer.

(5) The metaphor selects, emphasizes, suppresses, and organizes features of the principal subject by *implying* statements about it that normally apply to the subsidiary subject.

(6) This involves shifts in meaning of words belonging to the same family or system as the metaphorical expression; and some of these shifts, though not all, may be metaphorical transfers. (The subordinate metaphors are, however, to be read less "emphatically.")

(7) There is, in general, no simple "ground" for the necessary shifts of meaning—no blanket reason why some metaphors work and others fail.

It will be found, upon consideration, that point (1) is incompatible with the simplest forms of a "substitution view," point (7) is formally incompatible with a "comparison view"; while the remaining points elaborate reasons for regarding "comparison views" as inadequate.

But it is easy to overstate the conflicts between these three views. If we were to insist that only examples satisfying all seven of the claims listed above should be allowed to count as "genuine" metaphors, we should restrict the correct uses of the word "metaphor" to a very small number of cases. This would be to advocate a persuasive definition of "metaphor" that would tend to make all metaphors interestingly complex.[22] And such a deviation from current uses of the word "metaphor" would leave us without a convenient label for the more trivial cases. Now it is in just such trivial cases that "substitution" and "comparison" views sometimes

---

[21] This point has often been made. E.g.:—"As to metaphorical expression, that is a great excellence in style, when it is used with propriety, for it gives you two ideas for one." (Samuel Johnson, quoted by Richards, *op. cit.,* p. 93.) The choice of labels for the "subjects" is troublesome. See the "Note on terminology" appended to this paper.

[22] I can sympathize with Empson's contention that "The term ['metaphor'] had better correspond to what the speakers themselves feel to be a rich or suggestive or persuasive use of a word, rather than include uses like the *leg* of a table" (*The Structure of Complex Words,* p. 333). But there is the opposite danger, also, of making metaphors too important by definition, and so narrowing our view of the subject excessively.

seem nearer the mark than "interaction" views. The point might be met by *classifying* metaphors as instances of substitution, comparison, or inter-action. Only the last kind are of importance in philosophy.

For substitution-metaphors and comparison-metaphors can be replaced by literal translations (with possible exception for the case of catachresis)—by sacrificing some of the charm, vivacity, or wit of the original, but with no loss of *cognitive* content. But "interaction-metaphors" are not expendable. Their mode of operation requires the reader to use a system of implications (a system of "commonplaces"—or a special system established for the pur-pose in hand) as a means for selecting, emphasizing, and organizing rela-tions in a different field. This use of a "subsidiary subject" to foster insight into a "principal subject" is a distinctive *intellectual* operation (though one familiar enough through our experiences of learning anything whatever), demanding simultaneous awareness of both subjects but not reducible to any *comparison* between the two.

Suppose we try to state the cognitive content of an interaction-metaphor in "plain language." Up to a point, we may succeed in stating a number of relevant relations between the two subjects (though in view of the extension of meaning accompanying the shift in the subsidiary subject's implication system, too much must not be expected of the literal para-phrase). But the set of literal statements so obtained will not have the same power to inform and enlighten as the original. For one thing, the implica-tions, previously left for a suitable reader to educe for himself, with a nice feeling for their relative priorities and degrees of importance, are now pre-sented explicitly as though having equal weight. The literal paraphrase in-evitably says too much—and with the wrong emphasis. One of the points I most wish to stress is that the loss in such cases is a loss in *cognitive* content; the relevant weakness of the literal paraphrase is not that it may be tiresomely prolix or boringly explicit—or deficient in qualities of style; it fails to be a translation because it fails to give the *insight* that the metaphor did.

But "explication," or elaboration of the metaphor's grounds, if not regarded as an adequate cognitive substitute for the original, may be ex-tremely valuable. A powerful metaphor will no more be harmed by such probing than a musical masterpiece by analysis of its harmonic and melodic structure. No doubt metaphors are dangerous—and perhaps especially so in philosophy. But a prohibition against their use would be a wilful and harmful restriction upon our powers of inquiry.[23]

[23] (*A note on terminology*): For metaphors that fit a substitution or comparison view, the factors needing to be distinguished are:—(1) some word or expression E; (ii) occuring in some verbal "frame" F; so that (iii) $F(E)$ is the metaphorical statement in question; (iv) the mean-ing $m'(E)$ which E has in $F(E)$; (v) which is the same as the literal meaning, $m(X)$, of some

Bibliography

Among the chief texts entering into current discussions of metaphor are the following:

Monroe Beardsley, *Aesthetics* (New York, 1958), Chapter III;

Paul Henle, "Metaphor," in *Language, Thought and Culture,* ed. Paul Henle, (Ann Arbor, 1958);

I. A. Richards, *The Philosophy of Rhetoric* (London, 1936), Chapters V, VI;

Gustaf Stern, "Meaning and Change of Meaning," in *Götesborgs Högskolas Årsskrift,* Volume XXXVIII, 1932: 1 (Göteborg, 1931), Chapter XI.

Other discussions of interest, usually ranging beyond metaphor, include:

Owen Barfield, "Poetic Diction and Legal Fiction," in *Essays Presented to Charles Williams* (Oxford, 1947);

Cleanth Brooks, "The Heresy of Paraphrase," in *The Well Wrought Urn* (New York, 1947);

Scott Buchanan, *Poetry and Mathematics* (New York, 1929);

William Empson, *The Structure of Complex Words* (New York, 1951);

Martin Foss, *Symbol and Metaphor in Human Experience* (Princeton, 1942);

Isabel Hungerland, *Poetic Discourse* (Berkeley, 1958), Chapter IV;

Abraham Kaplan and Ernst Kris, "Aesthetic Ambiguity," reprinted in Ernst Kris, *Psychoanalytic Explorations in Art* (New York, 1952);

Abraham Kaplan, "Referential Meaning in the Arts," *Journal of Aesthetics and Art Criticism,* Volume XII (1954), 457-474;

Andrew Ushenko, "Metaphor," *Thought,* Volume XXX (1955), 421-435;

Philip Wheelwright, *The Burning Fountain* (Bloomington, 1954).

---

literal synonym, *X*. A sufficient technical vocabulary would be: "metaphorical expression" (for *E*), "metaphorical statement" (for *F(E)*), "metaphorical meaning" (for *m'*) and "literal meaning" (for *m*).

Where the interaction view is appropriate, the situation is more complicated. We may also need to refer (vi) to the principal subject of *F(E)*, say *P* (roughly, what the statement is "really" about), (vii) the subsidiary subject, *S* (what *F(E)* would be about if read literally); (viii) the relevant system of implications, *I*, connected with *S*; and (ix) the resulting system of attributions, *A*, asserted of *P*. We must accept at least so much complexity if we agree that the meaning of *E* in its setting *F* depends upon the transformation of *I* into *A* by using language, normally applied to *S*, to apply to *P* instead.

Richards has suggested using the words "tenor" and "vehicle" for the two *"thoughts"* which, in his view, are "active together" (for "the two *ideas* that metaphor, at its simplest, gives us," *op. cit.,* p. 96, my italics) and urges that we reserve "the word 'metaphor' for the whole double unit" (*ib.*). But this picture of two *ideas* working upon each other is an inconvenient fiction. And it is significant that Richards himself soon lapses into speaking of "tenor" and "vehicle" as "things" (e.g. on p. 118). Richards' "vehicle" vacillates in reference between the metaphorical expression (*E*), the subsidiary subject (*S*) and the connected implication system (*I*). It is less clear what his "tenor" means: sometimes it stands for the principal subject (*P*), sometimes for implications connected with that subject (which I have not symbolized above), sometimes, in spite of Richards' own intentions, for the *resultant* meaning (or as we might say the "full import") of *E* in its context, *F(E)*.

There is probably no hope of getting an accepted terminology so long as writers upon the subject are so much at variance with one another.

BIOGRAPHICAL NOTES

Biographical Notes

MONROE C. BEARDSLEY. Professor of Philosophy at Swarthmore College. Author, *Aesthetics* (1958).

MAX BLACK. Professor of Philosophy at Cornell University. Author, *Language and Philosophy* (1949). Editor, *Philosophical Analysis* (1950).

JOHN HOSPERS. Professor of Philosophy at Brooklyn College. Author, *Meaning and Truth in the Arts* (1946).

ARNOLD ISENBERG. Associate Professor of Philosophy at Stanford University. Author, articles in *Journal of Philosophy, Journal of Aesthetics and Art Criticism,* etc.

MARGARET MACDONALD. Late University Reader at Bedford College (1946-1952). Editor of *Analysis.* Editor, *Philosophy and Analysis* (1954).

JOSEPH MARGOLIS. Associate Professor of Philosophy at University of Cincinnati. Author, *Philosophy and the World of Art* (forthcoming).

FRANK SIBLEY. Member, Department of Philosophy at Cornell University. Author, articles in *Mind, Philosophical Review,* etc.

CHARLES L. STEVENSON. Professor of Philosophy at University of Michigan. Author, *Ethics and Language* (1944).

VINCENT TOMAS. Professor of Philosophy at Brown University. Editor, *Charles S. Pierce, Essays in the Philosophy of Science* (1957).

JAMES O. URMSON. Fellow of Corpus Christi College, Oxford. Author, *Philosophical Analysis* (1956) and co-editor of the late J. L. Austin's *Philosophical Papers* (1961).

MORRIS WEITZ. Professor of Philosophy at The Ohio State University. Author, *Philosophy of the Arts* (1950). Editor, *Problems in Aesthetics* (1959).

WILLIAM K. WIMSATT, JR. Professor of English at Yale University. Author, *The Verbal Icon* (1954) and co-author, *Literary Criticism, A Short History* (1957).

PAUL ZIFF. Member, Department of Philosophy at University of Pennsylvania. Author, *Semantic Analysis* (1960).